JACQUES MARITAIN
The Man and His Achievement

JACQUES MARITAIN
The Man and His Achievement

Edited with an Introduction by
Joseph W. Evans

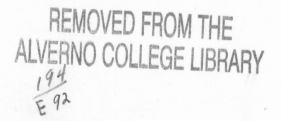
SHEED AND WARD – NEW YORK

Library of Congress Catalog Card Number 63-17143

The publisher wishes to thank the Bollingen Foundation for its kind permission to quote material from *Creative Intuition in Art and Poetry* by Jacques Maritain (New York: Pantheon, 1953).

Manufactured in the United States of America

Contents

Contributors

Yves R. Simon—died in May of 1961; from 1948 until the time of his death, he was Professor in the Committee on Social Thought, University of Chicago; author of numerous books, among them *Philosophy of Democratic Government, Community of the Free, Ontologie du Connaître,* and *Prévoir et Savoir.*

James Collins—Professor of Philosophy at St. Louis University; author of *A History of Modern European Philosophy, The Existentialists,* and *God in Modern Philosophy.*

Wallace Fowlie—Professor of French, University of Colorado; author of *Age of Surrealism, Clowns and Angels: Studies in Modern French Literature, Jacob's Night: The Religious Renascence in France,* and *Ernest Psichari: a Study in Religious Conversion.*

John J. FitzGerald—Associate Professor of Philosophy, University of Notre Dame; translated Maritain's *The Person and the Common Good.*

James F. Anderson—Professor of Philosophy, Villanova University; author of *The Bond of Being* and *The Cause of Being.*

Henry Bars—French priest, living in Perros-Guirec, Bretagne; author of *Maritain en notre temps* and *La politique selon Jacques Maritain.*

Francis Fergusson—Professor of Comparative Literature, Rutgers University; author of *Poems 1929-1961, The Idea of a Theatre, The Human Image in Dramatic Literature,* and *Dante's Drama of the Mind: a Modern Reading of the Purgatorio.*

RALPH NELSON—Assistant Professor of Philosophy, University of Windsor, Windsor, Ontario.

CHARLES O'DONNELL—American Consul General, Dacca, East Pakistan.

CHARLES JOURNET—Professor of Theology, Grand Séminaire, Fribourg, Switzerland; author of *The Church of the Incarnate Word* and *The Dark Knowledge of God;* editor of the periodical *Nova et Vetera.*

LEO R. WARD, C.S.C.— Professor of Philosophy, University of Notre Dame; author of *Blueprint for a Catholic University, Christian Ethics, God and World Order,* and *Values and Reality;* co-editor of *The Social and Political Philosophy of Jacques Maritain.*

JOSEPH W. EVANS—Associate Professor of Philosophy and Director of the Jacques Maritain Center at Notre Dame; co-editor of *The Social and Political Philosophy of Jacques Maritain;* translator of Maritain's *Art and Scholasticism and The Frontiers of Poetry.*

WILLIAM L. ROSSNER, S.J.—Professor of Philosophy, Rockhurst College, Kansas City.

Introduction

JACQUES MARITAIN has exerted profound influence on twentieth-century philosophy and cultural life. The author of more than fifty philosophical works and of countless articles which have appeared in journals and magazines of every description, he is widely regarded as the pre-eminent modern interpreter of the thought of St. Thomas Aquinas and as a highly creative thinker in his own right. The range and scope of his philosophizing are indeed impressive: among his works are *The Degrees of Knowledge, A Preface to Metaphysics, Existence and the Existent, Science and Wisdom, Approaches to God, Art and Scholasticism and The Frontiers of Poetry, Creative Intuition in Art and Poetry, True Humanism, Education at the Crossroads, Man and the State, On the Philosophy of History,* and *Moral Philosophy.*

Maritain was born in Paris on November 18, 1882, son of Paul Maritain, a lawyer, and Geneviève Favre, daughter of Jules Favre. Reared in an atmosphere of liberal Protestantism, he received his early education at the Lycée Henri IV, and it was there that he formed his close friendship with Ernest Psichari, grandson of Ernest Renan. The Renans and the Favres had been, in the nineteenth century, among the most representative of the great intellectual and political families of liberal and republican France. In addition to their lively passion for the world of ideas, the two young friends shared the same humanitarian interests.

Later, at the Sorbonne, Maritain studied the natural sciences, and for a brief time fell under the spell of teachers unshakably convinced that science alone could provide all the answers to the questions that torment the human mind. But it was also at the Sorbonne that he met his wife-to-be, Raïssa Oumansoff, a young Russian Jewish student who was to share his quest for truth and herself become an intellectual and poet of real stature. She was also to collaborate with him in a number of books. Maritain was one day to say of Raïssa (who died in November of 1960): "The best thing I owe to my studies at that time [at the Sorbonne] is that they enabled me to meet, in the Faculty of Sciences, the one who since then has always, happily for me, been at my side in a perfect and blessed communion."

Soon disillusioned with the scientism of their Sorbonne masters, the Maritains attended, at the urging of their friend Charles Péguy, the lectures of Henri Bergson at the Collège de France. Bergson liberated in them "the sense of the absolute," and, following their marriage in 1904, they were converted in 1906 to the Roman Catholic faith through the influence of Léon Bloy.

The years 1907 and 1908 were spent in Heidelberg where Maritain studied biology under Hans Driesch. He was particularly interested at the time in Driesch's embryogenetic theory of neo-vitalism, a theory then little known in France. Upon returning to Paris, Maritain undertook the task of directing the compilation of a *Dictionary of Practical Life,* both because of the financial remuneration and because of his profound desire to maintain that intellectual liberty which he thought he would have had to sacrifice if he had accepted a teaching position in any of the State schools. The three years spent in this pursuit were most fruitful for his development as a philosopher, for they enabled him to ponder with absolute freedom the philosophical problems which were gradually taking shape in his mind and on the solution of which depended his whole future thought. It was during this period also that Maritain turned to the study of the writings of St. Thomas Aquinas.

Maritain began his teaching career in 1912 at the Collège Stanislas in Paris. He also taught for many years at the Institut Catholique in Paris, and at a number of places in the United States and Canada —the Pontifical Institute of Mediaeval Studies in Toronto, Columbia University, the Committee on Social Thought at the University of Chicago, the University of Notre Dame, and Princeton University. From 1945 to 1948 he was French Ambassador to the Vatican. Upon completion of this appointment he began his lengthy association with Princeton. He returned to France in 1961.

Maritain's thought is based on the principles of Aristotle and St. Thomas, but incorporates many insights found in other philosophers, both classical and modern, and also profits greatly from data supplied by such sciences of man as anthropology, sociology, and psychology. Maritain urges us "not to confuse the philosopher's faculty of invention with the ingenuity that inspires the art of the dress designer." He defends both the notion and the reality of a *philosophia perennis,* and he sees it as having its most complete and articulate formulation in the thought of St. Thomas. And he holds that philosophy calls for a progress by *deepening insight,* as contrasted with the progress by *substitution* that more generally prevails in the sciences. On the other hand, he knows well that being or reality is difficult, that it is an inexhaustible depth, and that, conversely, the human intellect is a mendicant one, condemned to wresting the secrets of being slowly and arduously. As a result, Maritain is most attentive to the *other* philosopher, knowing that the thought of every great philosopher lives on a central intuition which genuinely gets hold of some aspect of the real, however poorly this intuition may be conceptualized. Finally, Maritain's feeding on the data provided by the sciences of man is prompted, first of all, by his recognition that truth in one realm is friend and solidary of truth in another, and secondly, by his conviction that the philosopher of man, at any rate, must have his eyes at every turn not simply on the *nature* of man, but also on his *state*—which state the sciences of man do much to delineate.

The aspect "Christian philosopher" is very marked in Maritain. For him, of course, "being a Christian" and "being a philosopher" are two different things, but they are not separate—these two different *habitus* pulsate together at the same immaterial node of the soul's energies. It is normal, then, that they interact, interpenetrate each other—"help each other to be." It is also normal that there be a certain agonizing tension—not conflict—between them: each takes on a certain thrust and force it would not otherwise have.

Maritain is admired even by those who may be of very different philosophical and religious convictions. He is admired not only for his life-long zeal for Truth and impassioned commitment to Freedom, but also for his exceptional qualities as a person—his humility, his charity, his fraternal attitude toward all that is. Increasingly he is being recognized as one of the great *spirituals* of his time.

It has been the desire of the contributors to this volume to focus attention on main aspects of Maritain's personality and achievement. We feel privileged and pleased to have as our opening article the essay by the late Professor Yves Simon—student, long-time friend, and dedicated co-worker of Maritain.

JOSEPH W. EVANS

University of Notre Dame
Notre Dame, Indiana

JACQUES MARITAIN

The Man and His Achievement

Yves R. Simon

1. Jacques Maritain: The Growth of a Christian Philosopher

IT IS ONE of my duties as a member of the Committee on Social Thought of the University of Chicago to help advanced students in the reading of philosophical classics.* When the program of a student has included *Art and Scholasticism* or *A Preface to Metaphysics,* I have sometimes felt that I was able to clear up difficulties which might have been insuperable had I not had the privilege of personal acquaintance with Maritain and with the historical circumstances of his development.

These remarks suffice to give an idea of the subjects that I shall try to cover. The period is roughly that of the precarious peace between the two World Wars. I first heard of Maritain about 1920, when I became a university student. After we came to this country, I in 1938 and he in 1939, we no longer met frequently as we used to do in Paris.

To perceive what the historical context means in the development of Maritain, let us compare his career with that of Bergson. Bergsonian philosophy can be well understood without much information about the person of the philosopher and the circumstances

* Professor Simon died on May 11, 1961, after a long illness. This essay was completed a short time previously.—Ed.

3

under which his research took place. In fact, few people know much about Bergson's life and his relation to the history of his time. The exposition of his philosophy is very orderly; you would think that the day he planned out his doctoral dissertation he already knew what he would be writing at the age of seventy. This is a unique feat in the history of philosophy. We may be interested in knowing what kind of life was his: for a number of years he taught in secondary schools, then at the Ecole Normale Supérieure, then at the Collège de France. He retired in 1918. With some information about philosophic programs in the secondary schools of the French Republic, about the functions and customs of the Ecole Normale Supérieure, about the Collège de France and about philosophic trends in the late nineteenth century, we have almost all that the history of the times can contribute to the understanding of Bergson. The case of Maritain sharply contrasts with that of his teacher. As one goes ahead with the reading of Maritain's works, he constantly feels the need for more information about the occurrences with which the composition of his books and papers has been connected.

I would like to start with a paradox and say that Maritain was the first non-scholastic among the disciples of St. Thomas. Not long ago it was quite customary to speak of scholasticism as if there existed such a thing as a scholastic philosophy provided with doctrinal unity. In fact, there are at least half a dozen philosophic systems which have an equal right to be termed "scholastic," although they clash violently on a number of fundamental issues. Let us ask of what subjects the word "scholastic" can be predicated relevantly. Certainly not of a doctrine, but of a set of problems— what is called in German *eine Problematik*—of a method, of a language, of a cultural form, and, finally, of the period in which this *Problematik*, this method, this language and this cultural form were prevalent. It is particularly to scholasticism as a form of culture that Maritain referred when he wrote that the philosophy of St. Thomas is called scholastic from the name of its worst ordeal.

A scholastic philosophy is a philosophy of professors, and Maritain holds that the professor is precisely the worst enemy of St. Thomas' philosophy. A scholastic culture is centered on what takes place between teachers and students, with little or no concern for what goes on in public affairs, in art and literature, and in spiritual life. It is this meaning of Scholasticism that we bear in mind when we set in contrast the Scholastics and the Humanists of the sixteenth century. These Scholastics were not always bad at expounding the rational, scientific and philosophic psychology of animals and man. But when there was a question of understanding man in the contingencies of history, in the indefinitely many accidents of his concrete existence, when there was a question of understanding what we now would call the existential man, they were rather poor, and the Humanists were much better. Interest in Scholastic philosophies was revived toward the end of the nineteenth century and the old conflict could be observed again. In fact, it had never died out. I know of liberal arts colleges where there is a tendency to center training about philosophy. Because of my professional interest, I might be expected to be enthusiastic about such programs. I am not. I rather think that on the college level it is man considered in the contingencies of his concrete existence who should be the main subject of liberal studies. Although there have been considerable changes in the attitudes and ideas of Maritain, one feature is present in all periods of his life: he has always been in warm contact with the existential man, and his excellence in the rational analysis of the soul has never interfered with his intuitive relation to men such as they are here and now, such as they have been shaped by history, by grace and by suffering, and such as they behave with regard to their eternal destiny.

These remarks lead us to consider Maritain's personal background. His family belonged to the most educated part of the bourgeoisie, and had connections with liberal Protestantism. He was born (1882) and raised in Paris. A city child, he may have retained some of the parochialism which is so common among

Parisians. Léon Bloy was instrumental in the conversion of Maritain and his wife to the Catholic Church (1906).

The personality and the work of Bloy remain obscure subjects on which there is little literature of any value. Léon Bloy was in some respects a great writer; he was a man who suffered immensely and expressed human suffering with extraordinary intensity. His Catholic faith was deep, burning and uncompromising, with a definitely mystical direction. Here, we are touching upon a point which matters decisively for the understanding of Maritain and of the movements in which he was active. At some time in the history of the Church (I shall not dare to venture a date, but I suppose it was no later than the end of the seventeenth century) the feeling spread that religion was principally designed to procure the perfection of morality. This pragmatic interpretation was extremely common toward the end of the nineteenth century. It was frequent even among sincere believers. Where did it come from? To a large extent from a more or less explicit conviction that there was a conflict between religion and science and that, accordingly, religion should be defended in terms of helpfulness and fruitfulness, rather than in terms of truth. The thing that science cannot do is to take care of human sorrows and weaknesses, whereas religion brings strength and consolation.

I am aware of the weak points of Léon Bloy. His really good books are few. As a stylist he is very irregular. Some of his eccentricities are shocking. In his writings, personal names of contemporaries or transparent pseudonyms designate symbolic characters who happen to be charged with the most shameful actions. How does the reader know that such and such a name or pseudonym designates a symbol rather than a real man? But Léon Bloy was animated by the most burning conviction as he fought moralistic and pragmatic interpretations of religion. Few men contributed so effectively to the shaping of an era of purer faith. Under the influence of such a man as Bloy, the faithful understood better that the center of Christian life is the beatific vision of the Divine Persons and that, in this world, there is nothing greater than the contemplation of supernatural truth in the charity of Christ. At this point it is relevant to note that the great epistemological work of Maritain, *The Degrees of Knowledge,* which includes long chapters on the natural sciences, ends with studies on mystical experience. This association—infrequent in the history of epistemology—expresses a disposition which has been that of Maritain ever since his early progress in philosophy and in faith. He knows St. John of the Cross as well as St. Thomas Aquinas.

From the beginning Maritain had the soul of a contemplative and that of an artist. I have some notion of the people whose company he liked, for, over a long period, it was my privilege to visit his home on Sunday afternoons. The living room was generally crowded, less by teachers or students than by writers, poets, painters, musicians, persons interested in mysticism, missionaries and friends of the missions. Most of the artists were of the vanguard description. Concerning Maritain's philosophical education, the important fact is that he studied under Bergson. The level of philosophical work in French universities was then at an all-time low. The predominance of neo-positivism and neo-criticism did not allow much philosophical thought to survive. Commenting on Bergson's doctoral dissertation, which is known in English as *Time and Free Will* but whose original title is *Essay on the Immediate Data of Consciousness* (1889), Georges Sorel wrote that the work of Bergson stood like a green and vigorous oak tree over the wasteland of contemporary philosophy. In Bergson's classroom a brilliantly gifted young man felt that philosophy was still capable of great accomplishments.

We noticed that one of the things of which "scholastic" can be relevantly predicated is a certain language. To be sure, some scholastic writers must be praised for having worked out a vocabulary equal to that of the exact sciences in precision and definiteness. But philosophic disciplines are things so human that they can hardly do without beauty of expression. The awakening of philosophic thought, as well as its communication, often requires the help of poetry. Scholastic writings are notorious for lacking the very qualities of style that philosophy needs if it is to be really alive and to achieve steady progress. This state of affairs was particularly shocking in France, where modern philosophy was founded by great writers. The school of St. Thomas badly needed a man capable of writing with art. Scholastic style is bad enough in Latin, but, when it is put in the vernacular, it is generally atrocious.

Maritain soon displayed qualities of intuitive, poetic and thought-provoking expression. However, the circumstances of his calling often made it impossible for him to get the best out of his talents as a writer. For one reason or another, most of his papers and books had to be completed within deadlines. Like Bergson, he could have won much glory in the art of writing. No doubt it has been in full awareness that he has consented to publish, for the service of men, many pages which fall short of the perfection of literary form he could have given them if he had been less interested in the urgent expression of truth. It is not always good to let souls wait until rough material has been polished, until long sentences have been nicely divided and until remarks placed in parentheses or brackets have been harmoniously integrated. In spite of difficult circumstances, there are pages of great beauty in all the works of Maritain. The long preface to the second edition of his book on Bergson demonstrates best his power as an artist. These eighty-six pages are a thing of beauty, where one could hardly find any defect.

Maritain has been and remains a nonspecialized philosopher. He has done important work in all parts of philosophy. He is the author of a treatise of formal logic, which was supposed to be followed by a volume of material logic that circumstances never allowed him to write. In several parts of his work there are essays belonging to the philosophy of inanimate nature, to the philosophy of life, to psychology; and everybody knows how voluminous is his contribution in metaphysics, ethics, and politics. True, of the many volumes which make up his works, only a few have the kind of unity that such a well-organized mind was capable of achieving. Not by choice, most of Maritain's books are made up of lectures and essays. He was often needed as a speaker and, rightly or wrongly, he always believed that he had no gift for extemporaneous speech. Almost all his lectures were written from the first to the last word. I am even tempted to say that most of the time what he did for his audiences was not to deliver a lecture but rather to read a booklet. A few weeks later the booklet, carefully revised and generally expanded, would be published as a journal article, and eventually, after considerable work toward completeness and greater accuracy, a few articles would be published in book form. Some of Maritain's best books would seem to be poorly constructed if we did not know that the real unit is not the book itself but each of the essays that have become its chapters. The great book entitled *The Degrees of Knowledge* (1932) is by no means a treatise on the degrees of knowledge. It is a collection of papers written as lectures about philosophy and experimental science, about the meaning of critical realism, about the greatness and the poverty of metaphysics, and about philosophy and mystical experience. All these papers have been revised with extreme care and the reader does not, at any time, feel that his expectation is frustrated by lack of order. *The Degrees of Knowledge* would be something completely different if it had been conceived as a systematic and complete treatise. I am not sure that it would have been better. The method actually followed by Maritain may have given him the best chance to fulfill his calling, which was not so much to treat questions without discontinuity as to awaken philosophical understanding in a great variety of domains and to demonstrate what the philosophy of St. Thomas is able to do for us in the difficulties, the possibilities and the yearnings of our time. Let it be remarked, however, that when Maritain wanted to write, not one essay after another, but a genuine book, planned as a book from the first day, he succeeded beautifully. The first edition of *Art and Scholasticism* is a masterwork of organization. In later editions, organization is somewhat weakened

by the addition of more papers on art, on poetry and on beauty.
But these papers we like to have under the same cover as *Art and
Scholasticism*. True, the disadvantages of short compositions disappear, for the most part, when they are put together according
to subjects. If we want to know about the theory of the sciences,
we are certainly going to read *The Degrees of Knowledge*. The
better informed will also read *Science and Wisdom*. But who would
suspect that there is a paper on this subject in a book entitled
Scholasticism and Politics? It is our hope that the Jacques Maritain Center at Notre Dame will accomplish the work of reorganiza-
tion which matters so much for the influence of Maritain in the
future. The task is worthy: let us not forget that since 1644—the
date of John of St. Thomas' death—there has been only one man
of genius among the followers of St. Thomas.

We now propose to describe the subjects where Maritain's gifts
of intuitive familiarity are at their best. This critic of Bergson, this
philosopher who spent so much of his life explaining and vindicat-
ing conceptual knowledge and who never missed a chance to use
those "scholastic distinctions" that ignoramuses mistake for vain
subtleties, gives evidence of a mind in which philosophic discovery
and progress are constantly enhanced by the intuitions of the contemplative, the artist, the believer, and the man of charity.

First comes metaphysics, which abounds in all of Maritain's
writings. For its central position, its thought-provoking power, its
liveliness and constant association of science and poetry, I recom-
mend *A Preface to Metaphysics* (original title: *Seven Lectures on
Being and the First Principles of Theoretical Reason*, 1934). Written in "spoken" language, these seven lectures were taken in short-
hand and later somewhat polished, but the style of oral exposition
was intentionally retained.

Maritain was still very young when he wrote *Art and Scholasticism. The Responsibility of the Artist* on the other hand was published in 1960. I expect him to write papers on art and beauty until

his last day. Thus, many are still to come if our prayers are listened
to. Let our attention now be directed to a paradox of great significance. That an artist should be interested in scholasticism, should
find a philosophy of art in St. Thomas, Cajetan, and John of St.
Thomas, and should use the principles of this philosophy to understand and explain what is going on in the vanguard of painting,
music and poetry in the twentieth century, will remain one of the
best surprises that ever confronted historians of philosophy. What
"scholasticism" meant when Maritain was a young man has become
hard to realize, precisely because of the work he has been doing,
for half a century, especially in the domain of the philosophy of
art. "Scholasticism" was never in vital communication with the
living energies of temporal communities. Even at its best it was an
academic and ecclesiastical affair. (The name of Descartes does
not appear in John of St. Thomas' *Courses* of philosophy and theology any more than the name of John of St. Thomas appears in
the works of Descartes.) At the begining of the present century,
"Scholasticism" suffered from having been deprived of genius for
two and a half centuries. The monks and seminary professors who
delivered and published courses of "scholastic" philosophy were
not all inept, and we should not find it below our dignity to learn
from such teachers as Zigliara and San Severino. Men like these
two really believe what they teach, and their erudition is useful.
Their metaphysical thought is by no means lifeless, but the thing
that they cannot achieve is to impart a new life to metaphysics. In
the great universities of the world it was generally taken for granted
that there existed no such thing as a science of metaphysics; no
professor of the Sorbonne or of the University of Berlin had ever
heard such names as San Severino or Zigliara. In fact, what was
going on in philosophy departments at the turn of the century was
generally not very important. The genius of Western nations was
producing masterworks in history, the sciences, technology and the
fine arts, but there was no communication between these domains
of intellectual vitality and the sound work that a few seminary

teachers offered to the world in a very particular language. It has been said that a word is "a little poem born of the people's spontaneity." Such poems are absent from the best as well as from the worst products of "scholastic" philosophy in the nineteenth century. After having read the first essays of Maritain on Bergson, Léon Bloy wrote in his diary that philosophy had quite a new appearance when it was treated by his godson. "[I have] read in the *Revue Thomiste* a paper of my godson Jacques Maritain, 'The Two Bergsonisms.' That I have little use for philosophy is well known: In my opinion it is the most boring way of wasting the precious time of our lives and its Hyrcanian dialect discourages me. But with Jacques Maritain things are strikingly different . . . . It never occured to me that the shabby jacket of a philosopher could clothe such a strong arm. The arm is that of an athlete and the voice expresses a powerful lamentation. I felt at the same time something like a wave of sorrowful poetry, a mighty wave coming from very far."

Together with metaphysics and the philosophic reflection on art, mystical life is one of the areas where Maritain is most at home and exercises, as it were effortlessly, his intuitive gifts. The importance of the studies on mysticism in *The Degrees of Knowledge* cannot be exaggerated. It is good that there should be a book in which the ways proper to mystical experience, as well as those proper to the positive sciences, are compared with those of philosophy and theology. It is good, in particular, that a philosopher should have taken the trouble of explaining to us how the sentences of a theologian and those of a mystical writer may express agreement at a very deep level although they sound contradictory. Such explanation could be given only by a philosopher familiar with the great epistemological notions of formal abstraction, degree of abstraction, standpoint, formal and material object, formal object *quod* and formal object *quo*. As already noted, Maritain knows St. John of the Cross as well as he knows St. Thomas. These two geniuses use considerably different methods of thought and expres-

sion. St. Thomas says that judgment about things divine may proceed by way of cognition—the result is scientific theology, the
sacred doctrine—or by way of inclination—the result is mystical
experience (*Sum. Theol.*, I. 1, 6.ad 3.). Maritain is familiar with
both of these ways. It is for very good reasons that the full title of
The Degrees of Knowledge is *Distinguish to Unite or The Degrees
of Knowledge.*

I have mentioned three areas marked by the excellence of intuitive familiarity. In other domains, Maritain did an immense
amount of work whose quality is often equal to that of the work
done in these three distinguished areas. The difference concerns
less the work done by the writer than the work to be done by the
reader. Granted that the case of a dull or lazy reader is hopeless
anyway, it should be said that in such a domain as art, understanding is powerfully aided by the intuitive warmth of the text. When
Maritain writes about mathematics, physics, and politics, what he
says may be deeply true and valuable in many respects, but the
reader is not helped by the warmth of intuitive familiarity as he
would be if the subject were art or mysticism.

The lecture on philosophy and experimental science which became one of the most important chapters of *The Degrees of Knowledge* was given about 1925. Here, while ceaselessly concerned with
uniting the efforts of the mind toward truth, Maritain shows by what
vital operations the study of the physical world splits into two
ways of thought: one is properly described as philosophic, and the
other is commonly called scientific. I am happy to say that an
important reason why I followed the teaching of Maritain more
than that of any other contemporary philosopher is precisely his
treatment of the relation between science and philosophy. In recent
years, controversies on those subjects have been violent, and Maritain's positions were attacked with a somewhat paradoxical zeal.
Why is it that while diversity has been asserted by the constant
direction of scholarly labor over generations and centuries, an
aspiration in plain conflict with the stream of history continues to

appeal successfully to many minds? When this question is clearly stated, it is easy to see that Maritain's position and that of his most intelligent opponents do not diverge so sharply as some believe. The truth is that the ideas expressed in *The Degrees of Knowledge* on the science and the philosophy of nature were only the beginning of a doctrine which urgently called for further elaboration, perhaps by its originator and certainly by his students. But after the publication of *The Degrees of Knowledge,* Maritain's enormous capacity for work was almost entirely dedicated to other subjects. As for his students, they were few, and they did not do the job.

The writings on politics may be, at the present time, the most celebrated and widely-discussed part of Maritain's work. It is important to remember that he came quite late to political and related subjects. Prior to 1926, his writings contain scattered allusions to political ideas which were in the air. Almost simultaneously we notice these new and consequential occurrences: for one thing, Maritain's creative interest comes to include the philosophy of societies; for another, from now on, a great part of his philosophic work will be concerned with the public events of the day. To ascertain the meaning of Maritain's writings in politics, to understand his dispositions as an observer of public events and the style of his expositions, it is indispensable to keep in mind that his career as a social and political thinker began when he was nearing forty-five. It is still more important to remember that the events which occasioned the new directions of his work were grave and, in more than one respect, heartbreaking. In 1926, the movement called *L'Action française* went into a crisis and soon was condemned by the Church. It is difficult to recount this strange story in its entirety (save in the roughest outline), much less to explain it. Some aspects of the case remain obscure and are likely never to be clarified quite satisfactorily.

By the time I went to Paris as a university student (1920), *Action française* was constantly gaining influence among intellectuals. It was a school of thought and a league rather than a party. Founded in the last years of the nineteenth century, its program was the restoration of traditional monarchy. But the word *program* is not strong enough, for the faith of the *Action française* people, and their readiness to take the words of their leaders were such that the restoration of monarchy in France (after a few years of daily excitement) had become the all-embracing solution to the problem of evil.

The daily paper, entitled *L'Action française,* was directed and, to a large extent, composed by two writers of great distinction, Léon Daudet and Charles Maurras. The son of a famous novelist, Daudet was himself the author of a few novels, but he was far better at writing memoirs and polemics. Maurras was the doctrinal leader of the school. It is hard to say what kind of thinker and what kind of man he was. In spite of highly dignified manners which resembled those of a philosopher, his interests were not philosophical in any technical sense. Rather, he was a classicist, an artist whose ideals were derived from Greek and Latin patterns. He could also be a powerful journalist. The deepest feature of his intellectual personality was perhaps the ideal of a state conceived as a work of art and governed by rules akin to those of the fine arts. The literary level of the whole enterprise was so excellent that if you had any feeling for French literature, you could have a pleasant breakfast every morning by reading the daily editorials of *Action française,* even though you might detest its ideas.

The movement was widely different from the various royalist groups which, despite the steady progress of republican ideas in nearly all parts of the nation, had never died out. It did not have the conservative, traditionalistic, upperclass, and aristocratic externals without which other royalist groups would have been inconceivable. With regard to religion, the make-up and the positions of *Action française* were somewhat paradoxical. It was the most outspoken adversary of republican anticlericalism and of the "secular laws" to which the French Republic was so firmly devoted.

Yet Charles Maurras was a complete agnostic. As a result of his cult of classical antiquity, he was known to have written a few pages of definitely pagan and anti-Christian inspiration. There were practicing Catholics among the leaders of the movement. Léon Daudet was one of them. Others were reputed to have no religion and even to be hostile to Christianity. In the years to which we are referring, the influence of *Action française* in the Catholic world was great. Most of the theologians who were friends of Maritain were also, almost as a matter of course, friends of *Action française* and indeed there was a time when a Thomist opposed to this movement looked eccentric, undependable, and rather ridiculous. Few cared to assume such an appearance.

In the summer of 1926, the Archibshop of Bordeaux published a letter exhorting the youth to keep away from *Action française,* whose influence was described, in very severe terms, as a danger to the essence of the Christian spirit. This document was shortly followed by a letter of the Pope to the Archbishop. While emphasizing the freedom of Catholics with regard to forms of government, Pope Pius XI approved the effort of the Archbishop of Bordeaux to check the influence of *Action française,* especially among the youth. An extremely bitter and violent crisis developed rapidly. On September 19, 1926, Maritain published his first political writing, a pamphlet entitled *An Opinion on Charles Maurras and the Duty of the Catholics.* At that time, what was meant to be obligatory in the Pope's directions was not entirely clear. But following the outright revolt of *Action française,* the daily paper as well as several books of Maurras were soon placed on the Index of Forbidden Books (December 29, 1926). The Catholics of *Action française* responded, roughly, in three ways. Some submitted reluctantly and kept their submission at a minimum. Others did not submit at all and for thirteen years remained in a state of rebellion. Many however submitted generously. To these the understanding of the case, so difficult at the beginning, came gradually. Out of an act of painful obedience, the loftiest kind of freedom was born for a number of souls.

Maritain never had had any formal connection with the now-condemned organization. But *Action française* had often praised him as a philosopher and had, indeed, contributed to the success of his early works. In 1922, the book *Antimoderne* was reviewed by Léon Daudet in his two-column, first-page editorial. As far as I remember, the job was quite well done and certainly helped to make Maritain known to a relatively large public. It is perhaps mostly because of the way *Action française* had recommended him that when the crisis came, Maritain felt it a duty to help puzzled minds and souls in peril. Prior to the condemnation of the movement, he had published the already-mentioned pamphlet on the duty of Catholics in which a sharp criticism of Maurras did not prevent him from voicing the hope that conditions of peace could still be provided. After the condemnation came *The Things That Are Not Caesar's* (original title: *Primacy of the Spiritual*). This book contained both theological studies on the relations of Church and State, and a timely, practical, apostolic, and fraternal message to beloved souls in the darkness of their ordeal. It soon became obvious to many that the effect of "Primacy" was profound and would be lasting. Today we realize that a new era had been opened, the characteristics of which were an ardent quest for theological enlightenment, an uncompromising sense of the intrinsic excellence and the irreducible worth of the temporal common good, and, finally, a burning zeal for the duty of helping, with all the resources of charity, humility, and knowledge, souls who could not wait, since they were engaged in a conflict involving eternity. In the years to come, situations characterized by darkness, by devotion to the temporal city, by an overwhelming sense of the primacy of things eternal, and by a loving understanding of the uniqueness of a personal calling in the midst of common anguish, were to occur again and again. The precedent set by *Primacy of the Spiritual* was to be followed by many more words ardently directed toward the understanding of what was going on in an immensely suffering world. Despite some appearances, and the very intense activity of theological wisdom and apostolic charity, the writings of Maritain would remain those of a philosopher whose effort always is, in some way or other, centered on problems natural, human, and temporal. Even in his strongest assertions concerning the primacy of the spiritual, Maritain would be faithful to the philosopher's calling with all that it implies regarding the natural character of the wisdom to be worked out in the midst of ordeals which involve our supernatural destiny.

The crisis of *Action française* ended only in 1939, with a formula of submission and repentance. Many things had happened in the meantime. I feel that I am no longer young when I see all around me boys and girls to whom the Spanish Civil War does not mean so much. It is already an old story. How many Spaniards died in this war? One million is a reasonable estimate, and a rather conservative one. The thing that I cannot say is what fraction of that million died on the battlefield. Beyond doubt, the ratio of those killed outside of all military action was very high. Whenever someone says that a huge amount of crime was committed only on the other side, he either lies or does not know all the facts. Besides the slaughter, the Spanish Civil War brought about, and not in Spain alone, an extraordinary indulgence in hatred and in the most debased feelings the human soul ever conceived. The French were close to the Spanish War in more than one respect. Lies about every subject that pertained to the ordeal of Spain were really atrocious. Spanish refugees who were pouring into France comprised all sorts of characters, from the most noble to the most undependable. We all felt that we had an urgent duty to do something about the misfortune of our neighbors and its international consequences. Maritain stood for mediation between the parties at war. So did I.

We met in committees with a faint hope that the crushing victory of one side and the slaughter of the other might be avoided. Anyway, committees were needed to organize some sort of aid for refugees. Besides works of relief, this much at least could be attempted: to save a few souls from systematic falsehood. Once more Maritain was taken into the world of action by the demands of truth and of charity. The effect of such circumstances on political thinking is obvious. Political philosophers and theologians have a tendency to oversimplify things and to derive obnoxious satisfaction from the host of illusions that their lack of experience renders inevitable. As the Spanish Civil War was going on, Maritain could not even be tempted to write papers or books on the abstract behavior of political and social essences. The circumstances made it necessary for his quickly-maturing political thought to stay in the midst of particular facts. The interest that he was then developing was especially concerned with historical trends. (His most important writing in this connection is his long preface to the book of Alfredo Mendizabal, *Martyrdom of Spain,* 1939.)

Indeed, a social or political essence cannot afford to exist without being marked by the contingency of factual situations. If we study, for instance, the relation between the temporal and the spiritual powers, let it be understood, from the beginning, that whatever is essential and necessary in this relation is always accompanied by features which do not belong in essential, necessary and universal fashion to the relation between the spiritual and the temporal. When such issues are considered practically—and this is the proper way to consider them, for they are practical issues—the feature born of contingency may be of decisive significance. Accordingly, it is most unreasonable to assume that a problem such as, say, the relation of Church and State, admits of basically identical solutions in Spain and in Ireland, or in the Spain of the seventeenth century and in that of our time. Generally speaking, to assume that an analysis of essences can ever suffice to take care of an issue modified by contingency, in other words, to assume that moral science can deal with contingent matters without being supplemented by the virtue of prudence, is a silly illusion which should not have survived the criticism of Socrates by Aristotle. But prudence, as philosophers and theologians understand it, is a kind of wisdom so hard to get, to keep and to manage, that under a variety of names mankind is likely always to nurture the ideal of a science which would suffice to trace our way in this world of contingency.

These are elementary remarks, and yet no more is needed to make the philosopher feel very uncertain about his role in human communities. After it is clearly understood that no scientific method will answer a question relative, in any way whatsoever, to contingent data, it soon becomes easy to understand that the philosopher, far from being able to answer *philosophically* the questions which puzzle his fellow citizens, may well be at a disadvantage and have particular reasons to remain silent. In order to acquire any kind of social and political prudence, a great deal of human experience is necessary. But a philosopher is a man who has spent his youth in libraries, in classrooms, in laboratories, in museums, and other such places where opportunities for human experience are at a minimum. It seems that the question is decided by these simple remarks: far from owing to his knowledge distinguished abilities for making judgments about the affairs of the community, the philosopher would be almost inevitably bound, by the circumstances of his career, to be a poorly-trained citizen, who should feel diffident when he is tempted to take part in public affairs. Of course, this would not prevent him from joining committees and exercising charity when, as a result of a civil war, hungry women and children are looking for help in a country where it is still possible to find food and shelter.

But this is only one side of the story, as I was led to understand by an incident of my own career. My first political writing, if I omit a few articles in my student years, was a short study on the Ethiopian War, or more exactly on the attitudes of French political thinkers toward Mussolini's war in Ethiopia. As this pamphlet was about to be published, I happened to describe it to an old friend whom I had known in groups formed for the study of international organizations. He was a man of sharp intelligence and fine education, a jurist by training, and a civil servant of high rank. Some prominent and noisy intellectuals had just given Mussolini the support of an enthusiastic manifesto. My friend listened attentively to my exposition. He interrupted me with this remark: "*You* are trained in the handling of abstract ideas." In another context this remark would have meant that a philosopher is restricted to abstractions and has no sense of political contingencies. But this is not what he had in mind. He plainly meant that to fulfill such a task as the defense of public conscience against corruption by politicians and intellectuals a few so-called abstract ideas, e.g., those of right, law, contract, community, authority, force, legal coercion, violence, autonomy, and civilization have got to be handled, and that in order that they be handled properly, philosophical training is necessary, or very helpful. To answer the question as to whether philosophers ever have a duty to take a stand with regard to temporal events such as a war, a revolution, a persecution, or the condemnation of an innocent person, we need only to understand the simple remark that my friend did me the honor of making on the occasion of my pamphlet. In order that the duties of prudence be fulfilled, it is sometimes necessary that the prudent man should have more than a commonsense ability to handle "abstract ideas." The need for such ability is still more obvious when there is a question of contributing as much truth as possible to the visions which animate a community, to its *ideology*—if this word can be freed from all unfavorable connotations.

Maritain was well trained in the handling of abstract ideas. Furthermore, he had a religious and mystical sense for the relation of time to eternity. He had all that prudence required, over and above the properly prudential qualities, in order that devotion to truth and justice should be worthily represented in a dialogue in which the most brutish appetites were both hidden and strengthened by the power of "abstract ideas" and of corrupt mysticism.

To accomplish the task we are trying to characterize, the understanding of historical trends is decisively important. An "historical trend" is the behavior of a social or political essence as modified by a situation which, in spite of its contingency, covers and governs a long period over large areas of human communities. When an historical trend is properly identified, it can be safely said that, as things go on, its characteristic features will be more and more unmistakably determined. And thus, within an order of things marked by contingency, we have to deal with a system which, as far as the purposes of action are concerned, assumes a character of necessity almost as definite as that of an essential type. It can be said, without any disorderly indulgence in metaphor, that the possible behaviors of a social or political essence are restricted to a small number of forms. Whoever has identified an historical trend has understood the law of the form which will predominate, again, over large areas and over long periods. Besides all that pertained to the immediate service of truth and charity against stubborn falsehood and hatred, the work of Maritain, in relation to the Spanish Civil War, consisted mostly in understanding what types of behavior had been assumed, in the lasting contingency of ages marked by such events as the Reformation, the Liberal Revolution, and Socialism, by such an issue as the relation between Church and State, and by such an ideal as that of the Christian state.

A student told me some time ago that he disliked in Maritain the constant association of the philosophic discourse with the apostolic concern. What my answer was I do not remember, but I think I know what it should have been. For one thing, I should have re-marked that most readers and auditors are themselves so interested in the connections between philosophy and religion that they do not want philosophical problems to be treated in isolation, that is, apart from the religious issues to which they are related vitally, though not essentially, in the longing of men for the truths which matter most in terms of human destiny. The thing which cannot be tolerated under any circumstances is that orders be confused, and that philosophic issues be treated according to revealed principles without a plain statement that we are no longer in philosophy. But such a confusion —a frequent accident, indeed, in the history of Christian thought— is particularly repugnant to a Thomist. In the discussions which have been going on for over thirty years on the notion of "Christian philosophy," Maritain has never failed to recall, against any possible misunderstanding, that this expression designates a *state* of philosophy, not an essence. If it designated an essence, it would be granted that philosophy receives premises from revelation, and of the great statements of St. Thomas concerning philosophy, theology, and their relationship, nothing would be left. When these positions are clearly formulated, the question remains as to whether it is desirable that philosophical issues be treated in a state of abstraction or in a concrete condition of association with the problems of our supernatural destiny. I would not hesitate to say that it is, to a large extent, a question of calling. I am strongly attracted by the method of isolation because it furnishes special guaranties of epistemological purity and logical rigor. To be sure, Maritain will never be tempted to use a revealed premise in a philosophical treatment. But there can be no doubt that his calling is that of the Christian philosopher who generally treats philosophical issues in the particular *state* that they assume by reason of their relation to Christian faith and theology.

Likewise, when we come to practical issues, it may be asked whether it is desirable that what is essential and scientific in them should be treated in the state of scientific isolation, or in association with problems of prudential nature. Again, the answer is, to a large extent, determined by one's particular calling. In order that we should, at all times, be aware of what we are doing, in order that epistemological purity be preserved, it is certainly desirable that some men should write treatises of political philosophy or theology where the consideration of contingency and the decisions of prudence play as small a part as possible. But what the calling of Maritain was is not dubious. We have seen that all his writings on political and social subjects were composed under circumstances which, purely and simply, demanded an extensive exercise of historical intelligence and prudential judgment.

In this long exposition, little has been said about the moral personality of Maritain. What would have been the use of expressing admiration for a man to whom I am well known to owe so much? By way of conclusion, I wish, however, to remark that there may well be a difference between the calling of a man and his choice. By "choice" I mean what he would have chosen if he had had his own way. I suspect that there have been many conflicts throughout Maritain's career between his choice and his calling. And I cannot think of a single case in which his calling was not preferred to his choice. Remote ages may find it relevant to remark that Maritain is the philosopher who, in case of conflict, never hesitated to fulfill his calling rather than to follow his choice.

James Collins

2. Maritain's Impact on Thomism in America

IN ANY THOUGHTFUL APPRAISAL of Jacques Maritain's work, there is a middle range of perspective which should not be overlooked. It stands somewhere between his effect upon American intellectual life as a whole and his quite specialized contributions to this or that philosophical discipline. This further dimension is his general influence upon Thomistic philosophy in its American form. It is bound up with his specialized work, and its consequences are felt in the American intellectual community at large. Nevertheless, we would be neglecting one of the major aspects of his achievement if we did not attempt to examine separately the pervasive impact of Maritain's thought on American Thomism.

The present essay is an independent reflection upon what the active presence of Maritain has meant and means for practising Thomists in our country. His significance for them can perhaps be brought out by developing three themes: the personal example of his philosophizing, the manner and range of his doctrinal investigations, and some crucial problems raised in the wake of his work.

1. *The Philosopher at Work*

The most elusive portion of Maritain's significance is the encouragement which he has given to Thomistic philosophical studies by the example of his own presence and labors. It is very difficult at this time to have a vivid grasp of the distance which Thomism has travelled in America since the survey made by Father Zybura in 1927.[1] The description he gave of the bleak condition of Scholastic thought was accurate enough, and was backed up in every particular by the replies sent in by non-Scholastic professors. From the Zybura report and the accompanying commentaries, it is clear that Scholasticism was regarded as a mental regimen entirely foreign to American education, as being practically inaccessible even to those conscientious scholars who would like to study it in English, and as having no demonstrable bearing upon the going concerns in philosophy.

This condition did not change overnight and in part it still describes the opinion of many American philosophers. However, a private correspondence carried on about fifteen years later with some of the contributors to the Zybura volume showed that, by that date, the situation was being modified in two important respects. For one thing, the leading American philosophers were now beginning to refer more specifically to Thomism rather than to a vague and global sort of Neo-Scholasticism. There was a growing awareness of a definite sort of philosophy having its sources in St. Thomas. Moreover, the majority of the correspondents mentioned explicitly their debt to Etienne Gilson for instruction in the history of medieval philosophy and to Maritain for providing a contemporary representation of the thought of St. Thomas. Through the writings of Maritain and Gilson, the leading teachers and writers in philosophy were coming to recognize that Thomism is not only a definite structure of theological thought but also involves philosophical evidence and argumentation. This did not entail any widespread acceptance of Thomism, but at least it opened the way for whatever serious philosophical discussion has occurred during the last twenty years between American Thomists and other philosophers.

Within the Catholic community itself, Maritain's presence in America has made more concrete and feasible the ideal of a Christian layman devoting himself entirely to the work of philosophy, whether as a Thomist or not. Maritain's fidelity to that vocation has encouraged laymen to devote their scholarly energy to work in the field of philosophy. It has also helped them to see that one can engage in rigorous and fruitful philosophical studies precisely as a Christian thinker who is also responsive to the influence of his faith. Although each individual has to work out his own mode of philosophizing in the Christian spirit, it is liberating to see this living intercourse between faith and philosophy, without there being any undermining of the assent and the evidence proper to each.

Maritain has not always been fortunate in his English translators, and his French prose itself is often very thorny. But a reading of his books is part of the liberal education of American Thomists, whose sources and customary terminology are in the Latin. Maritain is addressing contemporary men in their own tongue, exploring the resources of the living language for embodying classical doctrine, making the vernacular serve not only as a conveyor of old formulas but also as a means of reaching new insights. He brings out in practice a way of closing the gap which exists between accepting the general recommendation of thinking and writing Thomism in the living tongue and actually trying to do it. It has been said about certain German idealists and existentialists that it is kinder to their reputation to leave them in the original, rather than attempt to present them in English. Maritain is confident about the survival of St. Thomas in translation. But perhaps even more significant is his sense of responsibility for reworking the doctrine of St. Thomas in one's own French or English prose, so that the thought can be brought into familiar relationship with our daily experience and the course of scientific and artistic and social creations.

On this latter point, Maritain's import has not yet been fully grasped by American Thomists. They take it for granted that most Thomistic manuals are to be composed in plain English. Yet they do not always see how important it is both for the vitality of Thomistic thought and for its spread to use all the resources of the English language and literature in rethinking and expressing the doctrines. Maritain's own lifelong struggle with the naming word has not yet borne proper fruit, if we can judge by the slight concern shown by many American Thomists for style. Such a concern is too easily written off as a mere embellishment, easily offset by the soundness of doctrine. As a consequence, the articles and books on Thomism still lack the ring of native talk and the power of English prose. We do not have to possess the special poetic endowment of the Maritains to appreciate the need for keeping alive to the question of how to combine accuracy of statement with a firm and clean hold on the living medium of our language.[2]

There is another trait of Maritain's mind, however, which has had a formative influence on American Thomists: his personal enthusiasm for St. Thomas as man, thinker, and saint.[3] Here there is a convergence between Maritain and Gilson, and the effect of their joint impact is to produce in our country a warm and widespread attachment to St. Thomas in philosophical matters which lacks a parallel in Europe. Most American Thomists have not made the long journey from Bergson or some other contemporary philosopher to the Common Doctor, an intellectual experience which was decisive for Maritain himself. Nevertheless, they find that a personal appreciation of St. Thomas is indispensable for improving their understanding of his doctrine and sustaining their detailed analysis and use of his texts.

The problem which this attachment raises for American Thomists is whether it makes them so unresponsive to other philosophies that they cut themselves off, in a sectarian spirit, from the common concerns of the philosophical world and thus become ineffective. At least in Maritain's own case, it is clear that this is not a necessary consequence. There has been no atrophying of his relations with the contemporary world and no dulling of his responsibility for dealing with its common problems. Yet many Thomists have been slow to learn from him that there is no uniform and automatically effective resolution of the difficulty. It requires a personal act of synthesis to establish one's own working pattern for rooting oneself in the Thomistic sources in such a way as to remain actively involved in the philosophical investigations of our time. That this act is a free one and requires independent work, rather than imitation on the individual Thomist's part, is a lesson found in Maritain, but sometimes studied only with considerable reluctance.

2. *The Manner and Span of Inquiry*

The actual effect of Thomism on American Catholic education is a mixed one. At times, it results in an unfortunate nostalgic frame of mind which finds nothing worth investigating in modern philosophies and other intellectual movements, but yearns after a total revival of the intellectual situation of the thirteenth century. In the concrete, this sort of mind asks that only the philosophical efforts made by Thomists be regarded as philosophically sound and that their aim be to produce another *Summa Theologiae*. This attitude rests on several misunderstandings which can be pointed out. It misreads the historical situation of the High Middle Ages, which never experienced a period of unchallenged supremacy for St. Thomas or some other contemporary theologian. Furthermore, this outlook fails to take the uniqueness of history very seriously, since it is always waiting for the work of St. Thomas to repeat itself under only superficially different circumstances. Hence the tendency is to underestimate the intellectual resources developed in the modern world. Our prime responsibility in philosophy is taken to be historical recall made for its own sake rather than for the sake of approaching the problems of our own world with richer principles and perspectives.

On all these counts, Maritain must be regarded as a corrective whose critical import has not yet been fully appreciated. He underlines the fact that St. Thomas had to do battle for his teachings under conditions of constant criticism. He also regards as significant the grand scale on which St. Thomas engaged in close study and critical evaluation of the sources in Greek, Arabic, Jewish, and Patristic thought. The individual thinker who does creative work in philosophy must expect to receive criticism from other standpoints and must, in turn, devote considerable effort to an examination of the best positions available in his day. This throws some light on Maritain's reference to his own philosophical activity as a "Thomisticizing." By that term, he means remaining loyal to the full spirit of St. Thomas, apart from any connotation of narrowing down his intelligence and his sensibility. It means coming into methodical possession of the basic evidence concerning man and God as seen by St. Thomas, and using these truths as a center of evaluation and integration in regard to the philosophical problems facing contemporary man.[4] The office of the Thomist is neither to alienate himself from the tides of inquiry nor to exhaust himself in trying to bring about a massive conformity of thought. He must investigate such diverse positions as logical positivism and phenomenology, Freudianism and Eastern mysticism, appreciating the attraction of such movements, pointing out their aspects of shortcoming and failure, and incorporating their well evidenced views into a responsive and growing Thomism.

The connection between this conception of an open Thomism and Maritain's view of culture and history is not always seen. Human history is not a cyclic round but a creative thrust which involves newness as well as continuity. Since it does not advance through completely discrete leaps or through mere surface variation of the same pattern, historical becoming follows the course of analogically similar developments.[5] The rule of analogy holds good also for historical efforts at achieving a new realization for a philosophical system. Hence present-day Thomists have to respect the historical conditions under which alone they can fruitfully seek to restate the evidence used by St. Thomas. Their aim is not to provide a dim echo of what he once said, for the outcome of such a plan could only be a fraudulent kind of fidelity to the truth he served. What the Thomistic philosopher can try to do is to make a careful reading of St. Thomas, reflect on what the human mind has brought to light in subsequent centuries on some of the issues, and then make his own responsible inspection of the evidence and his own judgment about where the truth of it lies. He can expect that his final position will bear the marks both of his careful study of the Thomistic sources and of his independent inquiry into the present ways of man in nature, in society, and in search of God.

Maritain's approach to philosophical questions is not primarily a historical one. This is sometimes said by way of reproach, as though the only satisfactory handling of them is the historical mode. On this issue, one can easily get lost in a deluding verbalism. Every Thomist seeking firsthand knowledge must make a careful reading of the text of St. Thomas, as well as clarify its meaning in the light of all he can gather about St. Thomas' sources, methods, and discussions with contemporaries. In this sense, the thoroughly trained Thomist cannot avoid taking the historical approach. But there is a distinction between making a many-sided study of the sources and coming to one's own philosophical judgment in the light of them and whatever other aids one uses. This latter operation still remains to be completed, even after one has become well informed about the text of St. Thomas. And it is here that a legitimate diversity develops between the various ways employed to arrive at one's own philosophical judgment as a Thomist philosopher. Some minds reach this act chiefly through a comparative analysis and generalization of the historical materials in philosophy; others reach it chiefly through bringing Thomistic principles to bear upon problems as they present themselves in contemporary form. This difference in the ways of judgment is usually a matter of degree and not of exclusive opposition, although the individual mind ordinarily finds one of them to be more suitable to his capacities and special work.

Maritain follows the latter path. He teaches us how to use Thomistic resources of principles and evidence in treating the great problems in philosophy as they present themselves to our contemporary world.[6] We can profit by his example in this order without lessening our respect for, and often our real need of, the other path which leads through a critical and comparative analysis of the historical modes of philosophizing. To erect an opposition between the two means ordinarily employed for reaching philosophically grounded assent is needless and imprudent.

It will be helpful to probe a little deeper into one component in the dream of an anachronistic type of Thomism: its expectation of another *Summa* and its dissatisfaction in principle with anything else. As a practical state of mind, this means an inability to appreciate the worth of those Thomistic achievements which are actually brought forth or to contribute positively to our everyday understanding of familiar Thomistic statements and arguments. Once more, the difficulty springs from making an impossible demand for a repetitious and fundamentally univocal sort of intellectual history. A revival of Thomism in this sense cannot be accomplished under human historical conditions, and to wait for it means to sap one's initiative and critical probity. For a viable alternative, it is well to observe the spirit in which Maritain attacks a wide span of topics without pretending to be restoring the medieval synthesis.

What we have already called the middle range of perspective on Maritain consists precisely in taking a synoptic view of his works in their comprehensive scope. Even in a specialized sort of question, he does not lose sight of its wider context and its role in the whole process of philosophical inquiry. That is why *The Degrees of Knowledge* still furnishes the key for an understanding of his mind, despite the book's difficulty and the later developments made by him in existential metaphysics and social philosophy. All of Maritain's particular studies find their proper location within his gen-

eral study of the kinds and degrees of knowledge. They are treated
separately for purposes of scientific distinction and analysis, but
this is done so that they can be united together in the complex and
determinate order established by philosophical wisdom. The spec-
trum of human knowledges is broad and complicated: the task of
the philosopher is to inspect and test the structure of each strand,
respecting its own integrity and also striving to bring it into meaningful union with the others which supplement it. The philosopher
may well fall short of achieving an actual and full integration of the
several human knowledges, but at least he can set forth the typical
structure of each kind and indicate the principles for reaching
unification.

Maritain is not engaged in writing a twentieth-century *Summa,*
but he is performing the scientific and sapiential office of philosophy
in a manner that is at once guided by St. Thomas and alive to the
problems and conquests of our age. He retains his own vocational
difference from St. Thomas by always investigating as a Christian
philosopher, rather than as a Christian theologian who also philosophizes. This approach affects the kind of synthesis which he aims
at reaching through his type of analysis. Although the theologian
can very well profit by his findings and method, Maritain's own
work is formally directed toward a unification of knowledges which
can be achieved by means of a Christian philosophy. There is need
for a formally theological unification and perhaps for other ways
of reaching a synthesis, but it is the kind attainable through a
Christian philosophical wisdom for which he is responsible and to
which his study of the kinds of knowledge is internally adapted.

His respect for the limitations of his own approach is clearly
evident in his treatment of problems to which a Christian philosophy must remain open, without claiming to furnish a definitive
solution. One of these areas is mystical experience, both of a natural
sort and a supernatural sort. A Christian philosopher acknowledges
the reality of both types of mystical knowledge and does his best to
inspect their structure. Yet in doing so, he proceeds as a philosopher

trying to find a natural analogue for the mystical knowledge of the man of faith and trying to establish a set of relations between mystical knowing and our ordinary patterns of knowing.[7] He does not pretend to be dealing with the question in the same way as would the theologian of the mystical life. Maritain observes a similar self-limitation of his analysis when he deals with the principles of moral science. Even in taking his controversial position on an adequately considered morality, his purpose is not to render the work of the moral philosopher superfluous or to merge it with the functions of the theologian, as he develops his own science.[8] His intention is rather to determine the conditions and sources which must contribute to the principles in moral philosophy, at least as found in a concrete and plenary state in the Christian moral philosopher. The question of whether or not the factors specified by Maritain must indeed make the sort of contribution he envisages can be kept distinct from our present point, which concerns the self-limitation of the unifying activity of Christian philosophy in respect to the variety of human knowledges.

This characteristic insistence on the proper method and limits of philosophical wisdom does not make Maritain any the less aware of the profound influence of the Christian faith upon his philosophy. Here, the point of his example for American Thomists is a warning that they should not allow themselves to become prematurely stalled over the difficulties in the notion of a Christian philosophy, especially when that notion is kept at a very general level and separated from particular instances. It is much closer to our ordinary human practice to take an inductive approach to the question by reflecting on actual instances of men who philosophize in the Christian spirit and above all by gaining some experience on one's own. Maritain sees the reality of Christian philosophy partly in the philosophical aspects of the thought of St. Thomas and partly in observing the concrete influences at work in shaping his own acts of philosophizing. The Christian faith keeps his analysis of knowledge open to its full range of diversity, makes the question of a unifying wisdom very acute, and leads him to emphasize such particular aspects in knowledge as the mental word, the personal rooting, and the relation between knowing and loving. Yet it also leaves his mind free to tackle such issues according to the evidence and the order of reasoning proper to a humanly developed philosophy.

Perhaps no aspect of Maritain's approach has impressed itself so deeply upon American Thomists as his preoccupation with questions of knowledge and method. Four general features of this preoccupation are instructive for grasping the conditions for philosophical relevance in our century. First, the realist does make an ultimate reference of his findings to being in its existential act and real nature. But he must also respond to the difficulties raised by the long modern concern for epistemological and methodological questions. He has to dwell formally and in greater detail than did St. Thomas upon the ways in which we know natural being, existential act, and the forms of individual and social life. These noetic ways must be explicitly thematized in a Thomism which seeks the assent of contemporary minds. In the second place, however, Maritain's treatment of knowledge is postmodern in the sense that it does not revolve around the classical epistemological issue of whether the mind can reach out to the extra-mental world. He recognizes that this way of posing the problem of knowledge is bound up with Cartesian dualism and hence depends upon a particular set of metaphysical presuppositions, which need not be allowed to dominate the whole inquiry.[9] That there is no good reason any longer for permitting them to specify the entire approach to knowledge is the conviction of most philosophers who remain close to the natural and social sciences. The more a philosopher improves his acquaintance with these sciences, the more likely is he today to concentrate upon the going reality of knowledge in this or that scientific area. This calls for an analytic and descriptive study of the modes of knowing. It also raises the question of whether we can determine something in common to several of these modes and thus achieve their unity. Maritain adapts his approach to these conditions by making his account of the metaphysics of knowing and the unifying work of wisdom arise out of the actual analytic study of some scientific procedures.

In the third instance, Maritain does not permit his ultimate realism to impose a monolithic pattern upon all the ways of knowing. Especially in bringing out the difference between a philosophy of nature and a philosophy of science, he vindicates a place in realism for an analysis of the constructural activities of the mind which account for so many of the triumphs in the modern mathematical and physical sciences.[10] Even when Maritain's particular distinction between the empiriological and the ontological sciences is criticized, his influence among American Thomists has been decisive concerning the relation between realism and the scientific achievement of the modern world. Negatively, realism does not have to suppose that every cognitive activity of the mind must conform with the way in which the human intellect grasps being and makes the existential judgment. And positively stated, this is a factual question which can only be decided by taking a direct look at the several ways in which the human intelligence does operate in bringing forth the sciences and arts. The presence of constructs and their wide usefulness must be fully acknowledged, studied in precise detail, and then compared with the kind of judgmental acts and concepts which yield a knowledge of being in its existential act, its structure of natural change, and its moral reaches.

This leads to the final exemplar quality furnished by Maritain's study of method and knowledge. He has set a sound precedent for American Thomists by doing some field work in the various domains of knowing. Instead of proceeding by means of hasty deductions and synthetic vistas about what the types of knowledge must be and where they must fit into a scheme, he has continued throughout his lifetime to begin at the ground level with a descriptive acquaintance with what is actually being done in the particular area.[11] Part of the freshness of his mind comes from this willingness to remain receptive and to explore new regions on their own terms and with the aid of the best instances. This inductive and exploratory temper of mind, combined with a firm grasp on the metaphysics of knowledge, is Maritain's staying heritage for American Thomists. It is even more basic to appreciate this philosophical habit of mind than to agree with him on this or that particular point. For unless American Thomists approach their tasks in a similar spirit of inquiry, they will not be able to advance the philosophical work of understanding and ordering the various disciplines, facing the new and insistent problems of our institutions, and eventually leading men toward the truth about finite existents and God, the infinite act of existing.

3. The Wake of Problems

Our report on Maritain's significance would be incomplete if we did not indicate how he has stimulated many of the discussions in which the American Thomists are engaged. One matter which has interested them is the extensive use Maritain makes of the writings of John of St. Thomas. His appeal to this authority for a clear restatement of Thomistic doctrine has provoked a study of the relationship which exists between St. Thomas and his commentators. They are no mere repetitors of his teaching, but what they are actually doing with his thought depends upon the particular case. Sometimes, their work is to correlate passages and bring a doctrine to a more explicit, comprehensive, and ordered condition. But at other times, they are presenting their original solutions within the broad framework of Thomistic philosophy. The results of American research suggest that there may be a deep vein of new ideas introduced by the commentators in their treatment of analogy, abstraction, the kinds of concepts, and the constitutive notes of personality. To what extent these writers are making a continuous development of St. Thomas and to what extent they undertake some radical departures from him are questions which can be determined only through a careful comparative analysis. So far, only a start has been made with this problem. But the necessity for continuing to deal with it in order to clarify the kind of use which Thomists can make of the tradition of commentators is reinforced by the effective use which Maritain makes especially of Cajetan and John of St. Thomas.

The key distinction in Maritain between empiriological and ontological sciences has produced a revolution in the customary way of thinking about the distinction between the philosophical disciplines and the natural sciences. Some strict Aristotelians continue to regard the modern sciences as dialectical extensions of the same kind of inquiry found in the Aristotelian philosophy of nature. But continued analysis of the problem along lines suggested by Maritain has convinced many Thomistic philosophers of science that we must distinguish modern science and traditional philosophy of nature quite otherwise than by a mere dialectical extension or by a contrast between the special proximate causes and the ultimate causes.[12] The empiriological or constructural sciences are constituted by a quite distinctive kind of definition, set of principles, and mode of proof. They are not asking the kind of questions about the sensible world which will yield either dialectical or proximate answers in terms of the intrinsic causal principles of changing being. American Thomists are beginning to examine the method of quantitative correlation used so powerfully in the constructural sciences, both in regard to the physical world and in regard to the human psyche and human social forms. Maritain's pioneer work has enabled Thomists to take the modern sciences of nature and man as they are actually constituted. The problem of the unity of the sciences and their relationship to philosophy then becomes acute, but at least the discussion is concerned with the genuine ways in which the scientific mind today operates.

In the field of metaphysics, Maritain has led the way in emphasizing the existential meaning of being.[13] In conformity with his study of the kinds of knowledge, he has directed attention to the correlation between the existential act of the being and our existential judgment. Just as the act of existing is a unique perfecting of the being, so the judgment of existence is unique. It is not a mere product of a connection between concepts obtained previously through apprehension. In maintaining its distinctive character, Maritain has defended the primacy of judgment over the concept and has shown the need for a descriptive approach to the question of how we do form our existential judgment. His own provocative account emphasizes both the human and the intellectual nature of this type of knowledge act, both the need for sense perception of experienced things and the direct ordination of our intellect to the very being of things. In the wake of his analyses, American Thomists have been inquiring about whether our grasp of the existential act is strictly an intuition. They have also been re-reading St. Thomas in order to find a Thomistic meaning for "conception" which can be used to explain the way in which we can reflect upon and reason about our judgment on the act of existing, while nevertheless respecting the ineffable aspect of the existent being itself.

There is a bond between Maritain's treatment of recent existentialism and his approaches to God. His chief concern is not with the systems of the various existentialist writers but rather with the positive aspirations which can be detected in the movement as a whole. What existentialism in the popular sense has brought to formal expression is our common human awareness of the contingency of our being and the yearning of our heart for a reality which transcends the spatio-temporal in which we find ourselves. Maritain uses this basic conviction to suggest another argument for God's existence in addition to the familiar Thomistic ways.[14] Existentialism does not feed solely upon our sense of being contingent and placed in the universe of space and time, but also upon our sense of there being a certain disproportion between these metaphysical conditions and the yearning of our mind and heart for an eternal and immaterial good. Maritain argues that this awareness of a disproportion is a token of the eternal, exemplar reality of the divine mind, to whom we are related through memory as well as through inference.

Our concern is not with the details of this argument but with what it manifests about Maritain's challenge to American Thomists. He is hospitable to modes of reasoning to God which are not reducible to the five Thomistic ways. He suggests that there is a distinctively human awareness of contingency and disproportion which is not simply a variant upon the argument from contingent and necessary being, as defined in terms of the general philosophy of nature and the metaphysics of contingent existents in general. What the existentialists say about the distinctive mode of human contingent being, and what St. Augustine says about the rooting of human memory in an eternal reality not ourselves, are joined together in his argument. It has led Thomists to reopen the whole question of how to treat theistic arguments not readily reducible to the Thomistic ways, whether to regard them as probable rather than demonstrative, and how to explain the philosophical attractiveness (since Newman's time) of ways to God which are based on some distinctive aspects of man's being rather than on what he shares with all other material existents.[15] A moral argument to God has traditionally been appended to the five ways, but Maritain's example suggests that more attention should be paid to contemporary convictions about man which may contain at least some persuasive probable grounds of assent to God. That the task of searching for such grounds and testing their strength belongs to the Thomistic philosopher is one of Maritain's contentions.

In both his study of our knowledge of God and his esthetic inquiries of recent years, Maritain also directs attention to the problem of relating non-philosophical to philosophical knowledge. The actuality of this problem has been brought home to American Thomists, however, at two quite different levels. There is first the fact that we can have a knowledge of God quite apart from the philosophical demonstrations of the truth about His existence. Such knowledge is likely to include an element of faith and also an element of natural reasoning to God. The latter is an instance of natural non-philosophical knowledge which can remain in this condition and be valid without any incorporation into the body of philosophy, apart from the philosopher's reflective awareness of its reality. The work of relating these two kinds of knowledge is made more urgent by the presence of a similar problem in the philosophy of science and in the philosophical analysis of language. In all these cases, American Thomists face the need to clarify the relationship which should obtain between knowledge in the non-scientific state and in the scientific state, including philosophical knowledge. But Maritain also proposes still another meaning for non-philosophical knowledge in his teaching on a pre-philosophical intuition of being in its concrete existing reality. Precisely in its pre-philosophical condition, this intuition makes a founding contribution to his metaphysics of the existent, his special argument for God's existence, his view of moral principles, and his esthetic theory. Several Thomists are weighing the evidence which will indicate whether or not we possess such an intuition, as well as considering how a theory about it can be introduced into the common philosophical dialogue in America.

Are Thomists actively concerned with testing the detailed teachings contained in Maritain's esthetics? At this point in our description of Maritain's impact on American Thomism, we must observe that in many respects he remains a philosophical frontiersman who has blazed some new trails without finding sufficient manpower to follow through for the purpose of testing, consolidating, and extending his gains. Advanced investigations in the field of art and esthetics are practically nonexistent among American Thomists. Here is an area where guidance from classical sources is meager and where the individual inquirer is left pretty much on his own resources. As with the previous problem of style in philosophy, esthetic questions are not given their due importance. The twofold result is that one important way of access to minds is still closed off, and the Thomistic evaluations of works of art remain one-sidedly moral and deprived of their indispensable professional basis in inductive esthetic judgments.

Unfortunately a somewhat similar situation prevails in respect
to Maritain's social and political philosophy. It is welcomed by
American Thomists, especially for its warm defense of democratic
government and human rights, its stress on the religious and personal values in a sound civil society, and its discerning treatment
of such questions as the shape of education and the historical
vocation of the Jewish people. In addition, there has been considerable discussion of the precise import of Maritain's distinction between the individual and the person, which is basic for his conception of the common temporal good of men and their ultimate
religious ordination to God. But what is notably missing is a series
of studies in depth intended to evaluate and develop his leads on
such intermediate matters as the nature of race, people, and nation
and their relation to civil society and the state.[16] There have been
some excellent theological studies in this area. But the point of
Maritain's achievement is largely missed, namely, that the Christian
philosopher bears the responsibility for investigating a whole range
of structures in modern social life which are not simply reducible
to the relationship of Church and state or to that of man's temporal
and eternal ends. A Thomistic social and political philosophy can
be no exception to the rule that all vital philosophical developments
must build upon a careful analytic study of the actual ways of
things, persons, and social institutions.

Finally, Maritain's philosophy of history is itself in a tentative
form and has not yet inspired any thorough Thomistic work in this
region.[17] The absence of supplementary work here has led a few
of the younger American Catholics studying philosophy to conclude
prematurely that such inquiries cannot be carried on within the
context of Thomism. A more precise conclusion would be that
Thomists have not yet appreciated the urgency of their concentrating considerable research energies at this point. Especially the
work being done on the meaning of history by reflective historians
themselves, by analytic philosophers, and by the phenomenologists
and existentialists, has to be given a close examination. Then the

Thomistic resources on such relevant themes as human subjectivity, the human meaning of time, and the human ways of achieving community, will have to be reassessed and developed as a critical response to the suggestions made by these contemporary philosophies. This is precisely the sort of pioneer investigation carried on by Maritain in regard to recent philosophies of science, metaphysical doctrines, and standpoints in esthetics and morals. His general manner of conducting a philosophical inquiry contains potentialities for future studies in fields where he has made only a preliminary survey.

Summing up the impact of Maritain on Thomism in America, then, his presence continues to be a shaping and fermenting one. Philosophers do not live by doctrine alone but also by the encouraging example of actual thinkers, who show by their lives what it means to philosophize with all one's soul. His wholehearted devotion to the philosophical vocation is a beacon and often a consolation to others who venture on this path. Maritain's guidance is particularly important for Thomists who are learning how to think and teach and write under contemporary conditions. His way of philosophizing rests on a complex fidelity both to the philosophical tradition of Aristotle, Augustine, and Aquinas, and to the accomplishments and problems of our own time. This twofold orientation marks his major teachings on the division of the sciences, the act of existing and the existential judgment, the tension between person and temporal community, and the search for the unity of wisdom in our speculation and our practical life. While American Thomists are not merely repeating his positions, they owe him a primary debt in discerning the truths and facing the problems, even when this may lead to disagreement or to further exploration. The content and the spirit of Thomism in our country cannot be understood apart from the fructifying influence of Jacques Maritain.

NOTES

1. J. S. Zybura, *Present-Day Thinkers and the New Scholasticism* (St. Louis: Herder, 1927). The correspondence mentioned in the next paragraph is in the files of the Philosophy Department at St. Louis University.
2. In *Réflexions sur l'intelligence et sur sa vie propre* (third ed., Paris: Desclée, 1930), Maritain includes an appendix on philosophical language (336-341). He calls for a technical vocabulary which is precise and yet supple enough to retain its continuity with our basic human convictions or what he would now call our pre-philosophical knowledge. He also distinguishes between the technical language needed for a scientific formation of the mind and the style to be used in arousing true opinion in non-philosophers.
3. These aspects are combined in Maritain's study of *The Angelic Doctor* (New York: Dial Press, 1931), which for a generation now has given many English readers their first philosophical introduction to St. Thomas. A new translation, entitled *St. Thomas Aquinas,* of a slightly revised text was published by Meridian in 1958.
4. For an excellent statement of the philosopher's responsibilities both to truth and to philosophical dialogue, see the interchange between Maritain and Professor Sheldon: J. Maritain, "Philosophical Co-operation and Intellectual Justice," and W. H. Sheldon, "Professor Maritain on Philosophical Co-operation," in *The Modern Schoolman,* 22 (1944-45), 1-15, and 88-97, with special reference to Thomism and pragmatism.
5. J. Maritain, *Humanisme intégral* (Paris: Aubier, 1936), 150-51.
6. "I believe that its [Thomistic philosophy's] possibilities of invention and of progressive synthesis are inexhaustible, and that it is called upon not only to refute errors but also and especially to get to the very bottom of the problems which assail modern thought on all sides." J. Maritain, *Bergsonian Philosophy and Thomism* (New York: Philosophical Library, 1955), 20.
7. Maritain follows this method in his essay on "The Natural Mystical Experience and the Void," the very first sentence of which is the reminder: "This study is in the philosophical order." J. Maritain, *Ransoming the Time* (New York: Scribner, 1941), 255.
8. "Theology, in fact, strives for this continuity [with the beatific vision] for the perfection of its state as a science. Moral philosophy adequately considered, on the contrary, is *orientated* toward

natural and terrestrial evidence; and it is in this evidence, fittingly completed, that it asks to resolve, and actually does resolve, its principles." J. Maritain, *An Essay on Christian Philosophy* (New York: Philosophical Library, 1955), 88.

9. J. Maritain, *Three Reformers* (London: Sheed and Ward, 1932), 69-76.

10. Maritain observes that the conflict between the new Galilean-Cartesian mathematical approach to sensible phenomena and the older philosophy of nature was based on the tragic misunderstanding of thinking that they were both aiming at the same type of knowledge and hence that the conflict was inevitable, once the new results in modern science appeared. J. Maritain, *Philosophy of Nature* (New York: Philosophical Library, 1951), 41-42.

11. For instance, Maritain cites many social studies in *Man and the State* (Chicago: University of Chicago Press, 1951), and furnishes numerous "texts without comment" in *Creative Intuition in Art and Poetry* (New York: Pantheon, 1953).

12. The whole issue is reviewed by G. P. Klubertanz, S.J., "The Doctrine of St. Thomas and Modern Science," in *Sapientia Aquinatis* (Rome: Officium Libri Catholici, 1955), Vol. I, 89-104.

13. His position is stated succinctly in *A Preface to Metaphysics* (New York: Sheed and Ward, 1939), and in *Existence and the Existent* (New York: Pantheon, 1948). For a representative group of papers by American Thomists strongly influenced by the thought of Maritain and Gilson on existential metaphysics and theory of knowledge, consult the *Proceedings of the American Catholic Philosophical Association*, Vol. 21, 1946.

14. J. Maritain, *Approaches to God* (New York: Harper, 1954), 72-83.

15. The ways in which American Thomists are treating the problem of God can be seen in the *Proceedings of the American Catholic Philosophical Association*, Vol. 28, 1954.

16. These topics are outlined in chapter one of *Man and the State*. In *The Person and the Common Good* (New York: Scribner, 1947), Maritain gives his considered reply to some American criticism of his distinction between person and individual in respect to the common good.

17. However, *On the Philosophy of History* (New York: Scribner, 1957) is a good example of the way in which Maritain continues to probe tentatively into new areas and point out opportunities for further Thomistic research.

Wallace Fowlie

3. Maritain the Writer

IF I AM FAITHFUL to the assigned subject of this paper, I shall be
concerned not with what Jacques Maritain has written but with the
manner in which it was written, with his power and art as a writer.
And yet the subject matter and the style of this philosopher are
indistinguishable one from the other. The style is the man. The
style is his thought, his philosophy, his sensibility. I would make
the same claim if I were asked to write the life of M. Maritain.
The biography of this man does not conceal his work, for his
entire existence is that of an intellectual whose writings are the
reflections of a marvellously-ordered and spiritually-endowed life.
I merely plead that the kind of research I am undertaking here has
the characteristics of infinity.

His role in modern thought is unique and irreplaceable. He has
always written with perilous ease. Throughout his career he has
been solicited by philosophers, and by causes related to philosophy,
and he has almost never refused to speak, to write, to testify, to
correct. The purity of reflection is the mark of his intellect as it
expresses itself on so many delicate and profound and controversial
subjects. The exposition of whatever problem Maritain is discussing
may well be meticulous and lengthy, but then when his conscience
is quieted and he has fully exposed all aspects of the problem, his
thought begins to express itself in the abstractions of a philosopher.

46

On the greatest pages of Maritain these abstractions reach a dazzling luminosity. The words and the sentences seem to espouse his thought and preserve it in the perfection of the form they create.

I was about to speak of the rigors of his way of thinking, the rigors of his rational thought. But I am not sure that such a phrase says all that I want it to say. M. Maritain has a great affection for clarity of thought, for the limpid formula, for the expression which appears purely rationalistic. But he does not avoid obscurities when the subject calls for them. His long cohabitation with mystics and poets has taught him many lessons on the ultimate ineffectualness and inefficiency of language. He is attracted by the enigmas of man, by the most troublesome and the most persistent enigmas. The philosopher and the writer are one in his unwillingness to oversimplify what is complex and to explain what is only partially understood. Themes and concepts return in book after book of Maritain. In most cases they are the thoughts which have given him the most difficulty and for which he has therefore the greatest predilection. As he restates them, the form is modified, at times slightly, at other times radically. These modifications in form testify to an ever-deepening understanding of the concepts. Clarification of form occurs simultaneously with clarification of thought.

The sustained power of exposition in the writings of Jacques Maritain, and his determination, and even eagerness, to return over and over again to the same problems, give to this philosopher additional traits of the pedagogue. M. Maritain often resembles the pedagogue in the highest sense, the teacher who is speaking to pupils and disciples (in this case, readers) and who is reluctant to avoid any of the phases of his thought. The movements and the tempi of his language are various. He is able to attack swiftly and aggressively an idea he considers pernicious, and he is likewise able to deploy a slow painstaking examination of items which are important to review in order to reach a just conclusion. Every teacher, of the stature of Jacques Maritain, creates a manner of his own and forges a vocabulary of his own. The teacher's closeness to an audience of disciples almost inevitably leads him to a form of communication which may appear esoteric to those outside, to those unfamiliar with the permanent preoccupations and beliefs of the master. I firmly believe that Maritain's thought is accessible to all, but to gain access to this thought requires initiation to many subjects and especially to Thomism: both the philosophical assumptions of St. Thomas and the powers of synthesis in Thomistic thought.

The initiation I refer to is, in this case, an awareness the reader must have of the extraordinary depth of feeling expressed by Maritain when he writes. The degree of vehemence and love with which he writes makes him vulnerable to his enemies. He has grown used to this position of vulnerability. His major ideas are in their final statements extremely simple, but in order to reach this simplicity, he has ceaselessly to return to them and insist, by all the various ways he can discover, what their final simplicity is. This very insistence, which every good teacher has to employ because of the nature of his profession, may well give to M. Maritain's style a peremptory tone, a tone of self-assurance. But the initiates know that such words are not accurate to describe his style. A magnificent law inhabits this man and is the molder of his thought. Throughout all of his works he is concerned with the same doctrine which has to be explained and imposed if there is to be any justification for the leading ideas. There is without much doubt a certain monotony of intention throughout the pages of Maritain, and this monotony may at times seem unbearable to the non-initiate. Yet the source of this monotony is not dogmatism, as the novice reader might believe. It comes from the unity presiding over this philosopher's doctrine.

His thought is never at rest. The reader is first held and captivated by the animation of this thought so intent upon reaching elements of truth and endowing them with life and fervor. The work of writer is never over for Jacques Maritain. The world in which he lives is one of thought and passion, of mental activity which is tireless, and of passionate strength which never gives over to languor or debility. If the books are read one after the other chronologically as they were written, one has the impression of following a life which is being uninterruptedly restored and rejuvenated. One can be as struck by the perpetual mental activity of this life as by the thoughts themselves which this activity creates.

The range of his interests and speculations is so vast that the reader may at times have the impression that this philosopher is deliberately upsetting the rigors of composition and altering the usual perspectives of writing. But this is not true. The boldness of Maritain as stylist comes from the climate he creates in his books. It comes from the very form of his judgments. And precisely his judgment triumphs because of the extraordinary ubiquity of his thought. He is at all places where he should be.

The distances he covers are permitted because his faith is based upon the unity, the oneness of the universe. If he seems to move swiftly in all regions throughout the universe, it is because he is so anxious to comprehend and to explain the total solidarity of all things, to affirm their capacity to be together and to accept man in their midst, in a unified simultaneous existence. Maritain's vision of the world is that of an intelligible unity, the image and reflection of divine unity.

Maritain's is the vocation of the philosopher, that of being a witness of the world in its meaningful presence, and of welcoming the world by means of a language which attempts to reveal the truth of the world. For such a vocation one accepts in advance an inevitable and necessary solitude. Maritain's solitude is paradoxically that of a man who has had extraordinary friendships: Léon Bloy, Ernest Psichari, Marc Chagall. Like his friend Péguy, Jacques Maritain understood very early in his life the need for slow maturing, for a slow adjusting to the truths of his faith. His style comes from the patient assurance and the consciousness of a future which regulate his thought. He is a man who knew and accepted his vocation very early, and who thereafter lived by heeding the sentiment of this vocation and by preserving a fidelity to it.

If one accepts the proposition that it is impossible to discuss the style or the art or the power of a writer without involving his subject matter, then it may be permitted me to consider Maritain as a writer, in terms of two themes, of the two problems which have perhaps reached the largest percentage of his public: aesthetics and humanism. In his treatment of these two subjects, M. Maritain has revealed a sound knowledge of contemporary art and politics and an ability to explain them and illuminate them by means of constant reference to the philosophy of St. Thomas Aquinas.

Early in his career, his *Art et Scolastique* surprised simultaneously two worlds in Paris: the philosophers and the artists, the students of philosophy and the students of art. Both worlds realized that the author of this book was a metaphysician who seemed to look upon himself as if he were a contemporary of St. Thomas, as well as a man who had meditated for a long time on the paintings of Rouault, a revolutionary and totally modern artist. The principal ideas of *Art et Scolastique*, which first appeared in 1920, were examined further by Maritain in *Réponse à Jean Cocteau* of 1926, in *Frontières de la Poésie* of 1935, in *Situation de la Poésie* of 1938, and in *Creative Intuition in Art and Poetry* of 1953. In these five works, Maritain exposes his understanding of aesthetics under two general headings: the theories about art expressed by the scholastic philosophers, and the mysterious characteristics of contemporary art, especially in the realms of painting and poetry. Maritain's task was made difficult by the absence of any solid treatise on art by a scholastic. But in choosing and collecting the many disparate and scattered statements about art in the writings of St. Thomas and other medieval philosophers, he exemplified as a writer the skill of integration which is one of the characteristics of St. Thomas himself. The study of medieval art, as well as the study of certain texts of St. Thomas, taught Maritain many lessons on the artisan, on the dignity of the artisan's craft, and prepared the way for the philosopher's understanding of the artist and of what he will call the sublimity of the artist's vocation.

An entire generation of students and scholars are grateful to Jacques Maritain for the fidelity and precision with which he has defined and elucidated some of the most difficult of concepts. His manner of explanation is one of meticulous care in the art of defining, and at the same time, of joyous elation in the very discovery of definition. This rare quality of joyfulness adds a dimension to the exegetical passages of this philosopher. He thereby fixed the form of his thought into something quite unforgettable. I remember in particular, from my earliest readings of Maritain, his passages on the beautiful (*le beau*), on the transcendental character of the beautiful, on the particular kind of affinity which the beautiful has with God. I remember the delicacy and the details with which Maritain discusses the rules of imitation in art. *Ars imitatur naturam.* The skill of Maritain taught us what to understand concerning the doctrine of imitation; the love of Maritain for his subject taught us how important it is to understand this doctrine. The teacher in Maritain is never separated from the lover of truth.

The relationship between art and morality, for example, was one kind of lesson which he discussed in *Art et Scolastique* with an exceptional thoroughness and objectivity. But when he approached the immediate and specific problems of the modern artist, we realized that this philosopher-aesthetician was writing as one who felt deeply and personally the spiritual problems of his day, those which since the Renaissance have made the artist into an unhappy, and at times, desperate man. Maritain has not only studied the psychology of the modern artist, in contrasting it with the spirit of the medieval artisan, but he has also studied countless examples of modern art and the laws which seem to govern these works. These studies have helped him in his understanding of modern man and the tragedies of modern history, in the social and political sense. The exaggerations and the inhumanity of the political state are not without their counterpart in the drama of the modern artist.

He has always been able, as a writer, to formulate and project the dramatic qualities of his thought. In claiming that poetry must al-

ways remain within the realm of art, namely within the limitations
of something to be made, something to be created, he expresses at
the same time fear for the opposite, for such a poet as Arthur
Rimbaud, for example, who attempted to pass beyond the natural
frontiers of poetry, who experienced the temptation of knowledge,
of changing his being, of discovering a dialectic and a form which
would ultimately kill poetry and silence the poet. In his moving
analysis of the angelism of Rimbaud, Maritain defined and rede-
fined the rules of art and the temper of the artist, but he also
expressed, with the feeling of an artist himself, the spiritual drama
of this dilemma and its relationship with the general spiritual
anguish of modern man.

From his knowledge of Thomistic thought, Maritain was able
to point out the dangerous pretensions to "purity" which certain
schools and forms of modern art have made. More fervently than
any other writers, he described the significance of this "purity,"
the peril it implies in seeking to reach a state of independence from
morality. In a passage of *Art et Scolastique,* in which Maritain considers examples of the modern novel, he outlines a theory, or rather
a measurement of guidance for the modern writer, when he stresses
the importance of the understanding and spirituality of the artist
himself when he treats the problem of evil. It is the famous passage
on Proust, whom Maritain would like to have seen endowed with
the perceptiveness of a St. Augustine when he approached certain
themes in his work. By this kind of striking alliance, Maritain
teaches a great deal about the confusion of aesthetic and ethical
values which he looks upon as one of the besetting plagues of our
age.

The clarity and coherence of the writer's convictions are equally
apparent in the second theme in the work of M. Maritain to which
I should like to make reference: the philosopher's understanding
of humanism. History, for this humanist, is the long road taken by
man from the moment of his fall, to the moment of his redemption,
and which will continue until he is transfigured in the vision of

the Godhead. The Christian philosophy of history has been expounded by Maritain implicity and explicitly throughout his work with such a firm logic that he forces the will of the reader to pay heed to these illuminations and these arguments.

Because of historical crises and circumstances, Maritain, in order to define his understanding of history and his conception of humanism today, very often in his writing calls upon the contrasting Marxian view whereby history is interpreted as that force in the world which creates and forms man. This interpretation, antithetical to Christian philosophy, is sufficient in its prevalence today, to turn Maritain into a vigorous polemical writer when he attempts to offset Marxian doctrine. The vigor is polemical, but the style has such loftiness and sustained eloquence that no single category can adequately express it. In his life-long study of human freedom, Maritain finds it to be transcendent over the world. In his analysis of this doctrine, in the long harmonious sentences transcribing his thought, we often experience, as readers, something comparable to the very experience which he is describing: a transcendence and an autonomy of the human spirit. His writing, at its highest moments, is the realization, the making real, of the historical ideal of Christianity.

In his treatment of the richness of this theme, in his analysis of its multiple aspects, in the skill with which he orders and assembles the various problems and proofs and examples, Maritain demonstrates his fullest powers of dialectician and rhetorician. In discussing the place of man in the universe, he analyzes both the problem of the relationship between divine grace and man's freedom, and the problem of man's attitude toward his own destiny. Maritain feels, and has said on countless occasions, that new applications of the principles of Christianity are necessary today. His entire work might well be defined as the carrying out of this belief, the effort to explain once again the foundations of Christian thought and theology, and at the same time to explain, why in the light of today's history as well as of past history, the Christian can never reach the heights of Christianity, can never feel totally at ease in the temporal and eternal aspects of Christianity.

His feelings for the greatness of the Christian's vocation are strong indeed, but even more strong are his feelings for the limitations of the Christian today, for the distressing inadequacy of his efforts. The vibrant pages which M. Maritain has devoted to the place of Israel in modern history form only one example—but deeply characteristic of this philosopher—of the solicitude and the personal suffering he feels for the entire race of man. The plight and the struggles of Israel stimulate the entire movement of history. Maritain explains the dolorous waiting of the Jews and their anxiety, as signs that they do not have God, as signs that they refuse to receive the Incarnation into their hearts. But these passages on the mystery of Israel through the ages are easily applicable to any single Christian soul who holds back something in his own nature which should be offered with the total gift of himself.

In order to transcribe what he understands by the meaning of history, Maritain has created formula after formula phrased in words that will remain fixed in our memories for a long time. The sentence, for example, in *Humanisme Intégral,* where he asserts the dual aspect of history, its nocturnal, impure elements and its purity: "L'histoire est impure et nocturne, elle est l'histoire du mal mêlé au bien et plus fréquent que le bien. . . ." The history of evil is intertwined with the history of the world, but there is no reason, according to Maritain, for man to avoid contact with that history. It has to be participated in and understood in order to be purified. Only the Pharisee will avoid contact with the world's corruption and thus defer the world's salvation. "La peur de se souiller en entrant dans le contexte de l'histoire est une crainte pharisaïque."

The history of man seen as two simultaneous and contradictory forces: the deadening heavy weight of sin, on the one hand, and the illuminating spirituality of grace, on the other, is a Thomistic interpretation, for which Maritain has discovered vigorous fresh applications, sentences which often soar with a lyrical passion. They are the most difficult passages of the writing to translate into any other language, because they are indigenously French. They are inevitably the key passages, for which the philosopher found his most creative phrases. Like Bergson before him, Maritain writes books which can be understood in translation, but which can be felt only in French. Those passages in which he calls upon imagery and strong rhythm for the transmission of his thought, are precisely those which appear diluted in translation.

If the sources of the Christian philosophy of history can be traced to St. Thomas Aquinas, its fullest expression is to be found in the writings of Jacques Maritain. With this theme in particular, he reaches his full greatness as a writer, his deepest inspiration as a creative thinker. Ceaselessly throughout his books, Maritain evokes the presence of the Church in the history of mankind. In such books as *Humanisme Intégral, Du Régime Temporel et de la Liberté, Science et Sagesse,* and *Court Traité de l'existence et de l'existant,* he keeps insisting that if the Christian world knows sin, the Church is without sin. History is written under the permanence and the will of God. His plan is immutable and it allows the free will of man even to do wrong.

In his long career as a writer and thinker, Jacques Maritain has often expressed gratitude for the debt he owes to other writers and to friends. To some extent, his particular power as a writer has been developed thanks to certain exemplary forces. To Henri Bergson, first, who was perhaps the leading master for Maritain in his early years. If Bergson never professed Christianity, he often affirmed his love for Christianity. Moreover the literary gifts of Bergson, his rhythmic sentence and gentle eloquence, were transmitted to his early disciple. To Charles Péguy, Maritain owes especially the sense of the temporal vocation of the Christian. There has never been a fully satisfactory book written about Péguy. Maritain is probably the only man who could write this book. The third debt of gratitude, and perhaps the heaviest of all, is to his god-father Léon Bloy. The prophetic vocation of Bloy has been continued in Jacques Maritain. Bloy spent a good deal of his life in denouncing the luke-warmness, the fears and the prevarications of today's world. Because his faith was ardent and passionate, his sense of supernatural realities was extraordinary. He had the perceptiveness of a prophet and an almost terrifying knowledge of charity. In his friendship with Bloy, Maritain sensed especially the man's freedom of spirit and his desire for this freedom to inhabit all men.

It was not difficult for Maritain to adopt the affirmations he found in Bergson, Péguy and Bloy to the affirmation of faith he studied in St. Thomas. The writer's lesson which he learned from St. Thomas was the method he has applied faithfully to all of his work: *distinguer pour unir,* the need to distinguish carefully all the elements of a problem, in order ultimately to unite them. With every problem which Maritain has touched, he ends by fusing into an organic growth the supernatural life of the Church and the temporal life of the world. His humanism neglects nothing concerning man and nothing concerning God, because it is based on the double conviction that man is made from nothing and that man is made in the image of God.

As a philosopher, Maritain found his belief very early in his life. As a writer, he has never swerved from an effort to expound this belief, to explain it in the light of today's problems, to reiterate the Thomistic philosophy of existence which is agreement and reconciliation. Grace and nature, first, Maritain sees as the most important of the opposites which have to be reconciled. All the other important pairs follow logically from this first: faith and reason, the speculative and the practical, contemplation of God and understanding of the world.

Because of the many grievous dilemmas which Maritain has attempted to solve, his writing can seem at times to be a form of lamentation, a sorrowing poetic expression. But then it can change abruptly into a vigorous energetic form of polemics where passion is married to poetry thanks to his technical knowledge of scholastic philosophy. If he comes from St. Thomas, his position today as a philosopher is quite independent. The university world and the Catholic world have both come to realize this independent stand of the French philosopher. Whether he is speaking of Christian philosophy or of modern aesthetics, the accent of Maritain's voice is personal. The transparency and purity of his style lead one to believe that his nature is both that of a philosopher and a poet. All his life, he has been a reader of the poets, and his perceptive comments on the work of Baudelaire and Rimbaud and Cocteau are among the most precious he has bequeathed to future students of French poetry. Maritain knows and accepts the great claims of poetry: that it is the essential language, that it comprises the fullest extent of human expression, that it is the absence of speech as well as the written word.

John J. FitzGerald

4. Maritain's Critical Realism

NOETIC OR KNOWLEDGE THEORY, in the Thomism of Jacques Maritain, is neither the beginning nor the end of philosophical activity but rather its maturest state, marked by the mind's full awareness of the character, scope and value of human knowledge.[1] In the writings of Aristotle, Aquinas and the latter's most original and systematic commentators, Cardinal Cajetan and John of St. Thomas, Maritain finds a fully conscious, though not systematically elaborated, doctrine of knowledge.[2] In their historical periods, the knowledge problem had neither the central nor the separate status which it has acquired in the modern period as a consequence of the emergence and maturation of an autonomous natural science in sharp discontinuity with Aristotelian physics and the common-sense knowledge upon which it rested.

In response to the preoccupations of modern thought, Maritain has made explicit the implicit noetic of the Aristotelian-Thomist philosophy—disclosing, in the process, an irreducible diversity between perennial and contemporary metaphysics; a diversity found to be grounded in irremediable epistemological divergences. The aim of the present inquiry is to expose and relate the inner factors, factual and doctrinal, of the Maritain noetic and thereby exhibit something of its originality in and continuity with the philosophical tradition to which it explicitly subscribes.

Descriptive Analysis of the Knowledge Fact

In this context, epistemology is understood to be the critical investigation and evaluation of the nature and scope of the fact of human knowing—*le connaître*. The results to which such an investigation, correctly executed in accordance with the evidences and necessities of its subject matter, inevitably leads, in Maritain's view, are most appropriately designated *Critical Realism,* an expression entirely synonymous with the expression *Aristotelian-Thomist Realism.*[3]

From the outset, the investigation diverges from every sort of indirect realism, whether Cartesian, Lockeian or Kantian, and consequent idealism, by acknowledging the primacy and transcendance, in the act of knowing, of the real over knowing—an acknowledgment that yields forthwith the first truths of being and of human understanding in all its modes, pre-scientific and scientific.[4] Initially, scientific knowledge is construed in a large sense to include any systematic study as opposed to pre-scientific or common-sense knowledge construed as including the immediate evidences of external and internal experience together with their prevailing public interpretation as embedded in the contemporary vernacular. In this wide sense, common-sense or natural knowledge is the fruit not only of one's own experience of himself and the world about but also that experience extended, interpreted and expressed in current languages with their involved and changing cultural prejudices and predispositions. In this complex initial knowledge state only the invariant epistemic factors are relevant. Maritain characterizes the consciousness of these factors as "the natural metaphysics immanent in the human spirit."[5]

In the invariant constituents of its natural or prescientific state, human knowledge exhibits itself to attentive reflection as the mysterious though indubitable presence of a sensed reality to a sensing subject or knower. Though the sensory act originate and terminate in the sensing subject, it, and the sentient subject through it, are wholly oriented towards and completed in the presence of a non-subject or sensed object. Though, as a psychical act or sense perception, the seeing of this page be my act, the term to which this act relates me, the seen page, is neither myself nor my act. To be sure, not all known objects are sense data, but such as are not appear reflectively to be so related to things as sensed that, without sense perception and its immanent term, the sensed datum, knowing would not occur. The origins of the human knowing activity in sensory perceptions, particularly seeing and touching, are decisive for the development and value of that activity. For it is there that the first object of knowing is discovered as actually existing and actually existing as a concrete, singular spatio-temporal complex other than the existing embodied consciousness upon which it intrudes.

As signified in the predicate terms of the several existential or singular statements in which one asserts his actual knowledge of a sensed object, neither the singularities nor the actual existence of the thing signified in the subject terms is included. Considering the object upon which I type these lines, I say: It is white. It is rectangular. It is thin. It is paper. It is something. In each case, I see (reflectively) that these successive predicates express something of the object denoted by the subject term, but something of the object which has been and may be instantiated in any number of other sensed objects denoted by other subject terms. Reflectively, these respects, in which sensed things, the embodied self included, are related and distinguished by real likenesses and differences, are manifested in our knowledge from the outset in the non-sensible or conceptual presences of sensed things. Thus, one and the same thing, this page, as sensed, is concrete, singular and actually existing, but, as conceived, is abstract, universal and possibly existent. Though the unity and plurality of things as sensed and as conceived are diverse, they are seen not to be simply diverse in that one constantly and truly combines them in affirmations.[6]

The Thing-Object Duality

To account for these diverse but related immediate conscious presences (perceived, conceived and affirmed) of existing things, without prejudice to the integrity and autonomy in existence of both the real knower and the real known, Critical Realism re-examines the traditional distinction between a thing as thing and a thing as object. As a thing, this page is characterized by its continuing to be what it has been made to be when the initiating causes of its so being are no longer present. More generally, what characterizes any thing as thing is its being what it is and existing as such apart from its originating cause or causes. As initially presented in knowledge, that is, as first sensed, conceived and affirmed, an existing thing comes to be also an object, is present to and affirmed by a knowing subject in some one or more of the multiple aspects in and through which the knowing subject "lays hold" of it. At the beginning of the knower's complex elementary knowing act, that is, in its sensory component, a concrete, singular existent imposes itself upon the knower through the action of its qualities upon the sensory organs of the sensing subject. In this primal moment, the whole thing in its actual existence here and now is present to the knower as something there, now, shaped, colored, at rest or in motion. The single existent or thing exhibits a manifold of sense data or simple objects some of which, though perceived separately by one or another external sense, are grasped together as different aspects of one and the same thing by some unifying internal sense. In its manifold simultaneous and successive sensible presences, a sensed object, e.g., this page, is exhibited in the singularities and contingencies affecting it in its actual existence. But one's immediate knowledge of existing things, though stemming from sensation, does not present itself as terminating there.

In another, though simultaneous, phase of the elementary knowing act, the singular existent is found to be present in a manifold of concepts in which it is seen to be unaffected by (as abstracted from) the set of singularities and contingencies which it exhibited to the senses. Consider the predicate terms in the following descriptive statements: This page is white. This page is rectangular. This page is printed on. Does not each express of the thing, denoted by the subject term, not only diverse ways of being in which it presents itself in one's immediate perceptual experience but also such diverse ways in which the subject-thing is like innumerable other existing things, either actual or possible? Considered absolutely or in themselves, the *significata* of such predicate terms do not indicate the actual existence of the subject-things in which sensible experience shows them to be realized. They present themselves simply as analyzable and realizable values or ways of being so long as they are not restored, in the completing phase of the genetically basic cognitive act, the singular judgment or affirmation, to the actually existing sensed thing. In this context, the word white is a meaningful descriptive term of no actually existing thing so long as it has not been, as the predicate of a singular judgment, attributed to a subject term denoting this page or some other sensed thing from which the knower has conceptually derived or abstracted it. Thus, the simple reflective inspection of the ways in which a thing in its actual here-and-now existence is present in the fully conscious knowing subject and asserted in its basic complete elementary act of knowing, the singular judgment, suffices to establish the primitive grounds for this key distinction between a thing as thing and the same thing as object (sensed, imaged and conceived) as well as their inseparability. What it is to be page is exactly the same (whatever that is, whether simple or complex) as that in this surface, upon which these lines are written, which I assert in the predicate term of the judgment "This is a page." Realized or instantiated in this thing, the *significatum* of the word "white" has the additional involvements of actually existing and actually existing with all the singularities and contingencies affecting the concrete object to which I attribute it. Considered apart from its singular existential status in this concrete object or thing, considered, that is, in its static conceptual status as realizable in an indefinite number of things, actual or possible, the very same predicate term, without any alteration in its proper meaning, acquires or exhibits an additional set of traits exclusive of those which affected it in its concrete singular realization. Now it presents itself to reflective inspection as abstract, universal and immutable or static. In their common set of invariant meanings, the thing as thing and the thing as object (whether perceived or conceived) are not only inseparable but identical. In the sets of diverse features affecting this common intelligible whole, traditionally called the essence of the thing, the thing as thing and the thing as object are distinct.

This insight into the difference, not in meaning but in mode of being or existing, of every real datum, as sensed and as conceived in order to be affirmed, is the basic reflective evidence for the critical realist view of the truth of human knowledge as the conformity of what is asserted to be with what is; a conformity between mind and reality on the side of the mind's elementary complete act of knowing, the judgment or affirmation expressed in factual propositions, rather than on the side of that which is affirmed. One's affirmations, if true, are not indifferent to but indeed are measured by that which they affirm rather than conversely.[7]

How do such singular assertions of what the real is, in any given instance, present themselves? Responsibly uttered, they are fully conscious acts immediately accessible to reflective inspection, they present themselves as acts of the knowing subject in which he restores to the thing as encountered in his actual experience what, in conception, he has separated or abstracted from it. When inspected in its own rights, that which has been so abstracted always presents itself either as being or a mode of being, as that which is or the innumerable ways in which it is. In the statement "This page is white," one has rendered into language one's cognitive act of joining what it is to be this page with what it is to be white, expressing through the copula "is" the unity or identity (at least partial) of a notional diversity, namely, the notion of "what it is to be page" (a given state of affairs seen to include in fact but not to be reducible in fact to this other notion "what it is to be white"). In one and the same thing, denoted by the demonstrative pronoun "this," presented here and now to the knowing subject through visual perception, the knower has discerned not only "pageness" and "whiteness" but the pageness and whiteness of this thing—this white page. Described in terms of the reflective evidences which it conveys, the affirmation, "This page is white," discloses that the subject term "this" denotes a present sensed datum in and through a primary conceptual datum "page" to which, *via* the copula "is," is united the predicate term "white" denoting the same sensed datum but in the value of being signified by "white," that is, a sensible quality which, as conceived, includes no actual reference to this or any other actual subject. Analyzed reflectively in this way, such factual statements manifest the subject's conscious operation of conforming itself as knowing to an actual situation by combining in a terminal act, the judgment, what, in a prior act, conception, it had separated (mentally) from the existing real as sensed. The whole truth value of such affirmations consists not only in what the knowing subject does when it affirms something of any actually existing thing but also, and most particularly, in the subject's awareness that the union of subject term and predicate term which it asserts in judging corresponds to, because it is identical with, the union in an actually existing thing of what has been separately grasped by the knower in the diverse phases of his basic knowing activity. One first separates in conceptual thought knowable aspects of sensed things—not from the sensed things of which they are given as knowable aspects but from other knowable aspects of the same thing. Thus the predicate term "white" is not separated from that which is or can be white but rather from everything in that white thing which is not white. Of course, viewed in its own irreducible content, the notion white prescinds not only from all the non-white values of this or any existing subject in which, at the level of sense perception, one finds it concretely embodied, but even from the actuality of these subjects, that is, in a state of separation from all actual subjects. So conceptually isolated, such known values as white or whiteness do not however, according to Maritain, abstract from possible subjects. In this interpretation, things as conceived or concepts, such as white, include in their meaning the sense of what it is for anything to be white whether or not there are in actuality any white things. To be sure, the condition for the *de facto* conceptual presence of what it is for anything to be white is, in our case, that something white has actually been experienced. Here too is another evidence of the inseparability but distinction of thing and object—the inseparability which is the sign of the embodied mind's openness to bodily reality in its actual being and not simply in its psycho-physiological effects upon the knower.[8]

Transcendental Being, The Primum Notum

Another immediate conscious evidence, prior and relevant to the critical realist account of human knowing in its common-sense or pre-scientific phase, is the omnipresence and priority of being as the absolute value and term of one's knowing activity at every level (perceptual, conceptual, judicative and discursive) and in every mode (pre-scientific and scientific). At this point of our analysis, our interest is restricted to the omnipresence and necessity of this value of known things or objects at the pre-scientific empirical level —but at this level precisely in its function of providing in diverse ways the point of departure and the point of verification of all the sciences whether natural or philosophical. According to Maritain, epistemology or knowledge theory properly concerns itself with human knowledge in its highest and most certain achievement, that is, in metaphysics, taken in the classical sense of the science of being as being. Accordingly it presupposes and indeed conditions that science, may even be regarded as a part of metaphysics—not, to be sure, in the sense that it adds any new truths to one's metaphysical knowledge but in the sense that it gives new and deeper possession of acquired truths, especially those most general and certain truths of metaphysical science. This accounts for the centrality of the critical realist's insistence on being as simply and absolutely the first object of human intelligence in every mode of its activity, pre-scientific or scientific. The sense of this doctrine is that in knowing anything one knows forthwith, however obscurely, both being and its modes. The being, exhibited in one's intuitive empirical knowledge, is the being of this or that concrete actually existing thing. The value of being of such concrete existents is explicitly delivered in the transcendental concept of being. Reflectively inspected in itself, this value of things yields directly the principle of identity, that that which is is all that it is and nothing other than that which it is, the first principle of all that is and consequently of all that is knowable.[9] Though exhausted in none of its experienced instances, this first and principal object of knowledge is found in every known thing. Not that any known thing is or can be any other known thing but that every known or knowable thing is like every other to the extent that it both is and is knowable insofar as it exhibits the value of being, the value in virtue of which both the knower and the known are separated and related, the value in virtue of which all things that are, are one without any one being or capable of being in existence the other, the value indeed which is the ultimate ground of the unity of human knowledge at any moment in its historical and scientific development.

The Knowledge Fact—A Paradox

The first *de jure,* hence reflective, object of one's knowledge is being or that in sensed things in and through which they are not only situated in respect to one another and everything else but also in and through which what we know of them is meaningful and communicable. The systematic explicitation of the intelligible necessities inward to being provides the mind with the truths by which it can divide and unite all that it does or can know, including knowledge itself. For, on the one hand, in his knowing activities, the knower is said to grasp first and foremost that in the existing things of his experience (both external and internal) by which no one is any other and each exists, in some way, apart from every other. On the other hand, the very activity of knowing this involves that the knower come to be the other—the thing known or object—precisely in that which it is, hence in its very otherness. Thus, in knowing, one apparently achieves that which, by the first law of being and thought, the principle of identity, is radically excluded, namely, identity with other as other. The solution of this paradox provides a basic doctrine of the critical realist position.

Both the coming-to-be of something and the coming-to-be other of something that already is are familiar facts of human experience; facts accounted for in the tradition of the distinction between matter and form, between an existing subject of diversity and the diverse forms to which it is subjected. In such natural processes or changes, the product of the process, the other that came to be, was construed to be a composite whole or *tertium quid* distinct from, hence other than, its component principles. By contrast to the term of coming-to-be other in being, the term of coming-to-be other in knowledge is not a *tertium quid*—an existing composite irreducible to, hence other than, its component elements, knower and known. Indeed, the term of the knowing process is nothing other than the initial components, the thing known and the subject knowing, in such a state of being that both knower and known, without losing their ontological diversity, their essential existential otherness, acquire an existential condition other than that which in the natural order, the order of their first existential act, isolates and insulates them in their own respective first actuality.

By its natural first act or existence, called its *esse naturae,* this page in its whiteness and all else that it is is itself and nothing else. By its being known or by its existence in knowledge, called its *esse intentionale,* this page, in its whiteness, is present to and in the knower, not, of course, by the *esse naturae* which isolates it from every other existing thing, but by an *esse intentionale* or existential act which, relative to the natural existential act, is described as a meta-existence, an immaterial existence, a final actuality, which, without prejudice to the *esse naturae* which posits a thing in existence for itself outside of its causes, confers upon a thing, over and beyond its natural perfection of being what it is and not anything else, the meta-natural perfection of being both itself and other without contradiction. It goes without saying that things exhibit an *esse intentionale* only in the order of knowing. The *esse intentionale* clearly cannot be that existence by which the knower is all that he is and is nothing other than he is (that is, his *esse naturae*). In knowing this page then, I come to be it only to the extent that, in knowledge, it can be and is outside of its *esse naturae* but outside its *esse naturae* in an *esse intentionale* similarly extrinsic to my *esse naturae*. Indeed in coming to be the page to know it, I come to be more myself as a knower. Beyond the *esse naturae* which posits it and me in extra-mental existence, in existence in and for oneself, there must be the *esse intentionale,* which posits it and me in a state of identity which, because it transcends the *esse naturae,* overcomes or triumphs over the dispersion of the experienced real in a higher state of unity, higher because immaterial rather than simply material, higher because intentional rather than simply natural.

The same things, in this view, may and do occupy two universes, a universe of knowledge and a universe of existence. They exist both outside of the mind by their *esse naturae* and at the same time within the mind by their *esse intentionale.* Since human knowledge involves inseparably but distinctly the object known and the subject knowing, it may be described, on the part of the thing known, as the process in and through which the thing acquires an *esse intentionale,* and, on the part of the subject knowing, as the process in and through which the subject confers on things an *esse intentionale,* or simply the process of immaterializing things.[10]

The Metaphysics of the Conceptual Act

To account for the objective value of the conceptual representation of singular existents in their value of being and its modes, Maritain re-formulates a classical doctrine as found in the works of John of St. Thomas. There the non-conscious process of intentionalization, by which the knower actively assimilates itself to the sensed real, is accomplished through an inferred sequence of intentional entities whose necessity follows from the conscious evidences exhibited in the sensory, imaginative and conceptual phases of the immediate act of knowing. These entities, which John of St. Thomas calls "species," Maritain calls "objectifying or presentative forms."[11] They are simply those interior immaterial determinations of the knower in act in and through which an existing thing, other in its *esse naturae* from the knower, is interiorized and so present in the knower intentionally rather than as an accident in a substance. Interiorized in this way, the thing known or object exists with the same meta-existence (relative to the extra-mental or natural existence of the thing) as characterizes the knowing subject assimilated to the known object. Knower and known thus acquire an identical existential act which unites them without prejudice to the separate existential acts which separate them in natural existence.

At each successive level of assimilation of the actually existing real in immediate knowledge (sensation, imagination and conception) an appropriate objectifying form is posed as the necessary agency of the subject's assimilation of the object. At the level of sense perception,[12] the external sense receives from the physically external existent, stimulating the external sense organ, a first presentative form that specifies the sense power. To this specification, by which the sense power, through the joint agency of the sensible thing and the *impressed presentative form*, comes to be, in initial act, the sensed object, the sense power responds, in and through its own immanent act, and comes to be the sensed object in terminal act. At the same time, there is produced in the imagination an *expressed presentative form* of the sensible order, a sensible image, through which the sensed object is or can be present in the consciousness though absent from the external sense organ.

At the level of conceptual intellection, the intelligence discloses in the sensed things, thus initially assimilated through the sensible species, something of their potentially intelligible contents (being and its modes). This illuminative function, disclosing depths of meaning present in but not disclosed in the sensible presence, Maritain, following Aristotle and St. Thomas, ascribes to the active intellect. This capacity of the intellectual faculty is said to illuminate the sensible presentations (impressed or received objectifying sensible forms) and representations (expressed objectifying sensible forms or images) in the sense of making their potential intelligibilities actual—an effect accomplished only by leaving aside the concrete singularities of the sensible presences. In the act of disclosing the actual intelligibilities (the value of being and its modes) of the sensed real, the active intellect at the same time determines the apprehensive or receptive intellect through an impressed species of the intelligible order. This impressed intelligible objectifying form is nothing other than the potential intelligibilities of the sensible species made actual by the illuminative function of the active intellect. So moved or determined, the receptive intellect comes to be the object intentionally in first act. To this initial interior determination or actuation, it responds by producing within itself a concept, the *expressed intelligible species,* in and through which it raises the object to the peak of intelligible formation and actuality, and thus comes itself to be in final act the object. This recurrence, in the order of knowing, of the classical distinction between first (initial) and second (terminal) act, in the order of being, Maritain ascribes to the fact that in itself knowledge is found to constitute a complete metaphysical order. It is not surprising then to find transposed into the order of knowing the distinction between essential form and existence from the order of being and the distinction of operative form and operation from the order of action. Through its cognitive powers, the rational soul comes to be (intentionally) initially the object in first act in order that it may then come to be it in second or final act just as in the natural order nature exists before it acts.[13]

In this metaphysical context, the immaterial or objectifying forms are seen to perform two quite different functions. On the one hand, as ontological modifications of the soul, in and through the operative powers which they determine, these forms determine the soul in the same way that any form determines its appropriate subject. Such entitative modifications of one's own natural being are simply and solely dispositive conditions, prerequisite to but in no sense constitutive of cognition.[14] On the other hand, in their function as immaterial instruments of knowledge, they are in themselves nothing but the pure likenesses of objects; likenesses in no way akin to the likeness by which a photograph represents its subject but likenesses in the unique sense of being, in the soul, the object itself as separated from its proper natural existence and endowed with an intentional existence. In this, their proper intentionalizing role, these objectifying forms do not determine a power in the manner of a form determining a subject. On the contrary, they determine alike subject and object in that wholly immaterial or meta-subjective way by virtue of which the knower comes to be, initially in first act and terminally in second act, intentionally the object itself. In such a wholly immaterial informing, the soul receives or undergoes a determination uniquely in order to exert its own vital activity and thus bring itself in act to an existence not confined to itself. It is this act of purely immaterial information that constitutes cognition as such. Accordingly, knowledge, which exhibits itself immediately as an immanent vital operation, turns out, on analysis, to consist essentially, not in doing anything, but in being something; indeed, to consist in becoming and being minimally two things, oneself and other, and each otherwise than by an existence actuating a subject (an *esse naturae*). Such a mode of being, namely, *esse intentionale,* involves a union transcending the union of matter and form which constitutes a natural entity other than its constituents. It demands further that the known object be made present in the knowing power and its operation through an appropriate objectifying form. Finally and in particular, conceptual knowledge is accomplished through a mental word or concept— an objectifying form begotten by the intelligence within itself—in and through which the intelligence comes to be intentionally in second or terminal act this or that existing (actually or possibly) being in one or more of its intelligible determinations.[15]

The Metaphysics of the Concept

Following closely the position of John of St. Thomas, Maritain elaborates further the notion of the concept, or expressed objectifying form of the intelligible order,[16] in terms of a theory of signs which distinguishes sharply between instrumental and formal signs. According to this position, a thing is an instrumental sign when, being first known in and for itself, it consecutively makes known something else. In this sense, smoke is said to be a sign of fire, a portrait of its model, a word of its meaning or referent. In each of these cases, the instrumental sign is seen to be itself an object. A formal sign, on the contrary, is known, if at all, only in making objects known. If it is, in any sense, an object, it is such only consecutively to what it makes known and uniquely in making it known.

The concept, in its proper function of interiorizing in the knower one or another of the intelligible values of the extra-mental things encountered in sense experience, is said to be a formal sign and hence known only reflexively in and through that which it conceptualizes. As a formal sign, the concept presents itself or appears only as a second order reflex object or, in Maritain's phrase, only in disappearing before the direct or conceptualized object. Its whole being is its function of conveying the mind to something other than itself.

That which is known first and foremost in human knowledge is a given thing in one or another of its intelligible values and not, except in a second order reflection, the formal sign, in and through which the thing is rendered present in and to the mind. Just as in remembering it is not the objectifying form (conserved and used by the memory to recall in the present an existentially absent object) which is known, so in conceptual intellection, it is not the concept which confronts the mind and is known but the object presented to the mind through the concept. As formal signs, concepts are and function solely as the intermediaries in and through which conceptual intellection occurs. Such expressed species of the intelligible order or concepts are the only members in the class of formal signs —a unique class, cut-to-order, as it were, to the special requirements of any analysis which discerns and respects the proper nature of human knowledge. All the other signs encountered in our experience are instrumental in character. To ignore or overlook the irreducible originality of the facts of knowledge is to confuse these objectifying forms with instrumental signs as well as to contract the essentially immanent activity of sensation and intellection to the transitive activity of natural bodies. In both circumstances, knowledge itself vanishes.

The Formal and Objective Concept

In conceptual intellection, what conceptualizes and what is conceptualized, the formal sign (formal concept) and the conceived thing (objective concept), are distinct but related. In the concept, we have distinguished the entitative function, by which it is said to be a modification or accident of the soul, from the intentional function, by which it is said to be the formal sign, in and through which an extra-mental thing (actual or possible) is interiorized and grasped by the mind. As rendered mentally present in a formal sign, a thing is said to be a known thing or formal object. The object, thus grasped by the mind in and through the concept as formal sign, is the thing itself in one or another of its intelligible determinations, that is, as it presents itself at the term of the mental process in which it is transposed, initially through sensation and imagination, then through abstraction and conceptualization, from the extra-mental domain of natural existence to the intra-mental domain of intentional existence. As prior to and independent of this knowledge process, the thing is called the material object and as such exists outside of the mind by its natural existence or *esse naturae*.

One and the same object is thus found to be in two different existential states; the one, non-conceptual or extra-mental, is that of its natural existence where it is essentially individual and concrete, the other one, conceptual or intra-mental, is that of its intentional existence where it is essentially universal and abstract. Existentially polyvalent but essentially univalent, the object does not constitute with the thing two distinct terms but a single term or *quod,* which exists for itself in nature as *thing* and is grasped for itself in the mind as *object.* Consider, for example, that the *thing* is Peter who exists extra-mentally now in this place or that: this thing is not only man but also animal, substance, scientist or artist, ill or well. The object, in this instance, will be "man" which has simultaneously in Peter and outside of the mind a natural existence and in the mind an intentional existence. Though it is essential to Peter, the extra-mental *thing,* to be singular and concrete, and to man, the intra-mental *object,* to be abstract and universal, the object, existing in the thing with the *esse naturae,* singular and concrete, proper to the *thing,* and in the concept with the *esse intentionale,* abstract and universal, proper to the concept, remains in and of itself indifferent to both existential states. Accordingly, no unacceptable consequence results when in judgment one predicates an abstract universal of a concrete singular, when, that is, one asserts that Peter is man.

In contrast, the concept or mental word, reflectively discernible in one's thinking the object "man," presents itself as the *terminus in quo,* the interior term, that is, in which the object is intellectually perceived. Maritain finds a word of caution in order here as to the specious materialization and spatialization associated with the unavoidable descriptive terminology.[17] The conceived object is in no wise present in the concept as a material content in a material container any more than the concept contains the object in the manner of a vessel its contents. The concept is said to contain the object only in the sense that through it the object is present in and to the knowing subject. In proffering the concept as the completion of its immanent act, the intellect attains forthwith, in its own act, the object invested in the existential condition of the concept. And this is possible, only because the concept, in its status as formal sign, is nothing but the pure likeness of the object. Here again, as above, the notion of likeness must be purged of all material associations in terms of which it might be construed as a mirror image or as present to the mind's eye as a portrait to the eye of the body. All that remains therefore of the concept as pure likeness, purged of every analogy to instrumental signs, is simply its function of making known the object by bringing it to the peak of immateriality or spiritual interiorization.

Though, in the order of being, hence in its entitative function, the concept may be said to constitute with the object a pair of entities, in the order of knowing, hence in its intentional function, it constitutes no such pair with the object but is simply the object as known. As term or completion of conceptual intellection in act, the concept has as intelligible content the object itself. But this intelligible content which, as object, confronts or is posed before the mind, as concept, is vitally proffered by the mind and has for its proper existence the act of intellection itself. Thus to say that the concept is identical, in its intelligible constitution, to the object itself is not to say that the concept is that which is known but rather that the concept is the inner term in and by which the intellect comes to be in final act that which it knows. As formal sign, the concept is something known precisely and solely to the extent that it makes one to know what is other as other. As the immanent cause of the presentation of the object to and in the intellect in act, the concept is itself suffused in intellectuality in act. Indeed as terminating, in the sense of completing, intellection in act, the concept is one with intellection in completed act. For this reason, it is said that in the concept the object and the intellect are alike in ultimate act of intellectuality. The concept is thought or known, is *intellectum in actu,* only as signifying and not at all as signified term or object.

In its dual function, entitative as a modification of the subject which knows, and intentional as a formal sign of the object which is known, the concept then is in no wise two things but two formal values of one and the same thing; the intentional function relating solely to the act of knowing, the entitative function relating solely to the subject of this act, the soul in its natural existence (*esse naturae*). Arising in the soul as the utterance of the intelligence, already perfected by the *impressed species* and under the action of that created participation of the divine intellect, that peak of spiritual tension, naturally abiding in us and appropriately called the "activating intellect" (*intellectus agens*), this entitative quality or modification of the soul acquires the privilege of transcending its entitative function so that it is present in the faculty in the manner of a spirit. The intelligence, being in itself in vital act, confers this privilege upon the concept by concentrating, as it were, in this single focus, all its spiritual energy with the result that the concept is present in it not simply entitatively, as an informing form, but intentionally as a spiritual form absorbed, not in actualizing an appropriate subject to constitute some third thing, but in terminating the intellect intentionally—in the line of knowing therefore rather than in the line of being, and in just the measure that it expresses and immaterializes the object, making it thus not a thing but a thing *known.* Nonetheless, the immaterial form that is the concept and which the intelligence, rendered in first act by the *impressed species,* begets in itself, under the continuous action of the agent intellect, remains truly the object itself but the object immaterialized and intentionally present. Its whole specification comes from the object since both the intelligence which illuminates (the active intellect) and the intelligence which knows (the receptive intellect in final act) are initially and in themselves completely indeterminate. In short, the concept, in its intentional function, and the object can be distinguished only in that the concept is that which makes known while the object is that which is known, the concept is sign, the object is signified, the concept exists only in the mind, the object exists simultaneously in the mind and in the thing.

Abstraction and Some Ways of Knowing

As distinguished from knowledge in its pre-scientific mode, knowledge in its scientific mode may now be described in terms of the diverse ways in which the knower in act intentionalizes or immaterializes that which it knows. In continuity with the teachings of Aristotle, Aquinas, Cajetan and John of St. Thomas, Maritain explains the diversity of human sciences according to the diverse ways in which they immaterialize all or some of the only real beings directly accessible to human knowers, namely, physical realities, among which the knower finds himself included. Traditionally, this doctrine has been referred to as the degrees of abstraction.[18] We are not here concerned with its historical development or the disputed meanings of its various formulations. Rather we are concerned with the way in which, in Maritain's epistemology, it accounts for the distinction between scientific and pre-scientific knowledge, and, within science, the diversity of its basic types.

In its natural origins, at the level, that is, of immediate experience, human knowledge appears to be akin to animal knowledge in its most developed ranges. As distinguished from the higher animals whose knowing behavior appears not only to originate but also terminate at the same level, human beings, in their knowing activity, exhibit the additional elements commonly designated conceptual, judicative and discursive. This range of spontaneous or natural human knowledge can be conveniently viewed as intermediate between pure sense or animal knowledge and human science, the systematically developed mode of human knowing.

Just as scientific knowledge of nature, the world of things in which the knower finds himself, may be described as a development and perfecting of the obscure and indistinct knowledge of natural knowing, so this natural knowledge may itself be described as a development and perfecting of its initial phase or sense knowledge. Thus, at the level of direct or empirical conceptualization, sensed objects are exhibited in some of the manifold relations of likeness and unlikeness, dependence and independence, priority and posteriority, simultaneity and succession, by which their isolation as sensed singulars or elements in a context of sensed singulars is transcended and something of their complex unity in being is vaguely discerned. In direct conceptualization, the multiple, changing sensed aspects of an existing sensed thing in its sensed environment are transposed by the knower's natural or primitive abstractive power to a conscious domain in which both things and their aspects exhibit properties of uniqueness, universality and separation which are not seen in them as sensed. By virtue of this primal abstractive development of the sensed real in our initial conceptualization of it, the obscure and manifold order exhibited there can be simplified and clarified in classifications which, however arbitrary, as determined by practical psycho-sociological requirements, remain in some measure necessary.[19] At this level of the initial or primitive conceptualization of sensed things, the knower not only consciously discerns the manifold respects or inspects which existing things manifest to a knower naturally equipped to perceive them but also coordinates and subordinates or divides and unites them into quasi ultimate classes and sub-classes, genera and species. At this natural pre-scientific level, the abstractive process tends to separate the non-sensible or intelligible knowable elements and structures of things according to their generality or extensional universality. In Robert, James and William, it separates first the necessity of their being for as much as they are, then their being living, thinking, talking things, in short, the respects in which each one, so irreducibly different in his existential actuality, is seen to be reducibly alike not only to one another and everything else (at least as being) but to increasingly narrower groups of things—physical, vegetative, sentient, thinking bodies. In this initial or primitive and spontaneous inspection and analysis of sensed things, the mind abstracts increasingly general notions, of which the most striking feature appears to be the vagueness or obscurity which is seen to expand with their generality or inclusiveness. From Robert, James, William and . . . the collection of given individual men, the mind separates a vague notion of man; from man, dog, cat and . . . the collection of individual animals, the mind abstracts a vague notion of animal; from animal, plant and inanimate body, the mind abstracts the notion of physical body; and from all of these, the vague notion of being as the basic value of which they are so many divers modes. This first transposition by the primitive abstractive power of sensed things into the realm of increasingly general or inclusive and vague or potential ideas is traditionally called *total abstraction*. The significant feature of totally abstracted objects of thought is not at all the precision or incisiveness of their content but precisely their generality or predicability of an indefinite number of possible existents. However variant the stressed contents of the concept of man in diverse times and cultures, there is always, given the requisite individual and social development, a concept which purports to be descriptive of men and nothing else. In this conceptual order, things are traditionally said to be known first in their more general and vague traits before, by a subsequent consciously organized and reflective effort, being known scientifically in their more specific and necessary traits. In ordinary spontaneous knowledge, one knows men as talking and laughing animals before one knows them as systematic thinkers and, in principle, free agents. The notion of clothed animal is a totally abstract notion which truly presents to the mind a characteristic but not necessary trait of man in everyday experience. These initial conceptual presences of sensed things and their primitive arrangement in one's pre-scientific knowledge, though genuinely representative of things, is representative of them in any of their innumerable traits, whether superficial or profound; it being typical of the mind in this phase of its knowing activity to be more curious than critical, more desiring than discriminating. Through sensation and this, the first mode of conceptualizing, the knowing subject consciously confronts and explores the inexhaustible knowability of the real world in which it finds itself—the real world that from the outset presents itself as both one and many, enduring and changing.

The Generic Types of Science

Having, in pre-scientific knowledge, grasped the real in its diverse initial postures before the mind, the knower advances to the scientific mode when he strives to account for the invariant evidences given in immediate experience and its initial conceptualization. The history of Western thought provides the record of the mind's effort to penetrate and assimilate, according to its natural powers, the vastness and complexity of the universe of persons and things upon which it opens. Unlike the universe and its parts, of which it is man's account to date, this record is a product of man's conscious effort and, as such, embodies alike the successes and failures of those efforts. With the passage of time and the expanding participation in the scientific effort, the record achieves dimensions which transcend the capacities of individuals and begets all the vast paraphernalia of journals, libraries and learned societies. These agencies generate endless additions, to select and evaluate which the whole critical apparatus of modern scholarship has been developed. How, in this vast accumulation of records and this grinding machinery of criticism, is the perennially relevant to be discerned, formulated and communicated except through the formation and expansion of great traditions of learning—the custodians and developers of the genuinely valid elements cast upon the shores of the mind by the irregular tides of the human quest into the secrets of the universe?

Of the Greco-Judaeo-Christian Tradition, the Aristotelian-Thomist element remains one of the living components; the component which, in Maritain's view, is the only one in the Western intellectual tradition possessing an epistemic doctrine adequate to assimilate without distorting the diversities and originalities of man's successes to date in penetrating and grasping something of the unchanging, necessary structures of the real and our knowledges of it.[20]

As noted previously, the critical realist view of science presupposes the Aristotelian-Thomist metaphysics—that domain of inquiry in which to each and every known or knowable reality is assigned a set of necessary features stemming from its position in being. Accordingly, the critical realist doctrine is assigned to metaphysics, not as a material part but as a higher mode in which one not only knows metaphysically but is fully aware of the scope and value of this mode of knowing the real as distinguished from and related to such other modes as have emerged to the present. Philosophy, then, and particularly metaphysics, is not epistemology; rather epistemology presupposes philosophy of which it is nothing more than the fullest reflex possession. With these preliminaries, we may turn to the exposition of the Aristotelian-Thomist doctrine of scientific knowledge in its pure (speculative) as distinguished from its applied (practical) state.

As perfective of spontaneous or pre-scientific knowledge, scientific knowledge presupposes and develops pre-scientific knowledge, the knowledge, that is, of the real encountered immediately in one's sense and direct conceptual knowledge. But since one's ordinary knowledge is acquired not only through direct experience but also through the multiple agencies of instruction (linguistic and institutional) through which the immediate evidences of direct experience are interpreted in order to be used, science tends to control by correcting, where necessary, and expanding the received interpretations of the known facts. It is clear then that the total abstraction in and through which the vague intelligibilities of persons and things in the order of their relative generality are directly grasped by the mind, remains operative in the scientific as in every domain of human conceptual knowledge.

That which, in this doctrine, specifically distinguishes science from pre-science and non-science is the quality of the intelligibility of things as manifested in the scientific mode. This quality derives both from the metaphysical structure of the only existing things man knows immediately—himself and the surrounding world of physical bodies and events—and from the way in which he knows them in this structure. Though explicitly formulated in the works of Aristotle, this doctrine is extended and elaborated in the works of Aquinas and his commentators, Cajetan and John of St. Thomas.

In its terms, the scientific mode of human knowledge is distinguished from its other modes by the necessity of its object and the certainty of its conclusions. The scientific mode of human understanding is defined as a certain knowledge of things in their first causes. What is meant by "first causes" and how one comes to the knowledge of them as well as of the deductive consequences of this knowledge constitute the methodology of traditional philosophy, treated historically in the *Organum* of Aristotle and the classical commentaries on it.[21] That in this vast work which is of interest here, is the epistemological doctrine on the scope and value of the knowing activity which it analyzes and evaluates.

As known scientifically, things are divisible into three classes according to their relation to matter and existence. Some objects of scientific thought, those things known to natural philosophy, are found in the mind without the singularities which diversify them as they are encountered in their natural existence. In discerning these abstract universal objects in the concrete singular existents of sense experience, the abstractive intelligence ignores that in actually existing things which insulates each within itself and makes it to be, as it is in fact, other than every other concrete existent. That which in existing things principles their individuality or singularity was called "singular sensible matter." In abstracting from the singular sensible matter, the abstracting intelligence discerns in such things universal objects of thought bearing an essential reference to sensible experience in that they include the qualities and determinations, characteristic of each and every sensible existent—corporeity, spatial extension, temporal succession, qualitative diversifications and the mobility or changeability in respect both to their being and to these common ways in which they are found to be. That in directly perceived existing things, in virtue of which they are not this natural body or that natural body but simply natural body and as such extended in space and time, affected by diverse qualities and changeable both in their being and their accidents, was named "universal sensible matter." Thus, at the first level or degree of scientific abstraction, the existing things of immediate experience appear as objects of thought which, as separated in thought from individual sensible matter, are universal and unchanging, but, as including universal sensible matter, are essentially changeable. At this level of their scientific knowability, the changing things of direct experience fall under the competence of natural philosophy or natural science. As described traditionally, such objects can neither exist apart from (singular) sensible matter nor be thought of apart from (universal) sensible matter. Being related to matter and existence in this way is thus a distinctive feature of things as they appear to the intelligence, perfected in natural science and philosophy. Accordingly, the conclusions reached in such science and philosophy are subject to a rule of verification or resolution into sensible evidences, ontological or experimental, according as they are scientific or philosophical.[22]

Looking at things in the characteristic light of the first degree of scientific or, as the tradition puts it, formal abstraction, does not however exhaust or disclose all their scientific intelligibility. For the same things exhibit other intelligible necessities which, though inseparable from sensible (both singular and universal) matter in existence, are in thought separable from all sensible matter. Thus, for example, the dimensionless point, the line without thickness and the simplest figures, constructible from these, are thought objects, which, in the consideration of the mathematician, are considered apart from all the sensible or physical properties affecting them as instanced in sensed or imagined things. Such thought objects do not

abstract from that in existing things in virtue of which such things
can be related spatially and numerically in manifold ways. In the
vocabulary of the tradition, that which principles in existing things
these manifold relations was called quantity either continuous (for
abstract or geometric spaces) or discontinuous (for number series).
Thus, existing things, either actual or possible, offer themselves to
the consideration of the mathematician simply as orderable or ar-
rangeable in continua of points or numbers, spaces or series. Such
objects of thought are said to be abstracted from all sensible matter
—that in experienced things which principles both their singular and
common non-spatial and non-numerical qualities—but not from intelligible matter—that in things which principles the diverse ways
in which they can be related in respect to number and position. As
described traditionally, objects of thought, at the second degree of
formal abstraction, the level of abstraction characteristic of mathematical science, cannot exist apart from sensible matter but have to
be thought apart from sensible matter.

There remains, in the existing things of immediate experience, a
final and deepest structure of intelligibility encountered by the scientific mind when it considers in them, not that in virtue of which
they are necessarily changeable, nor that in virtue of which they are
necessarily orderable in respect to number and points, but that in
virtue of which they simply *are,* whatever their kind or mode of
being.[23] At this level of abstraction or scientific consideration, the
mind confronts an object of thought prior to, as presupposed by and
involved in, every other actual or possible object of thought. At this,
the third degree of formal abstraction, the mind discerns in and separates from the existing things of immediate experience, both external and internal, a completely immaterial or intelligible structure,
a domain of thought objects which involve nothing of matter,
sensible or intelligible, in their meaning. To be and to be thought,
such real objects can or must exist and be thought in complete separation from all matter, both sensible and intelligible. For some of
them are found to be that in every known actual or possible real

being without which such beings could neither exist nor be thought. For Maritain, as for the tradition, substance, act, potency, unity are all objects of thought which are found realized extra-mentally not only in the things of our initial immediate experience, natural bodies, but which also present themselves as necessary to anything that could possibly exist. Thus if it were the case that there existed orders of things outside of and beyond the order of bodily things, in which we find ourselves, then the things of these other orders, however else they might be, would involve necessarily, in their being and their intelligibility, these transcendental objects discovered in the existing things of our experience when the mind scrutinizes them in the third order of abstraction.

Beyond these transcendent objects, which are found to be necessarily involved in whatever is, there are other thought objects, God and spirits, the existence of which is not known immediately but mediately. Unlike the objects of thought just described, objects of thought which have to exist if anything, be it material or immaterial, is to be, these objects cannot exist in matter. Such are the credentials of their being that confinement in space and development in time, no less than realization in specifically identical but individually diverse instances, are radically excluded. These then are known, not through any abstractive operation but through a discursive inference from effects, known abstractly, to their necessary causes; inferences, that is, from the evidences of the being of embodied natures to the possibility (angels) and necessity (God) of beings of which we neither have nor can have any natural experience. Such entities are therefore said to be grasped not as terms of the mind's abstractive, but as terms of its discursive, activity; its discursive activity in the domain of the third degree of abstraction, inferring from the factual necessities of things in actual being to the *de jure* necessity of their causes (formal) and ultimately their cause (efficient and final) in being. The being upon which these inferred judgments of the metaphysical order bear is the being of beings (rather than the beings of being) grasped in a judgment of radical separation—a conclusion that asserts that these things that are and are known to be, and are known to be such as they are in the final analysis, by a being that is not they, is not of their order, however perfect they may be, and without which neither they nor anything can be or be thought.

So it is that, at the third level of formal abstraction, the philosophical intelligence enters into the things of nature only to be carried by what it finds to a supra- or meta-natural realm, a realm more congenial to the intelligence in its immaterial and spiritual actualities but more strange to it in the material instrumentalities of its embodied state. To be sure, the achieved understanding of this realm of possible and actual immaterial beings is the fruit of the whole Greco-Judaeo-Christian philosophical tradition in which Maritain finds his place as a contemporary, indeed a most articulate and original, contributor to its Aristotelian-Thomist current. As much as any living contemporary, Maritain has shown that the first and unchanging truths of things and our knowledges of them are not to be found outside of the living tradition of those few who have discovered and conveyed them. As in every age and with each man, the desire to understand what one knows through nature and cultural heritage is realized, if at all, not in isolation from but in living contact with the achieved results of others, past and present, so, today, the principal instrument of one's understanding of the being of things, in its absolutely necessary and universal meanings, remains the accounts of those who have seen and continue to see these truths; an understanding, limited and obscure in the beginning and at the level of the world of bodily things in which we find ourselves and where we first contact things, but expanding and clarifying as one presses the quest with integrity and discipline.

NOTES

1. Jacques Maritain, *Distinguer Pour Unir ou Les Degrés du Savoir* (hereafter designated *DS*), Desclée de Brouwer et Cie, Paris, 1932, pp. 145, 153.
2. *DS*, p. 161.
3. *DS*, pp. 156-157.
4. *DS*, pp. 142-150; Jacques Maritain, *Réflexions sur l'Intelligence* (hereafter designated *RI*), Desclée de Brouwer et Cie, 1930, pp. 289-305.
5. *DS*, pp. 158-159; 161-163.
6. *DS*, pp. 238-239.
7. *DS*, pp. 189-192.
8. *DS*, pp. 176-195.
9. *DS*, pp. 146-155; *RI*, pp. 45-47.
10. *DS*, pp. 166-167, 221-224.
11. *DS*, p. 224.
12. *DS*, pp. 225-226.
13. *DS*, pp. 226-227.
14. *DS*, pp. 220, 228.
15. *DS*, pp. 229-230.
16. *DS*, pp. 231-248, 220.
17. *DS*, pp. 164, 239.
18. Jacques Maritain, *Philosophy of Nature*, translated by Imelda C. Byrne, Philosophical Library, New York, 1951, pp. 12-44; *DS*, pp. 71-93, 106-120.
19. *DS*, pp. 54-58.
20. Jacques Maritain, *Science et Sagesse*, Labergerie, Paris, 1936, pp. 93-122.
21. *DS*, pp. 61-64.
22. *DS*, pp. 93-102.
23. *DS*, pp. 416-444.

James F. Anderson

5. The Role of Analogy in Maritain's Thought

"THANKS to analogical intellection, that natural marvel of lightness and strength which, thrown across the abyss, makes it possible for our knowledge to attain the infinite, the concept, divinely elaborated in the dogmatic formula, contains but does not limit, and causes to descend in us, in an enigmatic and mirrored but altogether true manner, the very mystery of the Deity which pronounces Itself eternally in the uncreated Word, and which has been told in time and in human language by the Incarnate Word." Thus wrote Jacques Maritain in 1929.[1] A few introductory notes—ontological preambles, we may call them—might help prepare the way for what is to follow.

"A philosopher is not a philosopher if he is not a metaphysician."[2] For Maritain, philosophy in all its branches is radically existential. And it is the intellection of being, and of the primacy of the act of being in all things, that lies at the root of the metaphysician's knowledge.[3]

Let the following remarks suffice to indicate the basic existentiality—and hence the fundamentally (I do not say formally) metaphysical character—of Thomist philosophy, both practical and speculative.

88

a. The entire perfection of human moral life centers around and depends upon charity. But there is nothing more "existential" than charity: Love concerns itself supremely with existents in their own personal existences, not with possibles or pure essences. Moreover, the moral virtue par excellence—prudence or practical wisdom— is the seat of judgments whose existentiality lies in their bearing upon particular acts to be brought into being, here and now.

b. Again, Thomist psychology is existentialist to the core. To cite but one of its central themes: Man's substantial and organic unity derives from the actuation in him of prime matter by a spiritual form which is an intellective soul whereby the human composite in its entirety and in all its parts is or exists.

c. Then, too, Thomist epistemology teaches that knowledge itself is a way of existing immaterially in which the knower "intentionally" is or comes to be the known.

d. Moreover, the whole Thomistic theory of causality is radically existentialist in that every sort of cause *is* a cause precisely by virtue of its existential contribution—its *influxum ad esse causati*.[4] Matter causes existence as ground of form, which of itself implies a relationship to existence since form is that by which a thing is determinately constituted for existence; the agent's action is an overflow into existence—an existential superabounding; and the end or final cause is the reason for all this existentiality as well as for the tendency of things to seek their own fulfillment in be-ing.

e. The Thomist philosophy of nature, furthermore, is basically an existential one because its formal subject is *ens mobile,* or that which exists mutably. And the entire hylomorphic doctrine, which is fundamental to it, is existentially oriented, prime matter and substantial form being conceived of as primary constituents of that which substantially is or exists.

f. In fact, even Thomistic logic—whose subject is the "being-of-reason"—is unintelligible without reference to the "being-of-nature" of which the "being-of-reason" is the correlate in the order of ideal existence. And the modes and conditions of existence enjoyed by things as objects of thought pose a perennial problem of cardinal significance in this logic.

There is no need to multiply examples. In Thomism, nothing whatever makes sense except in reference to existence or some form of it: without *esse,* nothing is; and if nothing is, nothing is intelligible.

One may, however, inquire as to the status in Thomism of the object indicated by the word "essence." Specifically one asks whether this name is used to signify the intelligible structure of things, and if things would be knowable to us unless they were intelligibly structured in ways accessible to the human mind. The answer is that "essence" does mean this and that without it nothing would be naturally knowable.

It is nevertheless crucially important to realize that the very notion of "essence" implies relationship to existence. True enough, the concept of existence cannot be cut off from that of essence: existence is always the existence of some thing—of a *what.* But even so, "essence" means precisely "that through which and in which a thing has existence."[5] "Essence," in the Thomistic sense, signifies capacity to *be* or *exist.* The basic Thomist teaching on "essence" is formally existential. Now we proceed to the center of our specific topic.

Analogy in Metaphysics

What Maritain calls the "intuition of being" is in itself a simple act, although it implies the judgment of existence. And it is this intellective act, he says,[6] which "makes the metaphysician." Analogy comes in precisely at this point. For it is impossible to grasp being in a properly metaphysical way without simultaneously apprehending its essentially analogous value: Being as such (which is the distinctive object of the metaphysician) is, as Maritain puts it, "grasped by a pure and genuine intuition only when its polyvalence or analogy, its essentially analogous value, is grasped *at the same time.*"[7]

Analogy is a property of the concept of being and of its predication because being is intrinsically present in all things in ways essentially diverse yet proportionally one. For Maritain, the primordial value of this concept lies in the fact that it makes accessible to the human mind "an entire universe of possible knowledge and intelligibility . . . which is not *one* thing, purely and simply one, but which is everywhere found in essentially different forms."[8]

Being confronts the metaphysical intellect as a purely intelligible object entailing an *ordered*[9] unity of diverse members participating proportionally though unequally in that common perfection which it is.

The fact can scarcely be overstressed that being is attained metaphysically only through apprehending its analogous or proportional diversification; as a metaphysical object, "being" is in every instance made known by the likeness of relations which the most diverse things have with it.

In metaphysics "being" signifies a properly analogous object whose analogicity is fundamental existentially and formal logically: things *exist* in various proportionally similar ways; therefore they are *known* in various proportionally similar ways. This sort of analogicity—"inscribed in the very nature of the concept of being"[10] —is the mark of analogy of proper proportionality. For Jacques Maritain the notion of being is analogical originally and in its essence; it is not a univocal concept afterwards employed analogically, as in analogies of attribution and of metaphor.[11]

The notion of being, though purely and simply multiple, enjoys a certain properly proportional unity, such that as each nature or essence is to its act of being so every other one is to its: the inseparable essence-existence pair constitutes the essential *structure* of the concept of being. Maritain sees the root of metaphysical analogy in the proportion of these two to each other in all things.[12]

Maritain notes the impossibility of thinking *being* without thinking *essence-existence,* and without thinking them as proportioned to one another:[13] in this ontologic unity and proportion lies the "substantial form" of that concept's intrinsic analogicity.

And according to him, it is just because "authentic existentialism" affirms the primacy of the act of existence[14] that it affirms likewise the inherently analogous character of the concept of being. For despite the inseparability of the notion of essence from that of existence, it is *existential* diversity which in the last analysis is the basis of the intrinsic analogicity of that concept.[15]

Now if, as Maritain has said, it is the intuition of being that makes the metaphysician, this metaphysically-generative insight has not for its *formal* object either the "vague being of common sense," or the "particularised being of the sciences and the philosophy of nature," or the "derealised being of logic," or the "pseudo-being of dialectics mistaken for philosophy." This formally metaphysical object, on the contrary, is being *qua* being; it is being, disengaged for its own sake, in the fullness of its own intrinsic values; it is, he says, being in all its *"analogical* and transcendental amplitude."[16] And he goes on to assert that it is the imperfect and multiple unity of being, as seen in this properly metaphysical light, which permits its unlimited extension to all its analogates, i.e., to all beings without exception.[17]

It can hardly be overemphasized that this object—being, including implicitly all its properly transcendental values—is simply unperceivable save in the light of its "irreducible proportionality or analogy" which is rooted in the fact that *"a* is to its own *act of existing (esse),* as *b* is to its own *act of existing (esse)."*[18] Thus, for Maritain, analogy is grounded absolutely in the being of things: "This," he says, "is precisely what judgment discovers, namely, the actuation of a being by the act of existing, grasped as extending beyond the limits and conditions of empirical existence; grasped, therefore, in the limitless amplitude of its intelligibility."[19]

As Maritain has so well explained, it is proportionality *or* analogy which alone accounts for the fact that this limitless intelligibility is intrinsically and properly realized in things: things *exist* always and only in *proportion* to their natures. And he is but voicing the thought of his thirteenth-century master in reminding us of the cardinal fact that "existence is the term as a function of which metaphysics knows everything that it does know."[20] For them both it is equally true that the name "being" refers not only to that which things are but also to their very act of existing.[21]

With these rudimentary and cardinal truths in mind one should not be surprised to read that "the worst metaphysical heresy is that which regards being as the *genus generalissimum* and makes of it at one and the same time a univocal thing and a pure essence." On the contrary, our author goes on to say, "Being is not a universal; its infinite amplitude, its super-universality . . . is that of an implicitly multiple object of thought which, *analogically,* permeates all things and descends, in its irreducible diversity, into the very heart of each . . . ."[22]

Analogy in Epistemology

Maritain's epistemology is an intrinsic part of his metaphysics because, with St. Thomas Aquinas, he conceives of knowledge as a way of *being* which transcends the limitations of material existence and reaches out to all that in any way is or can be.

This point is made clear through reflection upon the fact not only that knowledge consists in "becoming immaterially the other" but also that this "other" admits of no possible exception or exclusion: whatever is, is somehow knowable.

Just as Maritain's theory of being is analogical through and through, so of necessity is his theory of knowledge. That is why he envisages a proportional oneness, a unity of order, an organic hierarchy, of the degrees and modes of knowledge while insisting upon their specific diversity.[23]

There is *unity* because all knowledges, despite their variety and distinctness, are ways of being united with things "intentionally" by whatever means, whether by abstract conceptualization, as in science and philosophy; or by inclination, sympathy, congeniality, connaturality, as in the non-reflective, pre-scientific moral knowledge of the just man (who *lives* justice), in the mystical knowledge of the contemplative (who *lives* divine things), and in the poetic, non-conceptual knowledge of the artist.

There is *order* because knowledges fall naturally, according to Maritain, into an organic hierarchy, which extends from all the degrees and modes of rational cognition and wisdom[24] up to all the degrees and modes of supra-rational knowledge and wisdom.

He insists no less than his medieval master, moreover, that the modes of knowledge are to be viewed and assessed in various perspectives—in their subject-matters, in their specific formalities, in the ways of attaining their objects, in their ends. And yet he too maintains that they all present, amidst irreducible diversity, an ordered unity albeit a purely proportional one. And this of course is the mark of analogical unity in the most basic sense of proper proportionality.

It is clear that such an analogical community obtains among all degrees of abstract intellective knowledge, both the scientific and the philosophical, the practical and the speculative, whether derived from rational or supra-rational sources. For all these ways of knowing are one in attaining their objects through concepts.

But if there are non-conceptually mediated modes of genuine cognition, then these too must be embraced within the analogical community of knowledge. Now for Maritain (as for St. Thomas Aquinas) there are such modes of knowledge, which he designates by the equivalent expressions: "inclination," "sympathy," "congeniality," "connaturality."[25]

He states, however, that these two generic ways of knowing—the abstractive conceptually-mediated, and the non-conceptually mediated—are "entirely different types of knowledge."[26] Is there then any real link between them *as knowledges*? That is the question.

The question, I think, is answered in the light of the principle of proportionality or analogy. For Maritain's statement that these two are "entirely different types of knowledge" means only that they are other *in their mode*: although the manner in which these types are cognitive—and genuinely cognitive—is simply diverse, it is proportionally the same in both cases. The link between such modally diverse types of knowledge is a properly analogical one since they are ways of intentional-cognitive union, despite their irreducible diversity both as regards the objects they attain and the means through which they attain them.

In summary one may say that the principle of analogy is of prime significance in Maritain's metaphysics as well as in his epistemology (solidary with it) inasmuch as both are conceivable only in terms of the ordered unity of proportionally similar acts as *being*—of *esse reale* in the first case, of *esse intentionale* in the second.

Analogy in the Philosophy of Nature

Here too the notion of analogy plays a central role, though it looms less large than in the metaphysical world. The reason for this lies in the famous formula expressing the proper subject of natural philosophy, viz., *ens mobile*—mutable being. For if the *"mobile"* does limit the *"ens,"* the latter term nevertheless points to the ontological nature of this mode of knowledge and its consequent involvement in analogical ways of conceiving and defining its objects. As Jacques Maritain himself puts it: the proper, formal perspective of mutability is one "which restricts the notion of being without depriving it of its transcendental and analogical character."[27]

But does mutability itself account for the fact that the object of the philosophy of nature *is* analogous and is conceived of and predicated accordingly? It does not.[28] For that which makes any notion "analogical" lies fundamentally in the *existential* variety of its proportional realization. To understand this point is to see that the intrinsic possession of being, in diverse and proportionally similar ways, is precisely what makes the notion of mutable being analogous—makes it analogous, and properly analogous, not *qua* mutable, but *qua* being.

That is why it would be a mistake, in Maritain's eyes, to define the philosophy of nature "by saying that its specifying object is an object of thought of the generic order, such as *corpus naturale,* bodies and their properties."[29] In that case one would have failed to bring out the fact that the philosophy of nature "bears on being with the analogicity that being connotes."[30]

Nevertheless, one may well ask how the notion of being can really retain its proper analogicity under the restriction of mutability to which it is subject in the philosophy of nature. Is not being as apprehended metaphysically alone essentially analogous? And is not the notion of mutable being necessarily a quasi-generic one, because of its very restrictedness?

To these questions Maritain has not, as far as I know, expressly replied. But the answers are implicit, I think, in his doctrine concerning the "polyvalence" or "analogicity" of the notion of existence, understood as that primary metaphysical object which signifies "the seal of all perfection."[31]

For in the first place, mutability clearly does not restrict being in the sense of limiting it to a category of the Aristotelian type, viz., a form that is univocally predicable by virtue of signifying its object directly, *in precision from existence.* As Maritain repeatedly notes, the meaning of *esse* is always essentially analogous; analogicity is an inseparable property of *esse*; *esse* signifies that "act"— existing—whose polyvalence consists in the proportional unity-in-diversity of its presence everywhere.

It is no less clear, secondly, that being is inconceivable as a univocal genus, determinable by factors extrinsic to its own essential signification. (Being cannot be thought of as a "pure" form cut off from its "inferiors," for they too are and are beings.) The notion of being embraces all things (actually though indeterminately) within the scope of its essential meaning.[32] For Jacques Maritain (as for St. Thomas Aquinas) the philosophy of nature *is* a philosophy because it bears upon being. Its object, he says, "is always 'being,' which is an essentially analogous object of thought permeating all generic and specific diversifications, but 'being' restricted by the note 'mutable' or 'moving'—being insofar as it is mutable." *"That is why,"* he continues, *"we are confronted here with a philosophy."*[33]

If all this is true, then the answer to our question as to whether the notion of being retains its proper analogicity under the restriction of mutability is clearly an affirmative one. For Maritain, a philosophical science, as distinct from any sort of positive, phenomenalistic or empiriological one, is *formally* ontological in its principal bearing. Its object is therefore seen to be properly and essentially analogous even when its transcendentality is restricted, as it is in the philosophy of nature. An ontological way of knowing cannot but entail analogous conception by virtue of attaining to things in their *being*. This is the point that Jacques Maritain has kept constantly in mind when dealing with every sort of *philosophical* problem.

Allow me to add a few remarks concerning his views of the relevance of this principle of analogous unity to the problem of the relationship between the philosophy of nature and two other areas of knowledge: positive science and metaphysics.

As to the first—positive or "empiriological" science—he notes that the aspect of oneness-in-diversity (which is the hallmark of such unity) arises from the fact that while both have the same subject—*ens mobile*—and generically the same formal object—*ens sub ratione mobilitatis*—they are nevertheless specifically distinct as regards the "objective lights" or "formal perspectives" of conceiving and defining that are proper to them.[34]

As to the second—metaphysics—suffice it to say that this same principle of analogy plays a prominent part in Maritain's understanding of the order obtaining between these two ontological sciences. For here too formal distinctness goes hand-in-hand with complementarity: metaphysics "is in itself and formally independent of the philosophy of nature . . . but materially, and *quoad nos*, it presupposes it."[35]

"In the order of dispositive and material causality," Maritain observes,[36] "the wisdom *secundum quid* of the philosophy of nature, *considered at least in its first positions,* is a *condition* of speculative wisdom purely and simply of the natural order, that is, a condition of metaphysics." This "material dependence" of metaphysics upon the philosophy of nature excludes the possibility of our acquiring metaphysical wisdom except by means of analogizing from the sensible data of common experience conceived of ontologically in the order of the philosophy of nature. It is this latter science alone that makes it possible for us to discover in sensible things "analogical traces of deeper realities and truths which are the proper object of metaphysics."[37]

Analogy in Moral and Socio-Political Philosophy

Maritain has written very extensively on almost every aspect of practical philosophy.[38] Leaving aside the sphere of theoretical ethics—second only to metaphysics as concerns the central significance of the principle of analogy in it— and turning to the social and political realms, we find this notion everywhere lighting the way. For Maritain's whole conception of the nature of societies (whether natural or supernatural in character) is, like that of St. Thomas Aquinas, an analogical one: a society is an "order"; a social order entails not only plurality, diversity, and inequality of prior and posterior members, but also a certain oneness, which in them all (excepting only the Blessed Trinity) consists in a proportional community of diverse and unequal members or parts.[39]

Respect for the transcendentality and analogicity of the notion of order is expressly a first principle guiding Maritain's social and political thought—a respect rationally demanded because the notion of order "touches upon the notion of unity and thus belongs to the domain of the transcendentals, admitting all sorts of levels and degrees of realization," so that "it would be a prime disorder not to respect the hierarchy of divers orders, and make of the notion of order a diminished idea through considering it only in its inferior analogues."[40]

For Maritain the concept of order is simply basic to all social and political philosophy. But order is inconceivable, save analogically.

Now the fundamental position of the notion of order in Maritain's socio-political thought is shared by what he calls "the pluralist principle."[41] He thinks of it as the inseparable companion of that notion and avails himself liberally of its services: his whole philosophy of democratic order, in its most practical as well as its theoretical aspects, is understood to hinge upon this principle, analogously conceived and analogously applied. That is why he is able to maintain that "men possessing quite different, even opposite, metaphysical or religious outlooks, can converge, not by virtue of any identity of doctrine, but by virtue of an analogical similitude in practical principles, toward the same practical conclusions, and can share in the same practical democratic faith, provided that they similarly revere, perhaps for quite diverse reasons, truth and intelligence, human dignity, freedom, brotherly love, and the absolute value of moral good."[42]

Practical co-operation among men of good will living in a divided world depends upon the acceptance (even if it be only implicit) of this principle of analogous unity amidst irreducible diversity.[43] For such co-operation is possible only if men "distinguish properly between the rational justifications, inseparable from the spiritual dynamism of a philosophical doctrine or a religious faith, and the practical conclusions which, separately justified for each, are, for all, analogically common principles of action."[44]

An additional instance of Maritain's use of the principle of analogy in the socio-political order concerns his conception of society as communitarian and personalist: "It is not in a univocal manner," he remarks,[45] "that such a conception can be realized at different epochs of the world's history, but in an analogous manner." For although that history presents divers political regimes and specifically different types of common good corresponding to each of them, it has even so a certain unity and order among its various items and parts.[46]

It is the analogicity of the principle of the "common good" which, in Maritain's eyes as in those of St. Thomas Aquinas, alone makes intelligible everywhere (not only in the socio-political scheme of things) this fact of ordered unity-in-diversity. For order, at least in created things, implies a multiplicity disposed toward an end which is its "common good." Always, the many are to the one as parts to the whole; and the part is for the sake of the whole. And just as there exist innumerable kinds and instances of part-whole relationship, so is there an infinite analogous variety of the "common good," whose objective Prime Analogate is, of course, the single personal Whole that is God.

In dealing with every sort of question involving communities, societies, and persons it is well to bear in mind Aristotle's maxim that the good of the whole is "more divine" than the good of the parts. It was St. Thomas Aquinas who, as Maritain remarks,[47] applied this notion "according to the most diverse degrees of analogy"—and not the least significantly to the problem of the common good of human society.[48]

Not only is it useful and necessary for a sound social philosophy to bring to light the analogical diversity present throughout the realm of social and political regimes, but the same holds true as regards the philosophical study of types of culture and of Christian civilization; for here too the equivocist and the univocist errors must be avoided on pain of making everything unintelligible: "A philosophy of *equivocity* will imagine that with a change in time historical conditions become so different that they depend on supreme principles which are themselves heterogeneous: as though truth and right, the supreme rules of human action, were mutable. A philosophy of *univocity* would lead us to believe that these supreme rules and principles always apply in the same way, and that in particular the way in which Christian principles are proportioned to the conditions of each age and are realized in time should not vary at all."[49]

Rejecting these two erroneous approaches, Maritain explains

that "the true solution is found in the philosophy of *analogy*. The principles do not change, nor the supreme practical rules of human life. But they are applied in ways essentially diverse, ways answering to the same concept only according to a likeness of proportions. And this supposes that one has not merely an empirical and, we might say, a blind notion, but a truly rational and philosophical notion of the diverse phases of history."[50]

This notion he applies to the eminent problem of a new Christendom suited to the conditions of "the historic age we are entering" —a Christendom incarnating analogically the same principles as the prior ones but conceived of according to a type *essentially* distinct from them all: "A new age of the world will allow the principles of any vitally Christian civilization to be realized in terms of a new concrete analogue."[51]

Indeed it may be said that Maritain's whole conception of integral humanism, of Christian democracy, of the relations of Church and State, of pluralism in the structure of the body politic, as in the economic and the juridical spheres, and in education—that all this philosophy is meaningful only in the light of the principle of analogy (I do not say that this is the unique key to understanding it), since in every case one has to do with order, with the one and the many, with *proportional* unities amidst irreducible diversities.[52]

Analogy in Art and Aesthetics

In his epistemology of art[53] Maritain develops an analogical application of the general notion of connatural knowledge, conceiving of artistic, or in the broad sense, poetic, cognition as one of its specific kinds.[54] It is, he says,[55] "a knowledge through affective connaturality which essentially relates to the creativity of the spirit and tends to express itself in a work."

Maritain insists that this sort of connatural knowledge, like its other authentic forms, is genuinely cognitive: in it, "the object created, the poem, the painting, the symphony . . . plays the part played in ordinary knowledge by the concepts and judgments produced within the mind."[56]

Moreover, he conceives of "emotion," and its various roles, analogously: in art and poetry emotion is a vehicle of creative expression and is not to be confused with merely subjective feeling as a simple psychological state.[57]

Another striking instance of this same principle of analogy explicitly at work in Maritain's aesthetics appears in his conception of the relationship between the Fine Arts and Wisdom. The "curious analogy" here lies first in the fact that the Fine Arts, like Wisdom, are ordered to a humanly transcendent object, whose inherent value is likewise limitless: beauty is as infinite as being. It lies also in their common disinterestedness: both the Fine Arts and Wisdom are pursued for their own sakes. Then, too, their whole value is spiritual and they share in common a contemplative "mode of being."[58]

The extensiveness of Maritain's use of the notion of analogy in his aesthetical theory is evident from the fact that for him true art, as a virtue or *"habitus"* of the practical intellect essentially ordained to making, has always a purely *proportional* realization in diverse contexts: the Free and the Mechanical, the Liberal and the Servile arts are all truly arts despite the sharp distinctions between them. Indeed, were "art" not conceived of analogically its primordial philosophic meaning would be missed, because the very notion of "making" is itself intrinsically and properly analogous.[59]

If Maritain's whole philosophy of art and poetry is, from one point of view, dominated by the notion of analogy,[60] it is the same with his theory of beauty, which provides the metaphysical basis of that philosophy: "Like being and the other transcendentals, it (beauty) is essentially *analogous*, that is to say, it is predicated for diverse reasons . . . of the diverse subjects of which it is predicated: each kind of being *is* in its own way, is *good* in its own way, is *beautiful* in its own way."[61]

The analogicity of the notion of beauty, as "splendor of the form on the proportioned parts of matter,"[62] clearly appears not only from its transcendentality but also from an analysis of its basic ontological requirements of integrity and perfection, right proportion or harmony, radiance or *claritas*.[63] For all these must and can only be understood analogically.[64]

In order to understand that Maritain's whole philosophy of art and poetry follows the tradition of his medieval master in its metaphysical grounding, one need only reflect that the word "beauty" refers essentially to a polyvalent property of being as being. And yet one would miss the mark badly in failing to appreciate the distinctive difference of this "property" from all the rest: Beauty alone can be said to be "the radiance of all the transcendentals united."[65] For "wherever there is anything existing, there is being, form and proportion; and wherever there is being, form and proportion, there is some beauty."[66] Beauty thus synthesizes, in a certain fashion, all the prime transcendentals.

One must not forget however that the property of causing delight and joy, which is implicit in the idea of the beautiful and is to be understood in its full analogical amplitude, robs beauty of none of its objective reality. For beauty, as "the power of the real to reveal itself to our apprehension and in that vision to move us to delight, is *at once* a relation to a subject and an intrinsic constituent of things . . . ."[67]

In the aesthetical philosophy of Jacques Maritain, as in that of St. Thomas Aquinas, the notion of "knowledge through connaturality" is therefore clearly an analogous one, realized diversely in different contexts according to a certain proportional unity of meaning.

Analogy in Theology (Supernatural)

Coming full circle, we conclude with a few remarks about Maritain's conception of the theological relevance of analogy. Here again he is at one with St. Thomas in maintaining the cardinal significance of this principle. For Maritain well knows that if the principle of analogy alone makes possible in natural theology the contact of finite mind with infinite mind, this is all the more true as concerns the wisdom of dogmatic-supernatural theology, the first being the inseparable servant of the second.

The quotation prefacing this essay[68] sums up the matter admirably. And the rudimentary point of it all is contained, I think, in the following two propositions: (1) Proportional participation in the order of being grounds that unique form of intrinsic analogous predication called "proper proportionality"; (2) Without this grounding, affirmative dogmatic theology as a speculative conceptual science would remain unborn. Consider why.

The very notions used in the elaboration of dogmatic theology can be a means of true knowledge of God in His revealed nature only through their supereminent and infinite, albeit properly proportional, realization in Him. Were this not so, dogmatic formulae would have no proper value as formal vehicles of truth; at best their value would be improper and indirect, metaphorical or symbolic. They could not then be proposed to us as objects of genuine theological faith because such faith is directly and properly an *intellectual* assent to *truth,* for all that it is truth divinely revealed and not humanly accessible.[69] Now, the speculative science of affirmative or "cataphatic" theology is not the only form of theological knowledge: there is a negative, "apophatic" theology which is in its essence mystical contemplation, and which involves a trans-metaphysical degree of analogy or of "ananoetic intellection," viz., "the super-analogy of faith."[70]

The analogical instrument bestowed upon us by faith enables us to attain God with such non-metaphorical notions as fatherhood, sonship, generation, (three having the same nature, personal union with human nature, love of friendship between creature and Creator). This instrument is nothing other than a revealed analogy substituting for the vision of God in Himself. Through it, the human mind can enjoy a certain ananoetic knowledge which is supra-rational (not non-rational) as regards the uncreated Object wherein it terminates, while remaining conceptual and human in respect of the created objects through which it passes on the way to that Object.[71] Of course these created analogues—the father, the son, the redeeming of something wilfully forfeited or lost—form part of our human world.

Although the super-analogy of faith is humbler than metaphysical analogy because it is grounded upon such lowly human things, nevertheless we know through God's own word that it attains secrets about Him unknown to metaphysics. For *His revelation alone* has made it possible for the human mind to understand that such things as fatherhood and sonship have a transcendent and properly anal-ogous value, viz., "the value of analogy of proper proportionality."[72] "The names of Father, Son, and Holy Ghost are not metaphorical; they designate (yet without containing or circumscribing) what the divine Persons are intrinsically and formally . . . . Under its livery of poverty the super-analogy of faith conceals a supernatural vigour. By it we attain . . . the Divine Essence as it is naturally participable by no creature, and as no created perfection of itself can show it to our reason."[73]

The super-analogy of faith embraces also the images, symbols, and parables abounding in Holy Scripture, since in fact they are metaphorical analogies concealing and containing *analogies of proper proportionality*.[74] That is why they enable us to know (though improperly if taken literally) the intimate things of God: "They contain an authentically ananoetic significance (an anal-ogy of proper proportionality) which appears when we have re-course to other terms,"[75] although they too fall far short of expressing the exceeding richness of those Things.[76]

It is just because man is endowed with an intellect that his basic way of knowing is ontological: the intellect is made to know being even as the eye is made to see color. But "being" is the name of an intrinsically analogous notion. Analogicity therefore pervades all human conception of things in their being, even of the Divine Things proposed to us conceptually in the teachings of Faith. Throughout his work Jacques Maritain has kept constantly in focus this mark of "authentic existentialism."

NOTES

1. Preface to the second edition of *La Philosophie Bergsonienne* (Paris: Téqui, 1930), p. 15; Eng. trans.: *Bergsonian Philosophy and Thomism* (New York: Philosophical Library, 1955), p. 17.
2. "Un philosophe n'est pas un philosophe s'il n'est métaphysicien." J. Maritain, *Court traité de l'existence et de l'existant* (Paris: Hartmann, 1947), p. 37; Eng. trans.: *Existence and the Existent* (New York: Pantheon, 1948), p. 19. (This book has also been printed in paperback: New York: Image Books, 1956; we shall cite this last edition hereafter).
3. This is what Maritain means primarily by "the intuition of being"; it is an act of intellective knowledge which is at once abstractive and judgmental.
4. St. Thomas Aquinas, *In V Metaph.*, lect. 1 (ed. Cathala-Spiazzi, n. 751).
5. "Quidditas vel essentia dicitur secundum quod per eam et in ea ens habet *esse.*" St. Thomas Aquinas, *De Ente et Essentia*, cap. 1 (ed. J. Perrier).
6. J. Maritain, *Existence and the Existent*, p. 29.
7. *A Preface to Metaphysics: Seven Lectures on Being* (New York: Sheed and Ward, 1939), p. 63. (Italics added.)
8. *Ibid.*
9. See the conclusive study by Yves R. Simon, "On Order in Analogical Sets," *The New Scholasticism*, Vol. XXXIV, no. 1 (Jan. 1960), pp. 1-42.
10. J. Maritain, *A Preface to Metaphysics*, p. 64.
11. J. Maritain, *The Degrees of Knowledge,* newly translated under the supervision of Gerald B. Phelan (New York: Scribner, 1959), Appendix II, pp. 418-420.

12. *A Preface to Metaphysics*, p. 65.
13. *Ibid.*
14. *Existence and the Existent*, p. 13.
15. One thing alone prevents the univocal predication of *being*, viz., diversity with respect to the act of existing: *diversus habitudo ad esse impedit univocam praedictationem entis*, as St. Thomas puts it (*De Potentia*, VII, 7, resp.).
16. *Existence and the Existent*, p. 29. (Italics added.)
17. *Ibid.*
18. *Ibid.*, p. 40.
19. *Ibid.*
20. *Ibid.*, p. 41. This is necessarily so, because it is *esse* alone that makes whatever is to *be*, to *be* intelligible, to *be* all that it is: *hoc quod dico esse est inter omnia perfectissimum* (St. Thomas Aquinas, *De Potentia*, VIII, 2, ad 9).
21. E.g., see St. Thomas Aquinas, *In II Sent.*, d. XXXIV, q. 1, a. 1; J. Maritain, *Existence and the Existent*, pp. 42-43.
22. *Existence and the Existent*, p. 42. (Italics added.)
23. Cf. J. Maritain, *The Range of Reason* (New York: Scribner, 1952), "On Human Knowledge," chap. 1, pp. 3-18.
24. See Maritain's master-work, *Distinguer pour unir, ou Les degrés du savoir* (*Distinguish to unite, or the Degrees of Knowledge*), which is a vast exploration of this whole noetic field.
25. *The Range of Reason*, pp. 16-17.
26. *Ibid.*, pp. 3, 16.
27. *Philosophy of Nature* (New York: Philosophical Library, 1951), p. 119.
28. Though it is true indeed that the notion of mutable being could not be essentially analogous, i.e., analogous by proper proportionality, were "mutability" the name of a univocal genus.
29. *Philosophy of Nature, loc. cit.*
30. *Ibid.*
31. *The Degrees of Knowledge*, Pt. I, chap. V, n. 12, p. 218.
32. Cf. St. Thomas Aquinas, *In V Metaph.*, lect. 9 (*ed. cit.*, n. 889); *Quaestiones quodlibetales*, II, q. 2, a. 1 (3) (ed. Marietti).
33. *Philosophy of Nature*, p. 119. (Italics added.)
34. Namely, for the philosophy of nature: sensible being insofar as it is intelligible; for positive science: sensible being insofar as it is observable and measurable. Cf. *Philosophy of Nature*, pp. 135-139.

35. J. Maritain, *Science and Wisdom*, third printing (New York: Scribner, 1954), p. 36.
36. *Ibid.*, pp. 49-50. (Some italics added.)
37. *Ibid.*, p. 68.
38. His bibliography in this area contains some two hundred items, including books, essays and articles. See *The Achievement of Jacques and Raïssa Maritain: a bibliography, 1906-1961*, by Donald and Idella Gallagher (New York: Doubleday, 1962).
39. Cf. J. Maritain, *Du régime temporel et de la liberté* (Paris: Desclée De Brouwer et Cie, 1933), pp. 68, 89-95.
40. *Ibid.*, p. 89. (My translation.) These views are expounded and defended by Maritain with remarkable thoroughness and depth, above all in his great work *Humanisme intégral* (Paris: Aubier, 1936).
41. See *The Range of Reason*, Ch. XII, "The Pluralist Principle in Democracy," pp. 165-171.
42. *Ibid.*, p. 167.
43. See Maritain's Inaugural Address to the Second International Conference of UNESCO, "The Possibilities for Co-operation in a Divided World," in *The Range of Reason*, Ch. XIII, pp. 172-184.
44. *Ibid.*, p. 180.
45. *Humanisme intégral*, p. 144. (My translation.)
46. Cf. St. Thomas Aquinas, *In VII Polit.*, lect. 6; *Summa theologiae*, II-II, 61, 2.
47. J. Maritain, *The Person and the Common Good* (New York: Scribner, 1947), p. 19.
48. *Ibid.*
49. *Humanisme intégral*, p. 145. (My translation.)
50. *Ibid.*, p. 145. (My translation.)
51. *Ibid.*, p. 146. (My translation.)
52. His entire socio-political thought illustrates this point, but see especially *Humanisme intégral, Du Régime temporel et de la liberté, Man and the State, Religion and Culture*, and "Thomist Views on Education," in *Modern Philosophies and Education*, ed. by Nelson B. Henry (Fifty-fourth Yearbook of the National Society for the Study of Education; Distributed by University of Chicago Press, 1955), pp. 57-90.
53. Developed in such works as *Creative Intuition in Art and Poetry* (New York: Pantheon, 1953); *Art and Scholasticism and The*

Frontiers of Poetry (New York: Scribner, 1962); and *The Situation of Poetry* (New York: Philosophical Library, 1955)—as also in many essays.

54. Other species of it are found, for instance, in the domains of moral-practical knowledge—the just man ignorant of moral science *knows* what is good and what is bad—; in mystical experience—the "spiritual man" of the Gospel *knows* divine things through "suffering" them, not through theological science—; in the "know-how" of the athlete unable to explain his skill, etc. The generic notion of "connatural knowledge" extends to every type of true cognition attained through non-conceptual means.

55. *Creative Intuition in Art and Poetry* (New York: Pantheon, 1953), p. 118.

56. *Ibid.*

57. Of course both types of emotion are causal factors in the production of art: the creative—"intentional"—type being a formal factor, and the subjective type a material one. Cf. *Ibid.*, pp. 118-125.

58. Cf. *Art and Scholasticism and The Frontiers of Poetry*, pp. 33-34.

59. *Ibid.*, Ch. IV, "Art an Intellectual Virtue," pp. 10-22; Ch. V, "Art and Beauty," pp. 23-37.

60. *The Situation of Poetry*, pp. 51-52.

61. *Art and Scholasticism and The Frontiers of Poetry*, p. 30.

62. *Ibid.*, p. 25.

63. Cf. *Summa theologiae*, I, 39, 8; II-II, 145, 2, with 180, 2, ad 3.

64. Cf. *Art and Scholasticism and The Frontiers of Poetry*, pp. 27-30.

65. *Ibid.*, n. 66, p. 173.

66. *Ibid.*

67. Gerald B. Phelan, "The Concept of Beauty in St. Thomas Aquinas," in *Some Aspects of the New Scholastic Philosophy* (New York: Benziger, 1932), p. 126. (Italics added.) Cf. J. Maritain, *Art and Scholasticism and The Frontiers of Poetry*, n. 66, pp. 173-174.

68. See our opening paragraph.

69. See Maritain's magnificent pages in *The Degrees of Knowledge*, Pt. I, chap. V, "The Superanalogy of Faith," pp. 241-244.

70. See *The Degrees of Knowledge*, Pt. I, chap. V, "The Ways of Knowing and the Way of Non-Knowing," especially nos. 23-24ff.

71. *Ibid.*, Pt. I, chap. V, no. 26, p. 242.

72. *Ibid.*

73. *Ibid.*, pp. 242-243.

74. *Ibid.*, p. 243.
75. *Ibid.*, p. 243. E.g., to "eternal duration" instead of "the everlasting hills," or to "hypostatically united" instead of "sitting at His right hand."
76. *Ibid.* Cf. St. Thomas Aquinas, *Summa theologiae,* I, 1, 9.

Henry Bars

6. Maritain's Contributions to an Understanding of Mystical Experience

GREAT PROGRESS has been made in the last half-century in the understanding of mysticism. In order to grasp the origin of this, we would have to go back quite far into the past, to the very dawn of the modern world. Of course I am not speaking of the source of mysticism itself, for this source is situated still much higher (and in the last analysis it is outside of time, in uncreated Life). I am speaking of the understanding of mysticism, which we can discern as a religious fact and as a fact of culture in the world in which we live: this fact has its origin at the beginning of the modern age, in the sixteenth century. There took place at that time one of those instances of *prise de conscience*—growth in awareness—on which Jacques Maritain has so often insisted. As was to happen for Science—in the modern sense, and as distinct from Wisdom—at the time of Descartes, for art and poetry in the romantic period, so at the time of Saint Theresa of Avila and Saint John of the Cross mystical experience turned back on itself and came to know itself reflexively.[1] And far from paralyzing mysticism, this *prise de conscience* stimulated it. There was at that time a veritable mystical tidal wave throughout Europe; Henri Brémond studied it, with re-

111

gard to France, in his monumental *Histoire du sentiment religieux*.[2]
It was, as it were, a royal compensation which God gave to His
Church after the scission of the Reformation; and at the same time
it was a progress which was called for by the growth of the spirit
in time. But this "mystical invasion,"[3] after about a century, was
checked by forces of an opposite nature. The eighteenth and nineteenth centuries can be characterized on the whole as an anti-
mystical period in which "the level of religion was sinking."[4] There
were still mystics, but they were hidden (which, for them, is their
normal state) and the general interest lay elsewhere. The *prise de
conscience* therefore was naturally very much slowed down. There
were many works of "mystical theology" produced in the Church,
but these works had no part in the general circulation of the values
of the spirit. Culture was no longer animated by theology.

At the end of the nineteenth century, things began to oscillate.
While the causes are too numerous and too intricate for me to be
able even to enumerate them, I shall give two of them. I believe
that the strides made by History played an important role: As historians, especially historians of civilization and of philosophy, got
to know the past better, they were more and more struck by the
importance which the heroic spiritual life had had in the Middle
Ages and up to the end of the *Ancien Régime*. Above all, there
was at this moment a spiritual renewal which brought back into
the bosom of the Church a great many men devoted to the works
of the spirit. But these conversions were not principally "moral"
(sometimes they were even morally very imperfect, as was the conversion of Verlaine), but almost all of them had a mystical tone.
At bottom, it was the great religious movement of the sixteenth
century starting up again, after the pause of the Enlightenment and
of Naturalism. And there was to be a singularly fruitful conjunction—at times also dramatic—between this properly Christian
and Catholic mystical resurgence on the one hand, and the works
of independent historians and philosophers on the other.

Jacques Maritain also had personal reasons for becoming interested in mysticism. His first passion as a young philosopher had

been for Spinoza. Afterwards he had known Bergson and Bergson had led him to Plotinus. Much later Bergson was to ask Raïssa Maritain whether, for Jacques and her, as for himself, *"it* began with Plotinus?"[5] *It* was the path towards Christ.

Moreover, Maritain was led to the very threshold of faith by the attraction of the mystics. He did not begin the study of Saint Thomas until three years after his conversion; and it was not a method of rational dialectic which prepared his conversion, but a refraction of Catholic sanctity in Léon Bloy's *La Femme pauvre,* and then in the person of Bloy himself and in his train of pious protectors. Very early he tried to *understand* as philosopher the fact of mysticism. About 1912, together with his friend Charles Henrion, he "bombarded Father Garrigou-Lagrange with questions on the subject, to which the latter replied in his books."

In 1922 Maritain published his first essay on the subject, *De la vie d'oraison,* a book written together with Raïssa Maritain and intended for persons "living in the world and devoting themselves to the works of the intelligence."[6] The same two authors published many years later (1959) an essay, *Liturgie et Contemplation.* In between these two profound yet simple works there stretches a whole series of more technical works. "Mystical Experience and Philosophy" (1926) formed in 1932 the sixth chapter of *Degrés du savoir,*[7] which also contains "Saint John of the Cross, Practitioner of Contemplation." "Action and Contemplation" became the third chapter of *Questions de Conscience,* published in 1938.[8] In the same year, Maritain presented a report on "Natural Mystical Experience and the Void," which became the third chapter of *Quatre essais sur l'esprit dans sa condition charnelle* (1939; revised and enlarged edition, 1956).

It must be added that complementary views are expounded in many other works of the philosopher, especially those which are devoted to art and poetry. And Raïssa Maritain has written a study "Magic, Poetry and Mysticism," which is combined with other essays by her and Jacques Maritain in *Situation de la Poésie* (1939).

In every complex question, good method consists in starting from what is certain in order to advance towards what is less certain and to make the latter certain in its turn. The word "certain" can be taken in two complementary senses: first of all, that is certain which is well established in the order of facts, and secondly, that which is well illuminated by its causes in the order of doctrine. In both senses, orthodox Catholic mysticism contains remarkable guarantees: it has a continuous history, abounding in documents; and it has a coherent doctrine, expounded by authoritative masters. These two senses are complementary, for the historical development and the "homogeneous evolution" of the science of the interior ways has in the ordinary course of things ended in a doctrine which the Church has recognized as her own: in 1926 for example Saint John of the Cross was proclaimed Doctor of the Church.

Maritain knows mystical authors of all periods, but it is to John of the Cross that he has attached himself as to "the great Doctor of this supreme incommunicable wisdom"—just as Thomas Aquinas is for him "the great Doctor of the highest communicable wisdom."[9] Maritain's first major contribution to the understanding of mystical experience is his insistence that we ask the masters of lived mysticism for what they want to give us, what they are entrusted to give us, what only they can give us, and nothing else. This is a great lesson in method, and one that was not without profit. In 1925, Jean Baruzi had published a book on Saint John of the Cross which was full of understanding, knowledge and sympathy, but he thought he had found in the saint a philosophy of the neo-Platonic type and one even akin to the philosophy of Brunschvicg—and this in very good faith.[10] Maritain shows perfectly that John of the Cross is a "practitioner of contemplation," that what he teaches us is a knowledge in which "we can, no doubt, have masters and guides; but in this case they do not impart to us the objects of knowledge themselves. What they do transmit is a store of cognitions, counsels and rules which we need in order to have a certain experience, in itself, inexpressible, as is every experience."[11] In order to understand a doctrine, whatever it may be, it is necessary to be able to define the epistemological type to which it belongs. Saint John of the Cross represents a type relatively pure (and it is even for Maritain the occasion for defining "practically practical science"). Of course, there can be other types. For example, the Augustinian procedure, studied in *The Degrees of Knowledge* (Chapter VII), is defined by "the gift of wisdom making use of discourse," of speculative and principally theological discourse. But, before comparing two doctrines, like that of Saint Augustine and that of Saint Thomas, or that of Saint Thomas and that of Saint John of the Cross, it will be necessary to have situated each one in its specific attitude; and one will thus be led to recognize the validity of different "conceptual lexicons": Maritain's study of the "practicality" of Saint John of the Cross' vocabulary is a model of the kind.

However, the teaching of the "practitioner" is in no way pragmatic; it is saturated with speculative values, and in order to be rightly understood, it must be theologically interpreted. To wish to explain Christian mysticism without having recourse to the lights of Christian theology is at least as imprudent as to treat of modern physics without a sufficient mathematical inquiry; this is Bergson's error in his work, invaluable in other respects, on morality and religion, and especially in his interpretation of the mystics.[12] As for Maritain, it is indeed as philosopher that he has treated the problem, that is to say, "from a human point of view,"[13] as something "which is at the very heart of the human realm."[14] He thus treats the problem, not as a theologian, but as a philosopher, although not as a pure philosopher. His whole theory of "moral philosophy adequately considered" is here concretely engaged.

It is at the point of convergence of the teaching afforded by the great "practitioners" of mystical experience and a philosophical inquiry which knows how to have recourse to the lights of theology —not in order to attempt to "harmonize after the event," as has been very unjustly insinuated, Saint John of the Cross and Saint Thomas Aquinas, but in order to see better the single truth which they pursue in different ways and which they express in different languages—it is in "the thing itself" that philosophy will have a chance of discerning exactly what mysticism is. Here another distinction is necessary.

The definitions at which Maritain arrives are not, he tells us, obtained by an empiriological analysis but by an ontological analysis.[15] Of course this analysis starts from experience and observation, and in the end it will have to give an account of what has been observed. But it is not orientated towards the observable as such; it is orientated towards intelligible being and it is by means "of elements that constitute a nature or intelligible essence"[16] that it will give an account of experience. There are works of "psychology of the mystics" which have great value, and Maritain turns them to account, but it is to an "ontology" of mystical experience that he, for his part, applies himself. It is a question of situating mystical experience in the hierarchy of approaches which lead the human spirit towards the possession of Truth; this seems indeed to have been the deep-seated idea, the idea "at the back of the head" which presided over the conception of the philosopher's central work, *The Degrees of Knowledge*. Once mystical experience is defined and situated, it is possible to ask what its import is on the human world of culture.

In order to define mystical experience, one must seize it in its purity. Let us note first, to refresh our memory, that Maritain separates from the essence of mysticism all that the word may evoke of a "procession of phenomena, ecstasies, and extraordinary gifts belonging, when they are genuine, to what theologians call *charisms* or gratuitous graces."[17] Such a view, it must be added, is today quite common. One must also rule out all the "pre-mystical" instances, whether they belong to the properly religious order (Henri Brémond, for example, had a tendency to identify mysticism and prayer), or whether they belong to other orders, such as poetic experience.

When one gives ear to the Christian mystics, especially the masters, and above all John of the Cross, one admits without great difficulty the philosopher's definition: mystical experience is an "experimental knowledge of the deep things of God," or again "a suffering of divine things."[18] That is what the Saints tell us. But how is such an experience possible?

The explanation, Maritain says, is not to be sought in any intuition of God.[19] God cannot be seen piecemeal.[20] In the Beatific Vision, the intelligence will be completely satiated; here below it will never be. In mystical experience, God is known as much as He can be known in this life, He is known in Himself; but He is known through "union of love." It is the supernatural love of charity which alone can connaturalize the soul to Deity: this love becomes, according to the expression of John of Saint Thomas, the objective means of knowledge (*amor transit in conditionem objecti*). The soul suffers the touch of God Who makes grace fructify in love, and in this "suffering," which is still an effect of God but an effect at which the soul does not stop, God is experimentally known; He is touched and tasted as immediately as possible, although still (and even more than ever) in night, in a night which is illumination, according to the words of the psalm.[21] Such is the conclusion to which lead the converging teachings of Saint Thomas and Saint John of the Cross, who themselves were taught by the New Testament.

There results from this, in Jacques Maritain, a certain distrust as regards the term "contemplation,"[22] which he admits however we cannot do without and which is hallowed by mystical tradition. It *is* a question here of contemplation, if one understands by this word a terminal state in which the soul rests in its Good, a fruition of God. But this contemplation must be clearly distinguished from all that Greece and the philosophers have bequeathed to us under the same name. The contemplation of the philosophers is not truly an experience; it does not have love for its proper means; and it is incapable of attaining the Deity in itself.[23] The contemplation of the Saints is essentially an experience, and an experience of the

Deity. It is a Wisdom and the highest of Wisdoms, for it knows in itself the First Cause. But it is not as Cause that it knows It, but as Friend present in the soul.

Moreover, the soul has this experience only because it is delivered over to God, disappropriated. It is not the soul which leads itself, it is God Who leads it; it has renounced absolute self-mastery which was on the contrary the perfection of the Sage of the ancient tradition and of the Contemplative according to the ideal of the philosophers.

Maritain characterizes therefore entry into the mystical life as submitting to the regime of the Gifts of the Holy Spirit,[24] but here a distinction has to be made. The predominance, as to exercise, of the highest Gifts, those of Understanding and Wisdom, permits only infused contemplation under its typical forms; and it is according to these forms, the purest ones, that Saint John of the Cross taught the way of perfection, which is nothing other than the Gospel way. But the same Gospel way can be followed by souls who are no less holy than the first ones but in whom the active Gifts predominate, such as the gifts of Counsel and Fear of the Lord, and who therefore have contemplation only under a masked form. It is then a contemplation as authentic as the other, but which does not have the appearance of contemplating.[25] What is important, as a matter of fact, is not that the soul have the appearance of this or that, either in the eyes of others or in its own eyes, but that it really give itself up to the Spirit's guidance; and it can do this only through charity, that is, through a love given from on high, through a love which the creature is incapable of causing to well up in it, but which it can refuse to let well up. The whole philosophy of liberty is included in this negation.

A particularly important point of practical doctrine is thus established: supernatural mystical experience is bound to no condition of nature, to no particular temperament, or particular education, nor to any technique whatsoever. It is bound only to the Gospel way of life pushed to its ultimate consequences, and in particular

to "detachment from perfection in perfection itself,"[26] and finally
to the unforseeable choice of created liberty in its encounter with
uncreated love.

Jacques Maritain has sifted supernatural mystical knowledge, as
it is made known to us by the testimonies of the Christian mystics,
and the contributions he has made to the understanding of such
knowledge can be considered as permanent acquisitions. But he
has advanced a great deal farther—into regions where much remains to be discovered: in the direction of natural mystical experience and of the possible meetings between it and supernatural
mystical experience.

He began his study of mystical knowledge by thinking that there
was no natural mystical experience. The reasons he put forth
against its possibility in the first edition of *Degrés du Savoir*[27] retain
their value: an "experience of the deep things of God," a "suffering
of divine things" is impossible in the natural order—that is to say,
without grace and charity. Besides, the reflections he makes on the
method of non-Christian mystics remain true: grace can act outside
of a visible belonging to the Church; dubious or apocryphal cases
must be resolutely ruled out; finally, the role of the "separated
spirits" must not be overlooked.

Maritain however has not adhered to this negative position. The
mystics of India, especially, present him with a problem which
could not be resolved by any of the preceding answers: neither by
an anonymous action of supernatural charity, nor by illusion, nor
by the powers of darkness. Maritain listened to these witnesses,
tried to understand them, and finally proposed the answer which
is at once the most original and the most solidly based in reason.

His works on Christian mysticism and his works on poetry had
led him to examine thoroughly the question of knowledge through
connaturality and of its different types. He distinguished four types,
the last of which is subdivided in turn into two.

There is, first of all, the knowledge by way of practical inclination of prudential (moral) experience; Saint Thomas used it, by way of comparison, in explaining the "suffering of divine things." It can be combined with mystical life, but it is not a contemplative knowledge; it is a knowledge for right action.

Then comes the knowledge through intellectual connaturality with a certain type of objects, which is due to speculative *habitus*. In the wise man, such a knowledge can attain to a natural contemplation of things divine, but it is not a fruitive experience; it does not give the soul that repose in possession which characterizes mystical experience.

In the third place, there is a knowledge by way of creation, or poetic experience, which is indeed an experience (but of the created) and which disposes to contemplation (more than does prudential experience) but does not issue in it. It does not tend to silence and fruition in silence, but to the word and to an exultation in the word which is never satisfied by any work achieved but is always setting off again in pursuit of other works to be realized. However, since this poetic experience awakens to themselves the existential depths of subjectivity, it orients the one who has it in the direction of *an* absolute which is the absolute of personal existence. Such is the case, provided that this poetic experience does not seize the absolute and above all does not rest in it. I believe that, in actual fact, Maritain's works on the experience of the poet[28] have sustained and inspired his research on the possibility of a natural mystical experience properly so-called, which research, on the other hand, has been directly instructed by the fact of the mysticism of Yoga.

There is, finally, the fourth kind of knowledge, knowledge through connaturality, which is mystical experience considered in its widest amplitude, according to its general epistemological type. Can we now give a more universal definition of it than above, one that answers at once to Christian mysticism in the purity of its type and to Indian mysticism in the purity of its type, a definition not empiriological but ontological, "through the elements that constitute the intelligible essence"? We should say first that it is a contemplative or fruitive knowledge; it is not a knowledge "for action" or "for creation"; it finds repose in the object it knows. It is not a knowledge "by way of knowledge," as is the contemplation of the philosophers which "soars and does not stay at rest,"[29] but a knowledge "by way of non-knowing," which goes beyond concepts, and experiences the very reality that satisfies it, the absolute reality. Let us not yet say the Absolute, with a capital A: God alone merits this name. Let us say that mystical experience, in its most universal intelligible characteristics, is "the fruitive experience of *an* absolute."[30]

We already know that such an experience is possible through supernatural charity. But is it not also possible in the natural order itself? Yes, Maritain answers, this is possible. Only, this time, it is no longer a question of an affective experience (the natural love of God is incapable of connaturalizing the soul to the Deity), and it is no longer a question of an experience of the deep things of God, of a suffering of divine things. It is a question of a knowledge through intellectual connaturality whose term, attained in an experimental though negative manner, is the substantial *existence* of the soul.[31] This term is not the essence of the soul, for in the state of union with the body it is impossible for the soul to see itself. Moreover, it is not a question of seeing: this mystical experience is no less obscure than the other one. It is a question of experiencing, of tasting; and what is tasted, touched here as if it were naked, is the existence of the soul at the root of the powers which emerge from it, for the intelligence, in emanating from the substance of the soul, is informed by it as by an intelligible species.

However all this is possible only through a method or technique, of which Yoga supplies the example, and thanks to which the psychological swarming of acts is gradually destroyed. Normally, the soul has experience of itself (a confused experience) only through its acts. But it is here "the act of abolition of all act"[32] which, annihilating the whole interior multitude and paralyzing all operation, leaves the intelligence in contact with the sole object which remains to it: not the essence of the soul, whose intelligibility remains bound, but the *Self* itself. And in fact Yogis call "atman," or the Self, this absolute which they claim to attain.[33] The Void, in such a case, plays a role analogous to the role that love plays in supernatural experience: it becomes the formal means of the experience. And what is attained is doubtless no longer the Absolute, the divine Absolute, but *an* absolute, *esse* (the act-of-existing) in the pure state. But, since it is experienced in the pure state, without the limitation of the essence which exists and which is a created essence, what is known in it is "existence in its metaphysical amplitude, and the sources of existence . . . according as the existence of the soul, taken concretely and to the extent that it is an act of effectuation *extra nihil,* is something emanating from and suffused by an influx wherefrom it obtains its all."[34] There is present here, then, what Maritain had first thought impossible, a negative mystical experience of the presence of immensity itself. But it is also clear how natural mystical experience, each time it is not instructed and corrected by faith in the transcendent God, gives rise to monistic formulations.

To complete this brief exposition, let us see mystical experience within the structure of the human spirit and within human culture.

Supernatural or natural, this experience is at the very summit of the life of the spirit. Faithful to the tradition of his masters, Jacques Maritain sees in the Wisdom of the Holy Spirit a genuine science.[35] Proportionately speaking, I think that he would say as much of natural mystical experience. But it is necessary to distinguish the experience itself from the doctrine which teaches the ways of attaining it. Mystical experience is the supreme incommunicable knowledge; there will therefore be a difference of level between it and the "practically practical science" of masters such as Saint John of the Cross and Ramanuja.

However, each supreme in its own order, the two experiences are situated differently in relation to the other perfections of the spirit. Supernatural mystical experience is not the prolongation of philosophy: philosophy does not call for it as its complement and its necessary completion. No doubt every great philosophy is animated by a mystical aspiration,[36] inasmuch as the soul of the philosopher, who seeks to know through the highest and simplest causes, aspires—with a desire that is natural but by nature inefficacious—to see in Itself the Cause of Being that is God. But it is not in the prolongation of this aspiration that the experience of the deep things of God is situated: it is not as First Being that God is known in it; it is as Friend and as object of love. Upwards, between rational wisdom and the Wisdom of the Holy Spirit, there is discontinuity. But downwards there can be, and normally there ought to be, an influx of supernatural Wisdom and love of charity on philosophy. While leaving to the work of reason "the autonomy proper to it in the order of objective regulation,"[37] mystical experience, if it exists, illumines and strengthens the intelligence and enables the philosopher to see better what he can see precisely in so far as he is philosopher. Jacques Maritain explains admirably, as technician and as spiritual, this spilling over of the "objective irradiation" emanating from a first hearth in the soul, to the other hearths situated at lower levels. Moreover, love produces in the natural operation an effect which goes beyond it; it is thus that the syllogisms of Thomas Aquinas have a pacifying quality which is, as it were, the trace of his prayer.[38] It is thus, in another manner, that the poetic gift, in John of the Cross, becomes the instrument of the Wisdom of Grace.

On the other hand, since supernatural mystical experience is an experience through union of love, and since charity toward one's neighbor is inseparable from charity towards God, this experience has for a normal effect—for effect, not for end—to vivify human things, those of civilization and of political life itself, and to render man more human.[39] Not being esoteric in any way, this experience asks to descend into all states and all conditions, either under its typical form, or more often under its masked form. Although it is not ordered to the world but to the Kingdom of God, it is thus the greatest hope of the world, and the most hidden, the one that the world most ignores—which is to be expected.

With natural mystical experience, it is otherwise, for it pursues "the line proper to philosophical intellection over and beyond philosophy itself,"[40]—not without rupture however. But here, instead of the crossing of an abyss (where one is carried by the Spirit of God), it is an effort against the grain of nature, "an art of entering while living into death, into a death which is not evangelic death, intended to give place to the life of Another, but a metaphysical death, intended to winnow spiritual activities away from the body."[41] And this effort, Maritain says, is possible only because it answers to a more profound desire than the aspiration of the intelligence to see the Cause of being: the desire of the whole man, soul and body, to rejoin its sources.[42] The fact remains that such an experience is at the term of an ascending process in which philosophy normally plays its role. What can happen therefore is that philosophy may be swept up into the dynamism of the aspiration to deliverance, so that metaphysical speculation never succeeds in constituting itself according to a purely speculative mode, which is regrettable for metaphysics. Maritain has often noted that this was the case for India.[43]

It would be unjust, however, not to acknowledge that natural mystical experience, wherever it has existed, and especially in India, has exercised on the surrounding civilization a most valuable influence. The example of Gandhi would even indicate that this influence can extend even to the farthest reaches of effective political action[44] (but doubtless after having been secretly vivified by a current issuing from elsewhere: Gandhi knew the Gospel). An integral humanism will see in the mysticism of Yoga neither a decisive instance in man's pilgrimage towards the Kingdom of God, nor an efficacious remedy for the evils from which civilization suffers, but it will see in it a great testimony to "the highest natural aspirations and the weaknesses of our spirit."[45]

After having distinguished the differentiating characteristics of the two experiences, it is fitting to add that, concretely, many crossbreedings are possible, either among the two of them, or with one or another or several of the other types of knowledge through connaturality, in particular poetic experience. Maritain has made invaluable remarks on the subject. He thinks for example that the case of Plotinus—judged once by him with a kind of anxious and tender severity—will have to be reconsidered. On the other hand, his friends Olivier Lacombe and Louis Gardet are pursuing work in comparative mysticism that is full of promise.[46] Research in comparative mysticism is at the moment in full swing.

In conclusion, I would say that here as elsewhere Jacques Maritain has opened up new paths. Here as elsewhere he has opened up promising paths, not only owing to the accuracy and the soundness of the bases he has established, but also owing to an absolute fidelity to *all* the data of experience.

NOTES

1. *Liturgy and Contemplation* (New York: Kenedy, 1960), pp. 70-72.
2. Two volumes (Paris: Bloud et Gay), 1915-1933.
3. *Ibid.*, Vol. II.
4. *Réponse à Jean Cocteau* (Paris: Stock, 1926), p. 38.
5. *The Commonweal*, Vol. XXXIII (January 17, 1941), p. 319.
6. *De la vie d'oraison* (second ed., Paris: A l'Art catholique, 1924), Foreword; English edition: *Prayer and Intelligence* (London: Sheed and Ward, 1928).
7. *The Degrees of Knowledge.* Newly translated from the fourth French edition under the supervision of Gerald B. Phelan (New York: Scribner, 1959).
8. *Questions de Conscience* (Paris: Desclée de Brouwer, 1939). Cf. *Scholasticism and Politics* (New York: Macmillan, 1940), Chapter VII, "Action and Contemplation."
9. *The Degrees of Knowledge*, p. 311.
10. Jean Baruzi, *Saint Jean de la Croix et le Problème de l'expérience mystique* (Paris: Alcan, 1925). Cf. *The Degrees of Knowledge*, p. 9, n. 1.
11. *The Degrees of Knowledge*, p. 310.

12. *Ibid.*, p. 288, n. 1.
13. *Science and Wisdom* (New York: Scribner, 1940), p. 112.
14. *The Degrees of Knowledge*, p. 288, n. 1.
15. *Ransoming the Time* (New York: Scribner, 1941), p. 256.
16. *Philosophy of Nature* (New York: Philosophical Library, 1951), p. 75.
17. *Scholasticism and Politics*, p. 188.
18. *The Degrees of Knowledge*, p. 247.
19. *Ransoming the Time*, p. 264.
20. *The Degrees of Knowledge*, p. 270.
21. *Ibid.*, p. 261 et seq.
22. *Scholasticism and Politics*, pp. 188-189.
23. *The Degrees of Knowledge*, pp. 267-268.
24. *Ibid.*, pp. 259-260.
25. *Prayer and Intelligence*, Note IV; *Scholasticism and Politics*, pp. 186-187; *Liturgy and Contemplation*, p. 35 et seq.
26. *Quatre essais sur l'esprit dans sa condition charnelle* (Paris: Desclée de Brouwer, 1939), p. 176.
27. *The Degrees of Knowledge*, p. 268 et seq.
28. Cf. *The Situation of Poetry* (New York: Philosophical Library, 1955).
29. *The Degrees of Knowledge*, p. 268; *Ransoming the Time*, pp. 258-259.
30. *Quatre essais*, p. 132; *Ransoming the Time*, pp. 255-256.
31. *Ransoming the Time*, pp. 273-274.
32. *Ibid.*, p. 276.
33. *Ibid.*, p. 273.
34. *Ibid.*, p. 279.
35. *Science and Wisdom*, pp. 71-72.
36. *The Degrees of Knowledge*, pp. 240-241.
37. *Science and Wisdom*, p. 89.
38. *St. Thomas Aquinas* (New York: Meridian, 1958), p. 47.
39. Cf. *True Humanism* (New York: Scribner, 1938).
40. *Ransoming the Time*, p. 278.
41. *Ibid.*, p. 278.
42. *Ibid.*, pp. 261-262.
43. *Science and Wisdom*, pp. 708; *Bergsonian Philosophy and Thomism* (New York: Philosophical Library, 1955), pp. 38-40.
44. *Du régime temporel et de la liberté* (Paris: Desclée de Brouwer, 1933), p. 196 et seq.; *Man and the State* (Chicago: University of Chicago Press, 1951), pp. 68-71.

45. Cf., for example, two works of Louis Gardet: *Expériences mystiques en terres non-chrétiennes* and *Thèmes et textes mystiques* (Paris: Alsatia, 1953, 1958).

46. Cf. Olivier Lacombe, "La Mystique naturelle dans l'Inde," *Revue Thomiste*, 1951, 1; Louis Gardet, "Recherches sur la mystique naturelle," in *Jacques Maritain: son oeuvre philosophique* (Paris: Desclée de Brouwer, 1948). Lacombe and Gardet are preparing a general survey of natural mysticism, under the title *Mystique naturelle, l'Expérience du Soi.*

7. Poetic Intuition and Action in Maritain's *Creative Intuition in Art and Poetry*

Creative Intuition in Art and Poetry is the latest and most comprehensive study of those problems of the nature and meaning of poetry which have concerned Professor Maritain for many years. The title refers to the distinction between poetry itself and the arts —verse, painting, sculpture—whereby the poet seeks to embody the poetic experience he feels within himself. "There is no poetic experience without a secret germ, tiny as it may be, of a poem" he writes (p. 239). "But there is no genuine poem which is not a fruit growing with inner necessity out of poetic experience." Art and poetry are thus indissolubly connected; yet the distinction between them is of crucial importance for our understanding of the artist's psychology, and of the meaning and value of his work.

Inspiration, or "poetic experience" as Maritain prefers to call it, has been discussed since Plato. But Maritain shows that the full awareness of poetry in this sense, poetry as independent not only of faith, morals and philosophy, but even of the forms and esthetic criteria of all actual arts and schools of art, is a modern achievement. "As to the *prise de conscience* of *poetry as poetry*," he says (p. 256) "it was only in the course of the nineteenth century that

128

the phenomenon came about. Then, for some decades, one was able to contemplate a series of discoveries, failures, catastrophes, and revelations which were extraordinarily illuminating. I believe that what occurred after Baudelaire with respect to poetry had in the domain of art as much historic significance as, in the domain of science, the greatest crises of renewal and revolution in physics and astronomy."

Maritain is uniquely qualified to explore and assess the revolution which we call modern poetry. He lived the life of art in the time and place, Paris in the twenties, when an unparalleled galaxy of poets, painters and musicians was exploiting the "new self-awareness of poetry" in countless ways. Maritain knew intimately not only the art but many of the artists themselves, and what he says of poetry comes out of that rich and diverse life which he shared. But he shared it as philosopher, and in that respect also he is unique: who else has been able to use Thomistic insights and principles as he does, as a means of understanding the unprecedented modern world? It is his philosophy which enables him to place modern poetry in the context of a much older, wider and more central tradition. He completes the labors of the poets themselves, bringing their new self-conscious freedom into historic perspective, and into the light of knowledge as metaphysicians understand knowledge.

The purpose of the book, which its title describes, requires that any and all kinds of visual and verbal arts be taken into account. Maritain never forgets the vast accumulation available to the modern world, what Malraux called "the museum without walls": oriental arts, primitive arts from every corner of the world, as well as the harvest of our own long tradition. He keeps the reader reminded of all this by presenting, with each chapter, a selection of plates, and a collection of relevant "Texts without Comment": short poems, bits of philosophy and criticism, and gnomic utterances by poets themselves upon their mystery.

It should be clear from this brief description that *Creative Intuition* is not to be summarized or commented upon in a short article.

Its scope is too great; and moreover much of its value lies in its form and in the exact formulations reached from time to time. Maritain proceeds by his characteristic method of delicate dialectic, *distinguer pour unir,* as he calls it. His purpose is not to present an abstract thesis, but to lead the reader to new and more exact perceptions. And the best way to read his book is, therefore, as an "aid to reflection." A consistent vision of poem-making underlies the whole, but the best way to approach this vision is by way of some problem—whether of psychology or epistemology; *Geistesgeschichte,* or taste, or criticism—which the reader himself is struggling with. The book, if carefully questioned, will help the reader to think out his own problem, and so reveal one aspect at least of Poetry as Maritain understands it.

In what follows I propose to illustrate this process by asking the book a question which seems significant to me: What is the relation between modern poetry's new self-awareness and that conception of poetry as the "imitation of an action" which may be found in Aristotle's *Poetics,* and in another form in the *Divine Comedy?*

Maritain deals explicitly with this matter in his last chapter, "The Three Epiphanies of Creative Intuition." He is considering a question raised by Waldo Frank and Allen Tate: why Hart Crane, a lyric poet of great gifts, was unable to succeed with the longer, epic form he attempted in *The Bridge.* A few modern novelists have made long and elaborate prose compositions of some poetic validity, and poets of the past have succeeded with epic or drama. But contemporary poets formed in the modern lyric tradition, and enlightened by its strict self-awareness, though they often aspire to the larger forms, seldom master them. Why? Has poetry been revealed, once and for all, as essentially brief, as Poe taught? Is Croce right when he says that in the light of modern taste *The Divine Comedy* is not truly poetic as a whole, but only in bits?

It is in order to throw light on such questions as these that Maritain introduces the concept of "action." Frank and Tate had suggested that Crane lacked an adequate "theme" to unify *The Bridge.*

Maritain proposes to substitute "action" for "theme" as the clue to
the unity of the larger poetic forms. He explains that the theme—
the "moral of the tale"—"does not precisely relate to what the
poem *is,* but rather to what the poem intends or proposes, what the
poem *wills*" (p. 356). Action, on the other hand, does designate
the being of the poem, its inner life, or "movement of spirit," in
Dante's phrase. One may often abstract various themes from a good
poem. And there are plenty of clumsy moralizing poems in which
the ostensible theme is belied by the actual life we feel in them.

It was of course Aristotle who first described the arts as imita-
tions, in their various media, of action. The key word here is the
technical term *action.* Aristotle's doctrine makes little sense unless
one sees that by "action" he does not mean the incidents of the plot,
but an inner deed, a "movement" not of the body but of the psyche.
Our words *purpose, intention,* and *motive* refer to modes of action,
as that word is used in the *Poetics.* "Motive" is perhaps the best, for
it is the most general, including willed and rationalized purposes at
one extreme (Aristotle's "ethical motivation") and unwilled movements of spirit at the other (Aristotle's "pathetic motivation").
Action is an analogical concept, and real actions, as we observe
them, are each unique. The actions of poems and plays are unique
too. And only when one recognizes the particular movement-of-
spirit which the poet has felt, can one fully understand the art
whereby he has sought to imitate it: plotting, or the arrangement of
incidents which spring from the underlying motive; character, which
is "habitual action"; and the complex arts of words which also reflect the motives of the speaker. A long play or poem—even the
Odyssey—has one action, which is, however, developed in many
analogous incidents and characters.

Dante too (in *The Divine Comedy*) thought of action as the basis
or "inspiration" of the poet; and of his art as imitating action as
closely as possible. But he had never read the *Poetics,* and his Aristotelian philosophy came to him by way of the Fathers and Doctors
of the Church. He describes action in terms of love (*Purgatory,* 18,
Temple Classics ed.):

The enamoured mind falls to desire, which is a spiritual movement, and never rests until the object of its love makes it rejoice.

Now may be apparent to thee, how deeply the truth is hidden from the folk who aver that every act of love is in itself a laudable thing.

Because its material [i.e., love] may seem always to be good but not every imprint [i.e., the object that forms or actualizes love at the moment of attachment] is good, albeit the wax be good.

His work as poet of the *dolce stil nuovo* consists, not in following certain rules of *art*, but in imitating exactly the "spiritual movements" he perceives in his own inner being: (*Purgatory*, 24, my translation):

I am one who, when love breathes in me, take note, and in that mode which he dictates within, go signifying.

This is Maritain's distinction between poetic experience and art. We know with what appalling candor Dante noted love's modes in his own inner being, from the deluded motives of Hell, through the changing and suffering motivations of Purgatory, to the triumphant end in the *Paradiso,* when (Canto 1, Temple Classics)

as it draweth nigh to its desire, our intellect sinketh so deep, that memory cannot go back upon the track.

And at every point he imitated or "signified" love's modes in the modes of discourse—logical or rhetorical, poetic or dramatic— which best embodied that focus of desire and perception.

I have said that "motive" best suggests what Aristotle means by the "action" of poem or drama; and that is what Maritain means when he proposes to substitute "action" for "theme." But Maritain then reminds us that in Aristotelian philosophies of being and essence, matter and form, the potential and the actual, the concept of action has also much wider meanings (p. 358):

Philosophers distinguish between two kinds of action—"transitive action," through which one thing modifies another, and "immanent action," which belongs to the category of quality, and through which a living agent perfects its own being. Immanent action, which tends essentially to complete in actuation the agent itself, produces at the same time a certain effect or a certain fruit (the concept, for instance, in the intellect) which remains within the agent.

Assuming the Aristotelian notions of *act* as fulness or completion in being, and of *existence* as *actus primus,* primary act, and act of all acts, Thomist philosophy states that action or operation, either transitive or immanent, is *actus secundus,* an emergent terminative act, or a superabundance of existence, through which being asserts itself beyond substantial existence. For things are and exist before acting. Everywhere except in God, action is distinct from the essence of the agent and from its act of existing.

These notions show how Dante related the countless motives of his poem to a cosmological and theological framework. From another point of view, they enable us to see more clearly how the poet's creative activity completes or actualizes his own being. And, by analogy, one can see action as the *being* of the poem—to be further actualized, through the actions of the artist, in plot, then character, then language.

Maritain sometimes describes poetic intuition in terms of action, as, for example, on page 242:

In the first phase, then, in the phase of systole and unifying repose, all the forces of the soul, gathered together in quietude, were in a state of virtuality and dormant energy. And poetic intuition, still preconscious, was the only act formed within the preconscious life of the intellect, and was the secret reason for this silent concentration. It is not surprising that at a given moment this same poetic intuition, acting no longer in the manner of an hypnotic but rather of a catalytic agent, should make the virtual energies concentrated around it pass also to the act. Then, from the single actuation of all the forces of the soul withdrawn into their root vitality, a single transient motion will result, which manifests itself either negatively, by a breaking of barriers, or positively, by the entrance of poetic intuition into the field of consciousness.

One is reminded of Beatrice's explanation of the analogous (not, of course, identical) experience of beatitude (*Paradiso*, 28, Temple Classics): "the being blessed [*esser beato*] is founded on the act that seeth, not that which loveth, which after followeth." The stillness of perception precedes the "movement" of love; but both phases are modes of action.

But in his discussion of this matter in Chapter Nine (p. 365), Maritain writes:

I would say that there is for creative intuition three different states, in consequence of the spiritual spheres in which it acts.

In the spiritual sphere which is its own world—the creative night of the preconscious, nonconceptual life of the intellect—poetic intuition is in its pure, original, and native state, in its state of innocence and integrity, in its God-given state. And it passes into the work through the instrumentality of the *poetic sense*.

This, I take it, is that transition from the "act formed within the preconscious life of the intellect" to the moment when that inspiration is first consciously noted: Dante's "act that seeth." Maritain continues (p. 366):

Thus poetic intuition penetrates into the world of the early morning vision of the intellect, or of nascent logos. There, it is no longer in its connatural state, but in an alien state, peculiar to *the work as mentally conceived, the work as thought*. And then a certain objective virtuality which was contained in poetic intuition is, as it were, detached from it and brought to the act: poetic intuition passes into the work through the instrumentality of the *action* and the *theme*.

Notice that at this point he reserves the term "action" for *transitive* action—"motive" as one finds it in the play or poem. He is not thinking of the poet's being as act, nor of his initial act of perception, nor of the "act" he perceives. And Maritain proceeds to explain that the action itself (in this sense) may be developed "harmonically" to produce the larger forms of epic or novel. He writes (p. 369):

To sum up, I shall say that the poetic sense or inner melody, the action and the theme, the number or harmonic structure, are the three epiphanies of poetic intuition or creative emotion passing into the work.

Maritain's elucidation of the roots of lyric, epic and drama is of great value and originality. But I must leave that aside in order to follow the thin line of our reflections on "action," as Maritain relates that notion to poetry's new self-awareness. Does the modern lore correct, or supersede, the whole theory of poetry as action? If not, why does Maritain here in Chapter Nine present this newly-defined lyric awareness as more fundamental than action? There is great danger, at this point, of fatal blundering; let us note some of the reservations and distinctions with which Maritain has surrounded his account. For nowhere are his characteristic flexibility, tact, and intellectual humility more crucial; the reader must appreciate them if he is to avoid misunderstandings.

One must remember, first of all, that Maritain is talking about the *Epiphanies* of creative intuition, i.e., the way it *appears* to the poet at successive stages of his work. He is concerned to safeguard the validity of the poet's *experience,* lest the whole notion of poetry-in-itself be lost. And he knows that the whole wisdom of modern art bids the poet, *qua* poet, take poetry as a jealous god. At the moment of poetry's first appearance he does not dare to be aware of anything but *it*. He must quiet the feelings, the senses, and the mind, lest his intuition vanish, leaving him with a mere dry bundle of concepts to show for his infidelity.

Moreover, Maritain never forgets that the crucial phase of the creative process is subconscious or preconscious. And he knows that a theory of subconscious life—whether his own Thomistic one, or Freud's—can never be based on direct evidence. It must depend on two things: a general conception of psychic life, and a study of such dreams, unwilled gestures, and inspirations as seem to emerge from the subconscious and enter the conscious mind. In Chapter Three, "The Preconscious Life of the Intellect," he takes account of the point of view, and some of the concepts and discoveries, of contemporary psychology. The reader should remember that discussion too, in thinking over the meaning of the "three epiphanies." It is of the essence of Maritain's method to adopt various points of view, and to exploit various terminologies, in order to reveal poetic intuition as it were "in the round." And he can do this only because he does not make a fetish of *any* formulation of the problem. His philosophical concepts and structures are always regarded as more or less inadequate means to the intellectual perception itself, and in this respect his work is closely analogous to that of the modern masters of art whom he so greatly admires.

Thus when in Chapter Nine he closely follows the experience of the poet, he does not intend, I think, to abandon the other perspectives he has presented, but rather to correct and complement them. Nor does he ask the reader to do so. Thus he is acutely aware of the dangers in the cult of poetry-in-itself and in isolation; and he explores these dangers at length in Chapter Five, "Poetry and Beauty," and in Chapter Seven, "Poetic Experience and Poetic Sense." The new freedom of poetry in the widest sense—freedom, like that of modern science, from the notion of Being—has proved to be as dangerous as fission itself; perhaps more so, for the fission of the soul concerns us more intimately than the fission of the physical world. It is Maritain, as much as anyone alive, who has made us aware of this. And that is why he keeps us reminded, throughout the book, that Poetry, wonderful as it is, is not God, but only a gift dwelling most precariously in the human psyche.

If one tries to follow *The Three Epiphanies* with the relevant teachings of the whole book in mind, one can see that the underlying vision of *poetando*, is (though many-sided) consistent. But a question remains, about the relation of poetic intuition to action in the widest sense, which I think is particularly important in this generation. For it appears that poetry's self-awareness is an achievement which is now complete. Can any poet hope to go farther, under this dispensation, than Mallarmé and Valéry? Can anyone hope to achieve a fuller awareness than is to be found in *Creative Intuition*? The best contemporary poets, beginning with Eliot and including Hart Crane (with whose frustrations this discussion began), are looking for another way to understand poetry. And the question is, can they understand it as action without losing the precious essence? I have tried to show that Maritain, with his respect for the modern poet's experience, would doubt it. For to see the successive phases of *poetando* as modes of action would be to place it, at once, in a vast web of analogical relationships—between the poet and other beings; between his mortal being and his vision, between his vision and the work in which he embodies it. The poet's isolation would be gone: meanings moral and metaphysical, historical and epistemological would appear. He would be freed from the freedom of poetry-in-itself—a "freedom" which now looks airless and dark— but would he survive *as poet* in such a naked condition of mortality?

This question may be understood both as theoretical and as practical. One may gather, I think, from Maritain's whole book that he would answer the theoretical question in the affirmative: it is possible to understand poetic intuition both as ultimate, "in itself," *and* as a mode of action. The chapter on *The Three Epiphanies* may be read that way. And in his superb section on Dante (p. 370) he shows that Dante in fact did this. Dante seems to have been able to see his inspiration from many sides, in the round, without violating it; and to develop it "harmonically" on the vastest scale, yet in obedience to its most intimate promptings. But Maritain leaves the practical question, whether a modern poet could entertain the perilous notion of action and survive as a poet, unanswered. He knows that Dante's world and Dante's kind of belief—to say nothing of his genius—are inaccessible to us. And he respects the uniqueness of individual experience and the mysteries of art too much to pronounce upon them in a practical way. One should try to emulate this wisdom and this humility: the crucial questions, questions of concreate reality, are beyond us.

The reader will have noticed that in questioning *Creative Intuition* I have skirted a great many interesting matters without going into them at all. That may suggest, I hope, the richness of the book. One might ask it many questions, and receive many luminous answers. There is no substitute for reading the book itself.

Ralph Nelson

8. "Moral Philosophy Adequately Considered"

ALTHOUGH THE CONCEPTION of moral philosophy adequately considered is but a part of the complex which Maritain calls "Christian philosophy," it is undoubtedly the best example of the way in which philosophy can be affected by being in a Christian state. For Christian philosophy is nothing other than philosophy itself "in so far as it is situated in those utterly distinctive conditions of existence and exercise into which Christianity has ushered the thinking subject. . . ."[1] Philosophy is specified, that is, placed in a certain species, by its object alone, or by its objects alone if we bear in mind that philosophy is not one but a number of sciences. Nothing else enters in, neither the constructive operations of the intellect nor the play of the affections. Furthermore philosophy has its own principles and methods. But philosophy taken in this way, that is, as a nature, is but the result of a formal abstraction. Philosophy exists concretely in the intellect of the philosopher as a *habitus* or rather as a number of *habitus*. As such it disposes the intellect in a certain way and is a stable disposition changed only with difficulty. And existing concretely in the intellect of the philosopher, it exists with all the other spiritual energies in the soul. Hence philosophy, or the *habitus* of philosophy, can take on new characteristics or be modified by its existence within the soul. At this point we must consider the order of exercise or the state in which the *habitus* is placed. The question then becomes: Does the fact that a man is a Christian change the conditions under which the philosophical *habitus* is exercised? Maritain's reply is quite definite.

Taken concretely, in the sense of being a *habitus* or a group of *habitus* existing in the human soul, philosophy is in a certain *state,* is either pre-Christian or Christian or a-Christian, which has a decisive influence on the way in which it exists and develops.[2]

We are led to ask the exact way in which its state will have an impact upon philosophy when it is in a Christian state that philosophy is found. Maritain says that there are two ways in which the faith can influence philosophy—by providing objective data, and by supplying certain subjective reinforcements. Faith can first of all present the philosopher with certain data "which deal primarily with revealed truths of the natural order."[3] Such data have been missed or misunderstood by those who did not have the benefit of divine revelation, for example the great pagan philosophers. In addition to such natural truths, theology supplies other objective data which are concerned "with the repercussions of truths of the supernatural order on philosophical reflexion. . . ."[4] Maritain mentions as examples of the first kind of objective data the idea of creation, the idea of nature as capable of being perfected by a supernatural order, the idea of God as Subsistent Being Itself (He Who Is), and the idea of sin in the sense of an offense against God. And he says that the best example of the second kind of objective data is the metaphysical problem of the person which came to light through the speculation of theologians on the dogmas of the Trinity and the Incarnation.

Now there is another way in which faith aids philosophy and that is through certain subjective reinforcements. The philosopher is reinforced by the reception of "the superior wisdoms, theological wisdom and infused wisdom, which rectify and purify in the soul the philosophical *habitus* with which they maintain a continuity not of essence but of movement and illumination, fortifying them in their proper order, and lifting them to higher levels."[5] Such a reinforcement is possible within the soul because one *habitus* can affect another—for they are interconnected within the soul.

Now these are the ways generally in which philosophy can be modified and aided by being in a Christian state. Since we are concerned specifically with the problem of moral philosophy adequately considered, we will endeavor to understand what it means for moral philosophy to be found in a Christian state, and how it is modified and aided by being in that state. The word in the phrase "moral philosophy adequately considered" which requires explanation is "adequately." What precisely does Maritain mean by an adequate moral philosophy? Maritain employs this term with the meaning it possesses in the Thomistic definition of truth as *adaequatio rei et intellectus*. A moral philosophy adequately considered "is moral philosophy taken as constituting purely and simply (*simpliciter*) a true moral *science,* in a state which makes the mind of itself adequate to or in conformity with its object, that is to say, *human action.*"[6] A moral science inadequately considered would be one which is not adequate to this object and hence not a science in the Aristotelian sense of that term. It will be inadequate, says Maritain, if it is in ignorance of the concrete conditions within which human nature as it actually exists is placed in its journey toward its end. Historically we have been presented with two important examples of moral philosophies which are inadequate in this way: the *Nicomachean Ethics* of Aristotle and *Ecclesiastes.*[7]

Aristotle did not know the true ultimate end of man. In Maritain's words, "he remained placed at a viewpoint more essential than existential."[8] *Ecclesiastes,* on the other hand, is "the most eminent existentialist book which has ever been written."[9] It takes man in his existential condition as known through the light of the gift of science. Yet it abstracts from any supra-terrestrial final end. And for this reason *Ecclesiastes* remains a work of moral philosophy inadequately considered because it is a moral philosophy without a veritable knowledge of the ultimate end of man.

This question of man's end is one of the most salient ones in moral philosophy. The end functions as a principle in regard to operations or actions to be performed. The end of man is a principle of moral philosophy, although it is not the only principle. The moral philosopher seeks to know what the natural end of man consists in. Yet Maritain insists that the highest natural perfection which man can attain is the kind of possession of God afforded by a contemplation of His creatures, enabling us to know God as the cause of being —the famous *quia* arguments of the *Summa Theologiae*. But this "possession" is insufficient to insure the scientific value of ethics since it leaves man unsatisfied. Knowing God through His effects, we naturally want to know Him in Himself. Maritain concludes that man has no determinate natural end. There is no natural perfection for man, and to speak of an imperfect beatitude is to use the term loosely and improperly.

If it is true that the end in the realm of human actions to be performed plays the role of principle, and if there is no determinate natural end for man, we must of necessity ask how a natural ethics is possible, that is, how a purely natural ethics is possible and is adequate to its object. Now the knowledge of the true end of human life can only be acquired from theology, which tells us that this end is supernatural and consists in the vision of God, God seen face to face. "A purely natural moral philosophy adequate to human action *could have* existed, as the state of pure nature could have existed, but in fact neither does exist."[10] Man is in another state. "In fact, because of events which are of *capital* importance for the human race and for human nature, such as the creation of man in Adam's state of grace, the fall and the redemption, theological truths are indispensable for the full constitution of ethics and the object of morals is only adequately known in the light of these truths."[11]

Now accepting all that has been said, the moral philosopher can choose one of several positions. He can, of course, be satisfied with a moral philosophy which does not know the ultimate end of man. He then commits himself to a moral philosophy which is not a science. Secondly, he may, as many do, allot to moral theology alone a knowledge of human actions. In either case moral philosophy in the full sense of the word disappears. However, the second choice is in no way allowable since we cannot dispense with a natural way of knowing things relating to moral action, the use of human freedom. There is yet a third solution according to Maritain which consists in subalternating moral philosophy to theology. This solution would allow philosophy to retain its autonomy—which is not an absolute autonomy—while bringing it to a state of completion as a science. Maritain finds traces of such a position in Saint Thomas' doctrine of superior reason and inferior reason.[12]

Before we see the manner in which moral philosophy is subalternated to theology, we must examine certain differences between them. Theology is an uncreated knowledge. It is a wisdom whose *habitus* is rooted in faith. John of Saint Thomas spoke of it as a formally natural and virtually supernatural *habitus*.[13] It is a natural habitus because it is acquired by intellectual effort, by human work. It is not, however, merely an application of reason to matters of faith as if reason could prove whatever has been revealed. Theological truth is only possessed by the theologian when faith acts as the principal cause. Consequently a theologian who loses the faith, loses, by the same token, theological truth. Furthermore, whatever human knowledge is found in theology is instrumental. Reason is elevated and made able to produce effects beyond its proper power because it is used as an instrument by theology.

Philosophy, on the other hand, proceeds by use of reason. It is specified by an object naturally knowable to reason. The realization of the autonomy of philosophy was not complete in the Middle Ages since the emphasis was on reason as instrumental in the formation of theological *summae*. This latter fact also explains why the problem of the possibility of a purely natural moral philosophy never arose in the works of St. Thomas. The use of reason is not instrumental in philosophy, but the principal cause.

Now a comparison of moral theology and moral philosophy adequately considered should be made in terms of specification, in terms of their respective objects. In general both of them are concerned with human actions, but the fact is that two knowledges can "cover the same field and have the same object, human acts, and still remain two specifically distinct forms of knowledge. . . ."[14] To show the distinction between moral theology and moral philosophy adequately considered, Maritain has recourse to a distinction developed by Cajetan.[15] In general this distinction implies that there can be sciences which are generically the same, having what is called the same *ratio formalis objecti ut res,* while differing because each has a distinctive objective light or formal perspective, in Cajetan's terminology the *ratio formalis objecti ut objectum.* What does it mean to say that two sciences have the same generic object, but differ because of formal perspective? The generic appeal of intelligibility or *ratio formalis objecti ut res* of moral philosophy adequately considered, answering fully to the definition of science, is the ordination of freedom to the ends of human life. It is concerned with human acts as ordered to their actual end. Of course both moral theology and moral philosophy are concerned with human behavior as ordered to the ultimate end, and since this end is supernatural, there is a temptation to assert that theology constitutes the *only* possible science of human behavior. Maritain rejects this opinion which entails the absorption of moral philosophy into theology. What this proves, he says, is that no true science of human behavior can be established independently of theology. There is a diversity of sciences in this case because moral philosophy has an objective light which differs from that proper to moral theology. "It is *in so far as they are revealable* that theology weighs all truths of its own,—the laws of human action as well as the rest . . . ," while a moral philosophy adequately considered regards "human acts *in so far as they are capable of being regulated by human reason (suitably completed).* . . ."[16] While the objective light of theology is derived from the light of divine revelation, moral philosophy is a created or profane way of knowing within the practical domain. There is a manner of knowing things related to human life from a human point of view and theology can never be substituted for this kind of knowing. In this human way of knowing, reason is not instrumental, as it is in theology, but operates as a second principal cause.

If it is true that moral theology and moral philosophy are distinguished by reason of their respective *rationes formales objecti ut objectum* or objective lights, we cannot separate them because of the aid which moral philosophy derives from being subalternated to theology. For two reasons, as we have noted before but which we cannot overemphasize, a purely natural moral philosophy fails to attain the status of a true science, that is, one which is adequate to its object, in this case the direction of human actions to their end. First of all, a purely natural moral philosophy lacks the knowledge of man's true ultimate end, to which all his actions are to be ordered. This deficiency is critical because the end in practical philosophy plays the role of principle. Secondly, a purely natural moral philosophy lacks a knowledge of what Maritain calls the "integrality" of the existential conditions of human life. Theology is in possession of the knowledge which will correct and complete these *lacunae* in moral philosophy on the condition that moral philosophy is subalternated to theology. We must examine what "subalternated" means in this statement, that is, which mode of subalternation, using the well known division of John of Saint Thomas, is involved in this particular case. One point should be noted beforehand. The subalternation of moral philosophy to theology occurs in such a way that the former is completed and perfected by theology. It is not a question of moral philosophy needing theology in a radical or originative way.[17] In other words moral philosophy has its own methods and can attain many truths by following its own experiential way of knowing, but it reaches a point where it realizes its own ignorance and the limitations of unaided reason. At that moment the philosopher who is a believer will either be satisfied with a moral philosophy which does not know the ultimate end of man or he will want to subalternate it to theology, or—an unlikely step for him—he will attribute to theology alone the direction of human acts.

When moral philosophy adequately considered receives the knowledge of the ultimate end of man from theology, it receives a truth which is a principle for it. Consequently it possesses two sets of principles: those known through reason alone and those which it receives from theology. The principles received from theology then are not all the principles of the science of ethics. Because the knowledge of the end is a principle for it, moral philosophy is subalternated to theology according to the second mode of subalternation of John of Saint Thomas, subalternation by reason of principles. This occurs when one science takes its principles from another science, and where the subalternated science does not itself resolve its conclusions in principles which are *per se nota* or evident to it. Now if moral philosophy received all of its principles from theology there would be a subalternation purely and simply (*simpliciter*), but Maritain says that there is another type of subalternation by reason of principles which he calls subalternation in a certain respect (*secundum quid*). "Should a science perchance resolve its conclusions in principles naturally known, and yet occasionally borrow some principles from another science, it is said to be subalternate in a certain respect (*secundum quid*) to this science."[18] So moral philosophy is able to discover for itself certain principles, but it must depend on theology for the knowledge of others. Moral philosophy believes the received principles or rather takes them on trust; it does not see them. "Now every subalternate science considered as such accepts *on faith* and does not *see* the principles which it receives from the subalternating science."[19]

A consequence of the subalternation of moral philosophy to moral theology is a certain division of labor between them. Moral philosophy always considers human things under the aspect of the mystery of created existence. Moral theology, on the other hand, always considers human things under the aspect of the mystery of divine life. The center or axis is different in each case. Moral philosophy is bound up with the mystery of man and the "drama of his life as a creature of flesh and spirit."[20] With moral theology it is a matter of revealed truth and the mystery of faith. When theology, therefore, examines findings in ethnology, politics, sociology, and history, it will be from a different angle to that of the moral philosopher. There is a need for both a theology of culture and a philosophy of culture. Moral philosophy will take for granted that certain problems will have been treated in moral theology, such as questions relating to the infused virtues, original sin, and grace. In moral theology there will be nothing on political science as such, which has as its object the ordination of man and society to a temporal end. Finally we must bear in mind that the approach to the ultimate end will differ in each case. Moral theology will always regard the question from the viewpoint of the participation by man in the very life of God, while moral philosophy will regard it from the viewpoint of the completion and perfection of human nature.

We have mentioned already the two types of aid which theology renders to moral philosophy. It furnishes the latter with objective data which philosophers have overlooked or which were beyond their ken. In addition there are those subjective reinforcements through which the actions of men become efficacious. The knowledge of the ultimate end of man is one of the objective data, but it is not the only contribution. It is only through theology that we have gained an idea of sin in its full meaning of an offense against God. Christian theology gives an historical explanation of the fall of man from the state of integral nature through the sin of Adam, a sin of disobedience against God. We do not find a similar notion in the ethical thought of the great pre-Christians for whom sin was essentially a violation of a natural law by which human acts were measured. Through theology we know that man is in a state of fallen nature and that he cannot love God efficaciously above all things by his own resources. One cannot easily exhaust the importance of these doctrines for the moral philosopher. Perhaps we can show the importance of them, to some extent, by an examination of what Maritain calls the "immanent dialectic of the first act of freedom."[21]

Let us take the example of a child who refrains from lying, not because of the fear of punishment if he is caught lying, not because he doesn't want to offend his parents, but simply because he sees this act as evil. It would not be *good* to do it. Such a decision is what Maritain means by the first act of freedom. He does not mean that the act is first in a temporal sense, but it is morally an absolute beginning. Now prior to this act the child has no doubt received many imperatives and prohibitions from his parents, and through social habit he performed the ones and avoided the others. We prescind here from those cases involving religious education. Now when the child chooses the good for the sake of the good, he breaks out of the shell of determination under which he has previously existed. This act is not a signified act, not the result of a reasoning process, but a lived act. This means that we are dealing with a choice made by a person in whom there is not yet a development of the powers of reflection. The decision which the child makes is one that he can change later in life. Yet it remains an act of freedom which gives a basic direction to his life. Though it is a matter of being born to the spiritual life, we cannot therefore rule out the possibility of other births. In fact there are many births, deaths, and resurrections in the spiritual life. Now the memory of this first act of freedom may be effaced by time, possibly because the object of the child's act was itself trivial. The situation is similar to that of trying to fix the date at which the rational life was awakened in us. However, if this first act by which one breaks out of the shell of determination arrives later in life, there is a greater probability that it will leave a vivid impression, as does a moment of religious conversion. This awakening to the spiritual life can also take place through the experience of remorse, the self-reproach at turning from the good.

Maritain means by the immanent dialectic of this act its "secret dynamism" and its implications.[22] What movement occurs within

the soul when this initial act is performed? Maritain has drawn out
the implications of this act. The first implication of this act is that
the soul turns away from an evil precisely because it is seen as evil.
Hence the intellect distinguishes between good and evil and it knows
that one must do good because it is good. The second implication of
this act is that there is an ideal order, above the empirical order,
which involves an ought, an order which measures our acts. This act
implies the notion of a normality or law of human acts, a natural
law, which transcends the world of simple fact. The third implication, which follows closely upon the second, is that such a law can
exist and arise only from the Good itself. It manifests the existence
of the Separate Good Who is at the origin of the natural law. Hence
the initial act which chooses the good because it is good, tends in the
same movement toward the Separate Good. There is a formal orientation in the lived act itself, "not in signified act—to God as ultimate end of human life."[23] Obviously the child is not aware of these
implications, but they are embedded in the act whereby the child
decides for the good because it is good. "But by the same token he
knows God, without being aware of it. He knows God because, by
virtue of the internal dynamism of his choice of the good for the
sake of the good, he wills and loves the Separate Good as ultimate
end of his existence."[24] God is not seized as an object of the speculative intellect, as in a concept, but as the practical term of the
movement of the will. And this kind of implicit knowledge can coexist with a theoretical ignorance of God.

Now it is at this stage of the analysis that the philosopher who
does not avail himself of the knowledge which Christian theology
offers can go astray. For this act by which the child seeks the Separate Good, even though in a virtual manner, for its own sake, is not
possible without grace. This act implies that one loves God efficaciously above all things and this presupposes grace and charity in
the soul. Saint Thomas, speaking of man's ability to love God above
everything, states: "But in the state of corrupted nature man falls
short of this in the appetite of his rational will, which, unless it be

cured by God's grace, follows its private good, because of the corruption of nature."[25] Sanctifying grace enables us to love God with the supernatural love of charity, and to love Him as "the only true end existentially given of human life," while as *gratia sanans* "grace restores to human nature its ability to love God above all things as the creator of the universe—natural love virtually contained in the supernatural love of charity."[26] Furthermore grace restores to human nature its ability to ordain itself to God as its natural end, "an ordainment virtually contained in the ordainment to God as ultimate supernatural end."[27] In the state of pure nature, man could have loved God in this manner, but this state has never existed. It was also possible, as Saint Thomas says, in the state of integral nature. Through theology we know of the wound of original sin and the Redemption through Christ. Through theology we are made aware of the incapacities of fallen nature, the most striking of which is this inability to love God efficaciously above all things by our natural powers. Without grace we are weak in the face of those things which flatter our self-love. Maritain sums up what he has said in regard to the role of grace in the first act of freedom: "If the child decides upon the good in his first act of freedom, he is set free from original sin and receives sanctifying grace; but this is because, in order for him to decide upon the good in his first act of freedom, grace, insofar as it heals nature, was vouchsafed him."[28]

This problem discloses to us the poverty of every moral philosophy which attempts to constitute itself as a true ethics while ignorant of the principles of faith and theology. Such a moral philosophy cannot but falsify this act in trying to explain it. It does not know the true state in which man exists. The Christian who seeks to explain this act as a pure moral philosopher, leaving out all reference to grace, is in danger of falling into Pelagianism. For this first act of freedom is not possible without grace. The complete and true explanation requires the aid of theology, and once one admits this theological contribution, how can one maintain a purely natural moral philosophy? Only theology knows the true state of man, and it is not possible to direct human actions if one is in ignorance of their conditions of exercise.

When we turn to the subjective reinforcement which theology affords to subalternated moral philosophy, we encounter the doctrine of the synergy of the powers of the soul. For all its importance, Maritain is one of the few Thomists to so much as mention it. The term "synergy" is taken from biology, where it means the co-operation of many different functions which produces an effect of a whole. The example usually given is the interconnection of circulation, respiration, and digestion in the same organism. In man the union of soul and body is a substantial union which is effected by *esse* (the act of existing) which is at the root of this synergy. From the initial unifying dynamism of *esse* comes the connection of the principles within the existent subject, and especially the interconnection of the powers which allows us to use the image of a current or a stream. Within the dynamism of the existent there is an overflow of the superior powers into the inferior, an intercommunication in the existing being which does not destroy the distinctiveness of these powers. The principle of unity remains the same as in the case of the metaphysical principles of composite beings: there is distinction without separation, and this lack of separation implies an interconnection.

So far we have spoken only of the synergy or working-together of the powers of the soul, the vital connection which exists between them in the order of exercise. This does not mean that they are not distinct, for they are specified by different objects. If it is true, then, that the powers of the soul are interconnected in exercise, it certainly follows that the *habitus* which perfect these powers will also be interconnected. Maritain states this doctrine as being contained in the thought of Saint Thomas. "Nothing is further from Thomism than the idea of reason or philosophy working in isolation from other spiritual energies, and constitutionally opposed to participation in a superior virtue and to super-elevation either in the order of performance or, when the object requires it, in the order of specification."[29] The separation of one *habitus* from another would imply that they are isolated within the soul, having a kind of independence which is incompatible with their existence as accidents. The temptation is strong to conceive of the psychic life after a spatial pattern in which each faculty is a planet moving in its own path, always parallel and never touching the paths of the others. It is the Bohr model of the soul. It is an erroneous conception because the multiplicity found in the soul is a multiplicity of powers, *habitus,* and operations, all of which are accidents and not things. We have spoken of the unity of the soul itself, a unity which arises ultimately and intrinsically from *esse,* the act-of-existing. The numerical multiplicity of the powers, *habitus,* and operations of the soul is not to be taken in the sense of spatial multiplicity, but in the sense of transcendental number.[30] So the distinctions which arise from the order of specification do not eradicate the solidarities which are found in the living thing.

Let us now turn from the statement of the principle of synergic union, with its implication of a vital connection between the natural and supernatural virtues, and examine some of its applications. These applications are of capital importance for a moral philosophy which is to be adequate to its object. The first application concerns the relation of the natural moral virtues to the supernatural virtue of charity. Maritain notes, in a passage where he is presenting the thought of Saint Thomas on the problem, that the natural virtues are not virtues in a strict sense without the virtue of charity. By themselves the natural moral virtues would not have that binding connection which they require: for example the performance of an act of justice not only presupposes the virtue of prudence which makes one act rightly, and which is practical wisdom, but also fortitude and temperance, the former because one must know when to act, neither peremptorily nor too late because of fear, the latter because the passions must be submitted to reason so that concupiscence does not interfere with giving another his due. Each of these cardinal virtues is specified by a different object. All must be united in exercise, for they are directed toward the placing of a good act and must be as one virtue. Without charity, Maritain points out, these natural moral virtues could not be connected in the manner necessary for the performance of a good act. They would remain in the state of simple dispositions. A man may have true acquired temperance, continues Maritain, without charity, and it would be something more than the false temperance of the miser, say Père Grandet in Balzac's famous novel. A man can possess an acquired temperance, not vitiated by this kind of falsity, which will nevertheless remain in the state of a disposition and hence can be easily altered, unlike a virtue in the strict sense which is changed only with difficulty. It is true then of temperance, as with the rest of the cardinal virtues, that "without charity, they have no real connexion, they are not bound up together in one strong organism, because they are only connected *in statu virtutis*."[31] The point of this discussion is that the moral virtues must be interconnected, and if they are not interconnected, they cannot lead to the performance of good acts. They are not efficacious.

Maritain maintains that four important points are comprised in Saint Thomas' teaching on this question, in the texts from the *Summa Theologiae*.[32] In the first place Saint Thomas holds that no interconnection exists between imperfect virtues, that is to say, virtues which realize the concept of virtue only in an imperfect sense. Secondly, the acquired moral virtues, apart from charity, are virtues in an imperfect sense. They are only virtues in a certain sense (*secundum quid*), not purely and simply (*simpliciter*). The infused virtues alone are perfect virtues, or are virtues in the strict sense of the term, because they direct man to his ultimate end. The natural moral virtues, albeit imperfect, can direct man to a last end in a given order, such as the order of civil life, but cannot direct man to the absolutely last end. Thirdly, it thus follows that the acquired moral virtues are not connected. One can speak of a kind of connection of these virtues in prudence, though prudence itself is not a virtue in an absolute sense. Only through the virtue of charity, present in the soul in the state of grace, does prudence attain the status of a virtue without qualification. Not only does theology inform us of the true state of man and his need for grace if he aspires to love God above all things, but we know from it that the subjective dynamism is altered and fortified by the presence of grace. The objective datum of the necessity of grace has its correlative in the subjective reinforcement of the soul wrought by the virtue of charity, the effect of grace. Without charity, as we have seen, man cannot love God efficaciously above all things, and we cannot be deprived of the virtue of charity without being turned away from God as our supernatural end. Fourthly, a virtue in a certain sense (*secundum quid*) is an inclination to perform some action which belongs to the genus of that which is good. A virtue in the perfect sense is a "firm and stable quality which inclines of itself to the doing of a good work in a good way."[33] The first statement implies that imperfect virtues lead to the production of good only accidentally, in a hit-and-miss fashion. Certainly the imperfect virtues do not enable us to live the good life which is what ethics seeks to do.

Saint Thomas spoke of the man without charity as being a sick man who is deprived of those activities which moral health or normality allow, and which are the good connatural to man. The doctrine of St. Thomas is that man in the state of integral nature could desire and achieve by his natural strength alone the good proportioned to his nature, which is the good of the acquired virtues. After the Fall man is unable even to do this and is powerless to accomplish all the good of the natural order itself. This does not mean that Saint Thomas held the theory of total depravity, for even in the state of fallen nature man could do certain good acts through his natural power. Saint Thomas mentioned such activities as building houses and planting vines.

The second application of the doctrine of synergy which we will consider is also concerned with the relation of the natural virtues to the supernatural virtues. Here, however, we will discuss the relation between the acquired moral virtues and the infused moral virtues.

How does their co-existence in the soul in the state of grace affect them? Moral science is continued and completed by acquired prudence, while moral theology is continued and completed by infused prudence. Maritain says that in the case of a moral philosophy adequately considered, moral philosophy "is continued and completed by acquired prudence, as it exists in the soul in the state of grace, where it is joined with charity and super-elevated by its conjunction with infused prudence."[34] Acquired prudence, in this instance, is elevated by infused prudence, but not in an instrumental way. The infused moral virtues make the moral virtues correspond to the theological virtues and the supernatural end. The acquired virtues are not absorbed or eliminated by the infused ones. "It follows that in the just soul the acquired moral virtue coexisting with infused moral virtue forms with it a vital and synergic union."[35] The effect of the infused moral virtue is to proportion our acts to our ultimate eternal end.

Now what Maritain wishes to emphasize in this discussion is the ways in which the infused moral virtues can elevate the acquired moral virtues. One way consists in the instrumental elevation of the latter by the former and occurs when an infused virtue is exercised from a supernatural motive, as when infused fortitude resists temptation with the supernatural motive of conforming to the suffering and redeeming Christ. The infused virtue uses the acquired virtue as an instrument in the attainment of its own ends. Now the acquired virtues make our actions conform to the temporal ends of human life, the ends of political life. The goods of this order are goods proportioned to human nature. When a person in the state of grace exercises the acquired moral virtues to gain temporal ends, the acquired moral virtues are again elevated by charity and the infused moral virtues, but not instrumentally, since the initiative rests with the acquired moral virtues. This super-elevation is needed in regard to ends in the temporal order, for unless the ends of the political order are referred to the supra-temporal ends of human life, that order will lack the rectitude which is proper to it. In this latter case the acquired moral virtues function as principal causes, not as instruments of the infused moral virtues. Yet there is still an elevation of the acquired moral virtues beyond their natural point of specification. A politician who is tempted to betray his principles in order to protect his country will be fortified—if he be in the state of grace—by infused virtues which will make him trust in the providence of divine government. So in such a circumstance the synergic union of the natural and supernatural virtues, the acquired and the infused virtues, causes the acquired virtues to be elevated and become conformed, not only with man's ultimate non-temporal end, but even with those ends which are on the natural plane, the domain of civil life. The civic virtue of friendship can become charity because directed toward a higher end. Without the infused moral virtues, the acquired moral virtues are not even efficacious in their own order. The tendency of such virtues, lacking charity, will be to make the ends of the civil life, which are legitimate ends in a certain order, into absolutes, disregarding the prior claim and primacy of man's supernatural destiny.

The third application of the doctrine of synergy is found in the discussion of the ethics of thought: "What are the conditions and requirements of *right action* in the performance of the operations of thought?"[36] It is a problem in moral philosophy since it concerns the use of human freedom. Now granted that philosophy is specified by an object naturally knowable, or objects naturally knowable if philosophy is taken as a group of sciences, and granted that all affective dispositions are irrelevant when it is a question of the order of specification, are we to maintain that we can completely ignore these affective dispositions? Must we not also consider the order of exercise or performance? The distinction of the order of specification from the order of exercise implies among other things "that the *application* of our faculties to the task of discovering and elaborating truth is the work of the will like every *usus*."[37] The will moves the powers of the soul to perform their operations. So the intellect in the act of philosophizing presupposes an initiative of freedom and the effort of the whole soul with all that it encompasses. This means that the moral quality of the philosopher enters into play. We must give our attention to the role that the subjective dimensions perform in philosophical research.

The act of philosophizing involves the character of the philosopher. Pride, envy, vanity, gluttony and intellectual avarice, the preference of a dialectical virtuosity and of the false security of academicism to the mystery of being, the spirit of sectarianism and zealous bitterness, a taste for what is fashionable, self-satisfaction or satisfaction with a group or circle, the duplicity which turns against known truth, are fatal to the rectitude of this act.[38]

To counteract these many snares the philosopher requires the superior wisdoms: the wisdom of theology and the wisdom of grace. Maritain believes that finally the philosopher must needs enter into an experiential knowledge of spiritual things. To respect both the demands of the order of specification and those of the order of exercise is not an easy task and those who stress the objectivity of knowledge are often guilty of depreciating the conditions of its exercise. And although many contemporary philosophers place perhaps too much emphasis on the conditions of the subject who philosophizes, to the extent of denying the role played by the object in science, Thomists can often be criticized for ignoring the dispositions of the subject. The subjectivity of the philosopher must be purified, and this purification must come from the reinforcement given to the acquired *habitus* of philosophy by grace and the supernatural virtues.

In concluding this examination of moral philosophy adequately considered, we should take note of Maritain's conception of the philosophy of history. Maritain has recently pointed out that the philosophy of history belongs to moral philosophy.[39] While presupposing a knowledge of metaphysics and the philosophy of nature, it is concerned with the practical realm itself, rather than with the speculative. "The philosophy of history is the final application of philosophical truths, not to the conduct of the individual man, but to the entire movement of humanity. And therefore it is *moral* philosophy."[40] For this movement of humanity is towards the end of time, and the philosophy of history concerns itself with the actions involved in this movement. It treats of the evolution of mankind, not its biological evolution, but its moral one. Again we are confronted with the choice of taking account of the data of revelation or of proceeding as a pure philosopher. Since we must know the existential condition of man if we are to have a genuine philosophy of history, which, unlike the theology of history which is centered on the mystery of the Church, is centered on the mystery of this world, the philosophy of history too must become part of moral philosophy adequately considered. For the world is related to the Kingdom of God and the Church, just as nature is related to grace, although in both cases there is a difference of orders. A philosophy of history, being centered on this world, regards not only the supra-temporal ends of history and eternal salvation, as does theology, but the immanent ends of history itself. The pure philosopher who refuses to subalternate moral philosophy to theology, refusing all the data and the reinforcements which theology can give, cannot provide a genuine philosophy of history because "in his hands the philosophy of history is bound either to fail in its own expectations or to risk mystification, for in order to get at some level of real depth and significance it inevitably requires prophetic data. And where would the pure philosopher find authentic prophetic data?"[41] Only theology can provide such data.

Maritain's book on the philosophy of history is a tentative approach to the subject. His book is more an introduction to and outline of the philosophy of history than a full-scale treatment. It illustrates, from our point of view, how his notion of moral philosophy adequately considered has progressed from its first explicit exposition in *An Essay on Christian Philosophy*. The implications of this notion are far from exhausted. And the work of his lifetime has shown how deeply Maritain has realized the import of an epigram he placed in an early work: "The intelligence without faith and the gifts which accompany it, is not Rachel, but Leah, with sore eyes."[42]

NOTES

1. Jacques Maritain, *An Essay on Christian Philosophy* (New York: Philosophical Library, 1955), p. 30.
2. Jacques Maritain, *Science and Wisdom* (London: Geoffrey Bles, 1940), p. 79.
3. *Ibid.*, p. 80.
4. *Ibid.*, p. 80.
5. *Ibid.*, p. 80.
6. *Ibid.*, p. 109 note.
7. Jacques Maritain, *Neuf leçons sur les notions premières de la philosophie morale* (Paris: Téqui, 1951), pp. 86-88.
8. *Ibid.*, p. 90.
9. *Ibid.*, p. 86.
10. *Science and Wisdom*, p. 109.
11. *Ibid.*, p. 109.
12. *Ibid.*, pp. 155-161.
13. John of Saint Thomas, *Cursus Theologicus*, In Primam Partem, q. 1, disp. 2, a. 8, Ed. Solesmes (Paris-Turin-Rome: Desclée et Socii, 1931).
14. *An Essay on Christian Philosophy*, p. 67.
15. Cajetan, *In I Summa Theologiae*, q. 1, a. 3, n. III, V.
16. *An Essay on Christian Philosophy*, p. 76.
17. *Ibid.*, p. 89.
18. *Ibid.*, pp. 82-83.
19. *Ibid.*, p. 93.
20. *Science and Wisdom*, p. 120.
21. Maritain has treated this question in both *Raison et raisons* (Paris: Egloff, 1947), pp. 131-165, and *Neuf leçons sur les notions premières de la philosophie morale*, pp. 119-128. The former essay is included in *The Range of Reason* (New York: Scribner, 1953), pp. 66-85.

22. *The Range of Reason,* p. 68.
23. *Ibid.,* p. 69.
24. *Ibid.,* pp. 69-70.
25. *Sum. Theol.,* I-II, 109, 3c.
26. *The Range of Reason,* p. 71, footnote.
27. *Ibid.*
28. *Ibid.,* p. 74.
29. *Science and Wisdom,* p. 205.
30. Jacques Maritain, *Bergsonian Philosophy and Thomism* (New York: Philosophical Library, 1955), p. 255, esp. note 4.
31. *Science and Wisdom,* p. 146.
32. *Ibid.,* p. 145. Maritain is commenting on question 65, articles one and two of the *Prima Secundae.*
33. *Ibid.,* p. 149. Maritain is quoting Saint Thomas, *Sum. Theol.,* I-II, 65, 1c.
34. *Ibid.,* p. 210.
35. *Ibid.,* p. 211.
36. *Ibid.,* p. 206.
37. *Ibid.,* p. 206.
38. *Ibid.,* p. 207.
39. Jacques Maritain, *On the Philosophy of History* (New York: Scribner, 1957).
40. *Ibid.,* p. 17.
41. *Ibid.,* p. 40.
42. Jacques Maritain, *Antimoderne,* (Paris: Editions de la Revue des Jeunes, 1922), p. 41.

Charles O'Donnell

9. Jacques Maritain—Political Philosopher

THE PRESENT ESSAY is a study of certain of Jacques Maritain's political ideas most pertinent to the world we live in. It discusses first the relationship between politics and ethics so that we may distinguish at the outset the difference between success and justice as a measure of political action in our world. Secondly it considers Maritain's notion of a human order suffused by Christian principles. Finally the essay discusses the possibility of an international society. These topics are elaborated within the Maritain philosophical synthesis in order that in his words "the world in the making under our eyes may be reasoned out, judged and redressed."

Jacques Maritain has given us a philosophy of politics and culture which replies to totalitarianism and answers to the aspirations of free men. In this philosophy man has a life of his own in his family, church, labor union, enterprise or other association and also a life as a citizen member of a political society. According to this pluralistic view of politics and culture man pursues his freedom and happiness under authority. Man is born free and authority preserves this freedom. It is the Western tradition which Maritain recalls for us and helps us to understand in all its riches and dimensions. He presents to us a politics of political and cultural freedom which we need to act upon if we are to escape a politics of barbarism.

Politics and Ethics

Among the contemporary confusions about the fundamentals of our civilization few are as politically devastating as the failure to comprehend and arrange a proper order of things and ideas. An appreciation of the relationship between politics and ethics—the two principal practical philosophies—is one of the continuing problems in our times. The great debate on morals and politics which has been going on in the United States since the end of World War II has pivoted around unresolved feelings and ideas about morals and politics (I use the terms morals and ethics as synonomous). This disorder calls for fresh thinking.

Politics for Maritain is a part of ethics—that part of ethics which deals with man's existence in society and with what the aims of society ought to be—the good of the person as it relates to the political common good of persons in society. These moral goods are the supreme guides to political success in the long run. The position of Maritain rejects the so-called "realist" or power politics philosophy which measures politics by short-run successes accomplished with the help of technological triumphs.

In the view of Maritain, politics and ethics alike consider human affairs in two ways: "as they are" and "as they should be." "Realists" refuse to accept the idea that "should be" is a practical criterion. They regard the correctness of policy (which is a specific instance of politics) as determined essentially by the efficacy of the means for putting policy into action. "Realists" do not stop long enough to relate policy to moral purpose and consequences. The practical result of the "realist" approach is disorder and lost motion. Policy (the end of a politics) directs action and gets translated into action; the means (like tools) are left behind when the action is completed. Politics is efficacious for good or ill. What is required, as Maritain has clearly seen, is a measure of what policy "is" and "should be."

"Realist" morals favors what Maritain terms the technical rationalization of political power—that is, the maintenance of authority by whatever means (moral or otherwise) in order to ensure success. This doctrine in its most Machiavellian form is practiced by the totalitarians. In democracies a "realistic" formulation of this doctrine is that politics must succeed or risk the loss of a good (a truly good) cause. At the international level it is argued, for example, that the survival of a great nation must be assured by whatever means because such survival is essential to the well-being of the world as well as to a great nation. This argument represents a policy of confusion. *The principle* that a great nation *must survive* by whatever means serves the case of belligerent "realists" and pacifists alike inasmuch as it warrants either a preventive war or complete surrender to an apparent superior military power on the identical ground that we must at all costs survive.

The technical rationalization of means to ends, Maritain holds, guarantees success neither in the short run (which is the hope of the strong-armed men) nor in the long run (the hope of the pacifist and disciple of *laissez faire*). The power of evil which the technicians of success are ready to use, says Maritain, "squanders the substance and real energies of good." Maritain's idea is that if Machiavellian politics does not fail in the relatively near future, it nonetheless bears within itself the seeds of its own destruction. The spirit of technical rationalization of political power demands immediate success and seldom, if ever, is content with long-range results. Fascism and Nazism are prime examples of the kind of totalitarian successes which are measured by the lifetime of a dictator. On the other hand, the Soviet Union and Communist China may, to my way of thinking, prove to be examples of Machiavellians whose success may be assured for a long time although it is not guaranteed in the very long run. A succession of new-style Communist rulers may be able to go on for many generations strengthened by the unity and energy generated by the Communist revolution and its ideals. Moreover, as chance plays an enormous role in history, the Machiavellian tactics of the Communists may lengthen their fortunes, should weakness, ineptitude and division among free nations prevail. A united democratic world moved by a moral politics will, I believe, diminish and overcome the strength of totalitarianism.

If reliance on purely technical means cannot succeed for nations committed to non-democratic ideals, it will not help nations with democratic ideals. On the other hand, democracies are not doomed to failure, Maritain says, because they insist on acting justly against the ruthless employment of force and fraud. "The first condition" of good politics, wrote Maritain, "is that it be just." As Yves Simon shrewdly commented, "it is not impossible to cause what is just also to be strong—it is only extremely difficult." He might have added "and takes a very long time." The strength of the just, according to Maritain, can be accomplished by the employment of a moral rationalization of political life—"by a grown-up awareness of human needs . . . of the real requirements of peace and love and of the moral and spiritual energies of man." Mankind, even in the twentieth century, is only taking its first toddling steps in this direction.

The Western tradition is still afflicted by a puritanical urge to apply ethical norms in their full force to each circumstance as it arises. This affliction, which Maritain calls "hypermoralism," sometimes reveals itself in a hypocritical garb, and in that guise has given a bad name to morality as applied to political action. Hypermoralism by reaction generates cynicism and a so-called realism which are the enemies of morality and good politics. When moral principles are sincerely applied in a hypermoral manner, the judgments produced fail to take real life into account—they ignore man for what he is—a fallen and redeemed creature. In the international sphere hypermoralism, by insisting on absolute practical rules born of pacifism or militarism, produces misunderstanding among nations and thwarts the solution of many problems.

A realistic or existential politics for Maritain aims directly at the good of man in society. As long as the means are not bad in themselves but good in general, and generally proportioned to man's good, and for that reason bear the imprint of their end, such political means, Maritain declares, can be used. It is this rule which he says justified coercion and many intelligence and police methods. The principles of the lesser evil and the *fait accompli* play an important role in politics, national and international. These realist principles can be compatible with right order when they do not prevent political or cultural changes for the better, *circumstances permitting*.

Political prudence, the virtue which leads to right decisions in the here and now, must, according to Maritain, be possessed by political leaders to judge rightly in accordance with these realist principles. Those who govern, possessed of this virtue, will see to it that changes are made for the better when opportunities arise which will make the chances of success likely. This does not mean that virtuous (prudent) men alone, and apart from appropriate political structures, can make a good politics. Universal and absolute principles which have the character of moral ends do not fall because politics requires a realistic approach. Prudential judgments rest on these principles and on assessments of relevant social facts without excluding historical success. One of the triumphs of Machiavellian politics is that it has obscured the possibility of a moral, practical and successful politics. It is the long-run objectives which command the direction of a moral political order. A moral view is also a patient one.

The way in which principles are related to practice is especially relevant to reconciliations among the intellectually divided men of our world. In an address to a UNESCO meeting in Mexico City in November, 1947, Maritain concluded that men and women with wide differences, even downright opposition, in their views about the world, culture and knowledge can arrive at agreement based on common practical notions. Maritain believes it is vain to seek a common philosophical ground even in the free world. Instead he hopes that a sort of unwritten common law of human rights can eventually be agreed upon. Human rights, he holds, are part of the natural inclination of man in all ages. They belong to the moral conscience of mankind and have been formulated and made more precise through the ages, especially in the West under Christian inspiration. Agreement on a common body of such rights, he believes, can be reached even though each person believes in his own way of justifying such rights. Since the time Maritain expressed these views, the Western world has witnessed the beginnings of a practical common effort in programs for economic aid to under-developed countries. These programs have their origins in a practical acknowledgment of the existence of human economic rights which deserve protection. While much remains to be done, Maritain's idea that a workable agreement is possible in practical matters in spite of religious and philosophical divergencies has stood an historical test in the rapid development of aid programs.

The first and foremost principle which prompts men in a free society to act together in practical affairs is the sense of justice imparted by our Western heritage (and sometimes borrowed from us by the Communists). In its simplest terms justice means that in internal and external affairs political decisions should aim at giving each citizen, group or nation what is their due. In the largest sense what is due in external affairs is the recognition and respect for the common good of nations or for the nation over private-personal or group interests. It means, for example, religious tolerance and racial nondiscrimination. In the economic sphere it concerns the economic welfare of the masses. In politics it seeks to make men free citizens. The meaning of justice must unfold in history. It is the overshadowing obligation imposed on governments and private societies to attend to the historical demands of justice if they are not to be prey to the menace of power politics.

A close analysis of Maritain's thinking shows that over and above justice a Christian philosopher misunderstands his vocation if he does not grasp the significance of love in political and cultural life. The bond of society, and especially political society, is fraternal amity grounded in charity. It is probably not incorrect to say that this is one of the most unexplored and least understood aspects of politics. One of the deeper sides of this subject was touched on by Maritain when he reminded us that we do not love ideas—we love men.

Justice and charity are translatable into what Maritain terms the practical common principles of political action. The principles he suggests should be embodied in a Democratic Charter. The Charter of which he speaks is not to be understood as a formal constitutional document such as the Constitution of the United States. The Charter, I believe, is more correctly conceived as a conceptual framework to be gradually constructed by wise and practical men out of the abundance of their understanding of principles in relation to action. Men responsible for action in society, political or otherwise, who are aware of such practical common principles, will be enabled to make better decisions about concrete matters.

Such a Charter or conceptual framework will also give us a measure by which to judge the Communist world. When the Communists, for example, give real freedom to their poets to publish as well as write poetry, or permit their citizens to hold and practice religious beliefs without strong contrary pressures, they will begin to merit a measure of confidence among free peoples. Democracies have yet to develop a true accord on the common practical principles by which to judge our world. Within the free nations themselves the enlargement and enrichment of the freedom of a Democratic Charter will furnish an index of the destiny of democracy.

Maritain's accent on the steady pursuit of human well-being leads us to his central theme—that of a new Christendom—i.e., of a democratic Christian society which will begin to realize the gains to be obtained in a society governed by justice, caring about human rights and boldly engaged in creating a great commonwealth of peoples. The image of a Christian earthly city that Maritain holds before us is not an ideal of empire but a city of brotherly love and material well-being.

The ideal of a new Christendom has been attacked on two quite different grounds: one that it is an "absolute" and not an historical ideal and the other that it is an utterly historical or medieval ideal which Maritain proposes. Maritain has constantly presented the new Christendom as an historical ideal—that is, an ideal relative to a given age of history. As we have seen, his thinking on ethics and politics is of a piece with the view that a new Christendom is an historical and not an abstract ideal. The other idea, namely, that Maritain proposes a medieval ideal, is based on a misunderstand-ing of Maritain's observations that the culture produced in the past several centuries is in the process of dissolution. That he sees this dissolution taking place has not brought him to undertake the vain task of seeking to resurrect the medieval world. Maritain's criticisms of the Middle Ages should dispel any doubts on this score. The truth lies in a remark made some years ago that Maritain is not *anti-moderne* but *ultra-moderne*.

The New Christendom

The major political writings of Jacques Maritain, *Humanisme Intégral* and *Man and the State,* were published some twenty years apart. *Humanisme Intégral,* appearing in 1935, presented the ideal of a new Christendom which was foreshadowed in many of his political writings prior to 1935, notably in *Le Docteur Angélique, Religion et Culture* and *Du Régime Temporel et de la Liberté.* It was elaborated upon in certain of its aspects in writings published subsequently to *Humanisme Intégral.* In these later discussions Maritain referred to the New Christendom variously as a regime of Christian inspiration, as a democracy of Gospel inspiration, and to its manifestation as a heroic humanism or simply as a Christian humanism. In *Man and the State* he looked at the international dimensions of the new Christendom.

In its essentials a new Christendom is an image of the kind of a world Maritain believes that intelligent and good men would like to see made out of this world, and one in which they would want to live. The ideal of a new Christendom brings into focus the political common good of society as conceived in a Christian politics, namely the total good of persons and the cultural aspirations of all peoples. The ideal matters seriously because our world cannot be borne safely into the future on the wings of the enfeebled and divided tradition of liberal philosophy which still claims to inspire Western democracy. Valiant efforts to instill new life into this tradition, as exemplified in the sensitive and reasonable effort of a writer like Frederick Watkins in his *Political Tradition of the West*, have simply not caught on. The Western world, on the other hand, has no desire to leave the world to Communist "proletarians" to fight among themselves for technological supremacy after the "bourgeois world" has passed into history. A Christian political philosopher cannot leave the world in the lurch.

Maritain's outline of a "future" society can be made to appear as a never-never land. To so conclude would be wholly to misunderstand what Maritain has written. He does not suggest that we plan a Christianized Platonic Republic (which that philosopher admitted could only be realized in heaven). Maritain is talking to us about a human society which free men moved by a Christian inspiration are capable of organizing here on earth so that men and women can live out their lives on this planet more joyfully and more humanly than they now do. This is an immensely difficult practical ideal to realize. It calls for much understanding and love, the grace of God and the wise exercise of human freedom and authority. It is not a Communist-type utopia which is to arrive and survive because its inventors claim to have discovered the inevitable laws of history.

Maritain's ideal of a New Christendom may never come off because men can so exercise their options as to obtain another kind of life. An optimistic view of the chances for this society would lead one to believe that it could be realized relatively soon if men worked hard and fast enough for it. A realistic view (recognizing that most men act badly and that the understanding of political ideals comes slowly) suggests that a long time is likely to elapse before such a society could be realized. As totalitarianism grows apace, the ideal of a new Christendom becomes more urgent and necessary.

The new Christendom already exists in an inchoate and embryonic form—in islands of open-minded men, Maritain notes. It exists among all those who understand that to work for the establishment of new social forms consonant with the common good of men, it is necessary to maintain the primacy of moral values over purely technical values; the liberty of the spiritual with regard to the social and the eternal with regard to the human, to use Maritain's phrases. The kind of values which Walter Lippmann sees as the elements of his *Public Philosophy*—these contribute to a good human life. Many men of divergent political and cultural beliefs are contributors to the making of the new Christendom. Even Communism serves to remind us of our obligations to our society.

Maritain's ideal of a new Christendom is not a blueprint but a set of practical principles which suggest the principal features of the good society yet to be realized. The ideal as seen by Maritain has as its special marks those of a society which is "personalist, communitarian and pluralist"—a free society in which the general welfare and democracy are goals. It is these marks which command our attention.

The political philosophy of Maritain can rightly be said to have had its birth in the idea of the person. His earliest presentation of this idea was couched in philosophical-religious rather than in political terms. In the many essays in which Maritain has written about the person, he has showed the paramount importance of distinguishing in humans between individuality (which separates men from society and man from man) and personality (which specifies man's dignity and provides a bridge to society). Maritain discarded nineteenth-century individualism and laid the foundation of a politics of personalism on the substructures of Thomistic metaphysics. Regarding man as a person in society he once wrote, "Man as an individual person holds himself in hand by his intelligence and will; he not only exists physically but also spiritually in knowledge and love. He is in some way a whole—a microcosm." As man is not a closed but an open unity, Maritain went on, he tends by his nature to social life. His needs and his "radical generosity of spirit" (too often stifled by his own stupidities or by the political enemies of his soul) signify that he was meant for society. The human person, as Maritain sees him, requires a social and political life which is a whole (as the persons in the society are also wholes).

As described by Maritain the aim of political life is the common good—the good of the whole society. It is the good common to the perfecting of the whole society and also of the persons who are members of society. Political society by serving the common good redistributes goods to persons and aids their development. The unhappy fact of our contemporary world, I believe, is that our political societies only partially succeed in making this redistribution, and they do it very badly.

The common good looked at from the point of view of political society is the foundation of the authority of that society. The common good thus at once limits and empowers the action of authority. It is what an American political scientist would call a constitutional power. In the broad sense of Maritain's thinking, persons exercising authority for the common good do so in order to advance the virtues, civic and others, among the individual persons that make up society.

The persons of whom Maritain speaks bear the proper name of free men. Authority over persons aims at enlarging and advancing their freedom. For this reason Maritain refers to authority in his Christian democracy as the pedagogue of freedom.

Maritain began his speculations about freedom, as about the person, in a metaphysical context. He first elaborated his views on free will and freedom in the opening pages of the book known in English as *Freedom in the Modern World*. His metaphysical studies of freedom were accompanied by illuminating observations on political freedom. Maritain traces the totalitarian catastrophes of the twentieth century (in so far as philosophical ideas played a part in them) to the false conquests of freedom based on Rousseau's and Kant's mistaken ideas about the autonomy of the person and his freedom. These philosophers, says Maritain, divinized the individual and his freedom, thus leading logically to a practical atheism, to the disappearance of the notion of the common good as a concept of practical philosophy and to a falsification of the notion of authority.

In the good society—in a new Christendom—Maritain sees man progressively conquering freedom in social and political matters. In given historical conditions, he can become as independent as possible of *material* restraints (but not of the discipline of authority). The historical march of civilization, if it is to be a march and not a retreat, will lead to the conquest of freedom by men in society. Man as a person will have the opportunity to achieve his spiritual freedom. Political freedom will consist in a climate favorable to the pursuit of political and cultural perfection of citizens.

Speaking of authority, Maritain writes that political society, having its own reality, its unity and its life, is superior to its members as such and requires a hierarchical distribution of authority. The common good of a people in a Christian democracy has to be achieved, says Maritain, under conditions which philosophers denominate contingency and singularity (to use a looser phrase, "social change"). The agreement which men need to achieve common action requires an authority charged with the right to judge and command the operations of society. Maritain is careful to remark that authority, whether vested in elected or appointive officials, must be exercised for the sake of peoples regarded as persons (that is, as beings endowed with freedom).

Speaking of the interpenetration of freedom and authority, Maritain notes that social change can be orderly provided that such changes are subject to an authority which enhances the freedom of citizens and under which they exercise their freedom intelligently. A monolithic society or one that tends to be so exhibits characteristics of a static society—a deadly authoritarian uniformity is insisted upon and freedom, when not abolished, is rigidly circumscribed or smothered.

Maritain's ideal of a new Christendom is that of a society in which social change goes hand in hand with pluralism in political and cultural affairs. Social change is itself produced by a series of causes—by deliberate and free acts, by changes in the material conditions in which men live and by the incidents of chance. Governance of a society subject to these multiple forms of social change can lead to arbitrariness on the part of those exercising authority when they are chiefly influenced by the pressures of social change. In order to curb arbitrariness it is necessary to arrange authority in a decentralized fashion—so that multiple forces are pluralized rather than centralized. Pluralism is thus a true mark of the new humanism that Maritain hopes the world will eventually accept. Pluralism stamps this ideal with the seal of practicality and realism.

One of the philosophical roots of pluralism, as seen by Maritain, is to be found in the fundamental equality of men which manifests itself when men show respect for one another. "It is the natural love of the human being for his kind that reveals and gives life to the specific equality of men." This natural love very often makes its appearance in times of trouble when it brings men together to meet a common danger. Selfish complacency can be a great enemy of accord among men. Maritain regards inequalities among men as very real but quite secondary. Inequalities of ability, of acquired habits, and even those produced by the play of power in society, can generate unity in society when they represent a diversity of virtues and perfections. Political societies should aim at developing greater social equalities so that each person, whatever his abilities, will have an equal opportunity to perfect himself.

Social equality can come about in a plurality of organizations (industrial and business firms and associations, labor unions, a free press, etc.). At the head of a pluralist society is the political authority which has as its main business the care of the common good understood in its broadest political sense. Diverse social groups (natural and artificial) are subordinate to political authority but are as essential to the perfection of the good society as is the authority itself. The operative principle is that every function which can be taken on by a subordinate group in the hierarchy of societies ought to be performed by them. According to this principle there is more perfection in a whole made up of parts which are full of life and initiative than in an ensemble of groups which are only the instruments of a superior body. Subordinate groups can serve as permanent centers of resistance against arbitrariness; they can demand freedom and prevent the usurpation of political authority. The right of political authority to act for the common good serves in turn to limit possible excesses of power of subordinate groups and guarantees their freedom of operation. In a Christian democracy the checks and balances of a pluralistic society constitute a rational arrangement of freedom and authority.

To reconcile the practical conflicts which may arise between freedom and authority in societies, public opinion can play a moderating role. Maritain notes that educated and clever men are as often mistaken in political matters as are the ignorant; and that the errors of the unsophisticated are vulgar mistakes while those of the skilled are "intellectualized and documented." Maritain suggests then that what is most important is a right instinct. (Politically this instinct exhibits itself in a sensitivity to the general direction which affairs ought to take rather than in a perceptivity as to the appropriateness of the means called for.) This instinct can be cultivated by a good civic education. Politicians, Maritain thinks, are well advised to take into account any right instinct shown by the people. In so doing they acknowledge the significance of public opinion.

Another pluralistic institution which Maritain believes would be perfected in a new Christendom is the free press. Despite the dangers of excesses (and actual excesses) Maritain gives his strong support to a press undominated by government. He concurs in the proposals of the Freedom of Press Committee headed up by Robert Hutchins that the press ought to take responsibility for policing its own membership.

Maritain urges that religious diversity in the world today be accepted as a social fact. Christians, without giving up their religious convictions, he says, are obliged to love other persons whatever their religious beliefs. In countries whose citizens belong to various spiritual traditions the members of diverse religious denominations would co-operate in matters of common social and political import. Government, Maritain insists, should encourage religion without giving a privileged position to the members of any particular denomination; and the way in which civil society would support Christianity would consist above all in giving the maximum of freedom to preach the Gospel and in looking to the many activities inspired by the Gospel to contribute to the furthering of the common good.

In the complex area of economics Maritain has proposed pluralistic solutions with particular insistence. Not only does he feel that the working man must be more able than he is to speak for himself in a capitalistic society, he has urged that labor be given property rights, i.e., shares in business and other forms of participation in the management of business affairs which would diversify ownership and the control of economic wealth. He has likewise insisted that these diverse economic institutions produce not for their own sake or for the sake of material consumption but in order to contribute to the well-being of all members of society. Galbraith in his *Affluent Society* expresses a somewhat similar point of view with regard to the economic objectives of our rich society.

Maritain's new Christendom is not a substitute city of man molded to the liking of those who think that science and technology have inherited political power. His ideal of a new Christendom is a

vision of a society open to all the good things of science and technology, open to the past, and above all concerned with the spiritual
and cultural freedom of men. This ideal should arouse men actively
engaged in day-to-day affairs to think more seriously about what
they are striviing for. A long look ahead will be helped not by
prophecy but by the practical employment of the principles of
knowledge and goodness of those who will give the world a new
direction—towards a good society.

International Society

When Jacques Maritan wrote *Humanisme Intégral* in the early
thirties he was apparently not thinking about the new Christendom
as an international society. He was looking at its internal principles
and structures. To the extent that he conceived his ideal in geo-
graphic terms, he was thinking mainly of Europe. As far as one
can judge from externals, Maritain's more recent interest in international political affairs seems to stem from his wartime experiences, his assignment as French Ambassador to the Vatican, and
his reflections on international subjects while in the United States.

Maritain favors "one world." He believes that in time (probably
not our time) the only feasible arrangement for a world order lies
in a world government having direct jurisdiction over peoples rather
than nation-states. Maritain does not think that such a world government can be realized for some time to come. He thinks that it
is nonetheless worth talking about. He does not agree that discussions about a world government which may not happen for a century or more should discourage interim solutions to long-range
problems. Maritain is wholly sympathetic to practical, interim and
even piecemeal solutions of national conflicts. He supports the
United Nations as well as other international efforts to bring about
greater unity among nations. He looks at world order as a practical
philosopher.

For Maritain the nation-state is not a permanent category. He regards the nation as an ethnic cultural community of men which does not by its nature have political authority. With many other contemporaries he feels that one of the greatest obstacles to peace in our day is the linking of absolute state sovereignty to the rights of nations conceived as states. The nation-state is, according to Maritain, an historical form which can pass without destroying the cultural character of nations or the proper autonomy of political societies. Maritain contends that no political power, either national or international, can be absolutely sovereign—that is, a wholly unlimited power—for such power belongs to God alone. No wonder that sovereign states and their rulers attribute God-like qualities to themselves. For the time being there is little else save the opposing force of other states capable of thwarting the tendency of states to assert their supreme domination and supreme amorality. Maritain holds that nations or combinations of nations organized as political societies can rightly claim autonomy and legal supremacy within their territorial limits. National states which are democratic and are therefore subject to popular control can be open societies— societies which, as a matter of principle, can work together with other nations to achieve an international common good.

Maritain has written relatively little on the problems of the atomic age. He has expressed the belief that the traditional arguments which justify war are no longer applicable in the atomic age. On this issue he appears to be at odds with other Catholic thinkers such as Father John Courtney Murray. He is at one with Father Murray and others about the urgency of doing everything human and just to achieve a peaceful world. He places some of his hope for peace in our days on the good sense of democratic states and on the gradual development of good will and fellow feeling among peoples.

In line with Maritain's thinking it is proper to observe that, important as is the careful attention we pay to daily events and problems, a prudent diplomacy is not enough. The well-being of nations will not be the sure result of tactical victories over unending crises.

Nor will better international organization guarantee peace. Diplomacy and international organization must more and more go back to the sources of human freedom and look to the principles on which they can hope for success; they must develop the wisdom to know what they are aiming at. We not only need a national purpose, as George Kennan argues, we even more desperately need an international purpose.

Significance of Maritain's Political Philosophy

Jacques Maritain's is one of the too few Christian voices making themselves heard in our century about the great political and cultural issues of the day. Maritain speaks as a philosopher in a non-metaphysical age (whose mind quickly tires of great issues). He has dared to examine the metaphysical roots of basic political problems. Maritain is a Christian philosopher to whom non-Christians will listen. The very uniqueness of his position may be taken as a hopeful sign that a revolution in Christian political thought is at hand.

Maritain has contributed many things to that thought. He has in fact laid down the main lines of a Christian political philosophy for our times and for the future. He has tapped the mainstreams of Thomist philosophy and directed it into channels which make that thought significant for us. Modern man is threatened by totalitarianism and is still not confident in his knowledge of how to cope in a practical or theoretical way with the forces let loose by this new political and cultural heresy and the great advances in science and technology. The pragmatic temper of our times prompts the West to a technical rather than a moral solution—for one thing it looks so much easier. Maritain has rightly seen the need for both moral and technical means of realizing the ends of a democratic and civilized life. In the socio-technical sphere he recognizes the growing importance of an expanded knowledge of social facts about all societies on our globe. In the philosophical area Maritain's studies of the person, freedom, authority, the nature of evil, and the moral conscience of men are in the first rank of importance for the future of political action as well as thought.

Maritain's politics is a treasure-trove of illuminations and perceptions which should revolutionize Christian scholarship in this field. Maritain has shown the way to a greater open-mindedness on the part of Christian political thinkers. He has reminded them that the study of politics is a subject worthy of the highest efforts of Christian scholars. Above all, Maritain has offered inspiration and guidance to the practitioner of politics in the national and international arenas.

10. Maritain's Sense of History

THE TITLE OF THIS ESSAY can give rise to three questions: Does Maritain's philosophy enable him to take full account of becoming and evolution? Does it enable him to appreciate the work and the task of the historian, to define with exactness historical knowledge? Does it allow him to come to any conclusions, without undue extrapolations, as to the meaning of the human adventure, its origins, its destinies?

R. G. Collingwood[1] thinks that if Herodotus, "the Father of History," had no immediate successors, it is because his genius, which impelled him to save from oblivion and to assess the events of the past, went counter to the general tendency of Greek thought, which was turned, on the contrary, towards the immutable and the imperishable and was therefore fundamentally anti-historical. The same author explains[2] that this tendency did not come from any incapacity of the Greeks to seize becoming; it was rather their keen and painful perception of the inconstancy of things that led them to escape from contingency in order to raise their eyes towards that which is lasting. A similar phenomenon is found, according to Mircea Eliade, in the myths of archaic peoples: their constant return to archetypes is their sole means of escaping from the vertigo of time. On both sides, with the Greeks as well as with the Primitives, it seems that a conscious refusal of history turns minds toward a philosophy of permanence and of being.

Aristotle's becoming aware of the distinction between being-in-act and being-in-potency enabled him to dominate the fatal conflict which divided Parmenides and Heraclitus and fully to integrate becoming into a philosophy of being. But Aristotle was not able to attain to the idea of creation; his belief in the eternity of the world did not enable him to free himself from the cyclical conception of becoming and of history. It will take the Judaeo-Christian revelation to bring to men the notion of the no longer cyclical, but linear and vectorial, character of time, and of the progressive movement of history. The acceptance of time and of history, writes Maritain, noting some observations of Eliade's in his book *The Myth of the Eternal Return,*

far from being matter-of-course in man, is for him a difficult and dearly paid achievement. Man is naturally frightened by the irreversibility of his own duration and the very newness of unpredictable events. He refuses to face them. Hence the negation of time by archaic civilizations. . . . Acceptance of time and of history was a conquest of Christianity and modern times. But this very acceptance would be of a nature to drive man to despair if he could not decipher some trans-historical meaning in the awful advance of time into the night of the unknown, thronged with perpetually new perils.[3]

We have just read that the acceptance of history has been a conquest "of Christianity and modern times." As a matter of fact, the Judaeo-Christian revelation speaks to us of a progress and a fructification of time with respect to Sacred History. It is concerned neither with the history of the cosmos nor with the progress and fructifications of the temporal work of man. On this point, Saint Thomas continues to think, along with his predecessors and all of antiquity, including Ecclesiastes, that there is nothing new under the sun. From its beginning, in fact, the philosophy of being was bound up with the science of the Ancients. One did not distinguish, at the first degree of abstraction, the plane of the philosophy of nature and that of the experimental sciences. All seemed to form but one single block.

But then there appeared a new way of knowing nature, prepared by the works of the Parisian Doctors of the fourteenth century, of Leonardo da Vinci and especially of Galileo. The place of the new discipline, mathematical physics, had been indicated by Saint Thomas in speaking of optics and of acoustics. But this science had not as yet been born. When it finally arrived on the scene, and when it seemed, as Descartes put it, that it was going "to make us as masters and possessors of nature,"[4] it overthrew at one stroke the whole edifice of the ancient science. But as this latter was joined to the philosophy of being, it was thought that one was confronted with a dilemma: either to choose Wisdom or to choose Science. It was the latter, and the philosophies of compensation it proposed, that won the day.

Such was the intellectual tragedy that was enacted on the threshold of our modern world, and which is still far from coming to an end.

No one has had a keener grasp of it than Maritain nor described it with as much penetration. He has not ceased in his studies, constantly deepened, on the relationships between philosophy and the sciences, to show at what price an accord was possible. In assigning the legitimate place of modern physics and the experimental sciences in the hierarchy of the degrees of knowledge, he has worked on the one hand to free them from the false philosophies which try to annex them, and on the other hand to open up for the philosophy of being infinite horizons in research.

Thus, for example, the question of the part of necessity and of contingency in the cosmos needed to be examined again:

The ancients attributed to the celestial spheres a *divine and eternal structure,* and sometimes there is the temptation to look upon the universe as a *machine* whose plan of construction would have the value of an essential structure, and would impose on all its events the same necessity as a geometrical essence imposes on its properties (the Spinozist conception of nature). But in reality it is quite otherwise: the world of the stars and in particular the solar system are the result of a long evolution governed at once by the exigencies of nature and of matter and by an immense succession of de facto conditions. . . . *The universe has resulted from the long historical evolution of a multitude of factors in interaction.* . . . The world is not a clock, but a republic of natures. . . .[5]

Similar re-examinations are indispensable in the biological order:

. . . the substantial form, in the realm of life, could be considered as protruding, in its virtualities, beyond the capacities of the matter it informs in given conditions, like, for example, an architectural style or poetic idea which we might imagine as thrown into matter and working it by itself. In short *the substantial form would then be viewed as an ontological impulse realizing itself in various patterns* along the line of a certain phylum. Yet such evolution could, of course, only take place within the limits of the phylum or the ontological species in question.

Secondly, concerning the hypothetical origin of the various phylums themselves, if we now take into account the transcendent action of the First Cause, we may obviously conceive that (particularly in those formative ages when the world was in the state of its greatest plasticity, and when the divine influx was penetrating nature and completing the work of creation) that existence-giving influx of God, passing through created beings and using them as instrumental causes, was able—and is still able—to heighten the vital energies which proceed from the form in the organism it animates, so as to produce within matter, I mean within the germ-cells, dispositions beyond the limits of that organism's specificity. As a result, at the moment of generation a new substantial form, specifically "greater" or more elevated in being, would be educed from the potentiality of matter thus more perfectly disposed.[6]

In the erroneous perspective of Darwinism,

man appears not only as issuing from a long evolution of animal species
(this is after all a secondary question, purely historical), but indeed as
issuing from this biological evolution *without metaphysical discontinuity*, without at a given moment, with the human being, something
absolutely new beginning in the series: a spiritual subsistence implying
for each generation of a human being that an individual soul is created
by the Author of all things and cast into existence for an eternal destiny.
Supported by revealed dogma, the Christian idea of man has not been
shaken by Darwinism.[7]

Similar re-examinations, finally, are called for on the plane of
human development. Supported, for example, by the data of ethnology, but as interpreted in the light of what philosophy teaches
us about human nature, the philosopher of history will be able
to disengage a vectorial law, that is to say, a law of capital importance concerning the linear development of history, namely,
"the law of the passage from the 'magical' to the 'rational' regime
or state in the history of human culture."[8]

To our first question: does a philosophy of being such as Maritain's enable him to do full justice to becoming, to evolution, to the
movement of history?—we see what the answer is. Let us turn
now to the second question.

Does Maritain's philosophy enable him to appreciate the work
and the task of the historian, to define with exactness historical
knowledge?

A difficulty presents itself here. Everybody considers history as
a science and speaks of the historical sciences. For Aristotle, on the
contrary, history cannot be a science. It tells us of what has happened, and therefore of the singular. Poetry, which proposes what
is likely to happen and disengages in some manner the lessons of
history, is already closer to philosophy.[9] The one tells us that
Croesus and Polycrates ended up in bankruptcy; the other will disclose that great fortunes are close to great catastrophes. Whom must
we believe? Aristotle or the Moderns?

When it is said, on the one hand, that the Greeks, with Herodotus and Thucydides, elevated history to the rank of a science, one is thinking of the work which enabled them to substitute for legends and myths the coordinated and documented account of the past. And this is right: everyone will agree that in this sense *history is a science*. "History," writes Henri Marrou, "is indeed a scientific knowledge, specified by its proper object—the human past—and its methodological technique (heuristic, criticism, interpretation), itself determined by this object: human reason adapts itself to the difficult missions which are entrusted to it, but it is always the same reason that acts and whose work we observe."[10]

But, on the other hand, there is agreement today that historical truth is entirely different from the truth of the mathematical or natural sciences. This is not to say that the historian has to create historical truth; his role is to help us to discover it, to render more intelligible the *object* by rendering more intelligible the *subject*. Historical truth is—it too—a conformity with being, but with *singular* being. The historical elucidation never provides us with a *raison d'être* drawn from what things *are* in their very essence. In this sense, if one takes "the words 'science' and 'scientific' in the broad Aristotelian sense (intellectually cogent or demonstratively established knowledge) which covers, in a quite analogical way, both *philosophy* and the *sciences* of phenomena,"[11] one will have to acknowledge, with Aristotle, that *history is not a science*.

These precisions give rise immediately to an important remark:

Since history is not concerned with abstract essences to be brought out from the singular, but with aspects of the singular itself to be picked up as particularly important, it is clear that the manner in which the historian directs his attention is a determinant factor in the process. And this direction of attention itself depends on the entire intellectual setting of the subject. So the entire intellectual disposition (I do not say, except in a most indirect and remote manner, the affective disposition, for the historian is not necessarily a poet, though perhaps the perfect historian would be a poet)—the entire *intellectual* disposition of the subject (the historian) plays an indispensable part in the attainment of historical truth: a situation which is totally at variance with scientific objectivity, where all that pertains to the subjective dispositions of man, except as regards the virtue of science, disappears or should disappear. For the historian it is a prerequisite that he have a sound philosophy of man, an integrated culture, an accurate appreciation of the human being's various activities and their comparative importance, a correct scale of moral, political, religious, technical and artistic values. The value, I mean the *truth,* of the historical work will be in proportion to the human richness of the historian.[12]

Maritain cites Marrou here: "The more the historian is intelligent, cultivated, rich with lived experience, open to all the values of man, the more he will be capable of finding things in the past, the more his knowledge will be susceptible of richness and truth."[13]

What are the relationships between history and the philosophy of history?

Good historians—because they have personal experience of the contingencies, complexities, and uncertainties of historical work, nay more, of the element of relative non-intelligibility that is involved in history— have a natural distrust for the philosophy of history. . . .

And yet, they cannot help recognizing that, once the problem 'does the pilgrimage of mankind, triumphant and heart-rending by turns, through the duration of its history, have a value, a fecundity, a meaning?' has been posed, it cannot be eluded.[14]

We see the twofold task that imposes itself on the philosopher: on the one hand, to turn aside the false philosophies which claim to explain history rationally or to reconstruct it according to necessitating laws; on the other hand, to work towards the elaboration of a philosophy of history which cannot be genuine "if the general philosophy it presupposes, and of which it is a part, does not recognize *the existence of human free will* (together with the other

properties of the human person) and *the existence of God:* the
consequences of these two truths being that human history implies
a double kind of contingency, on the one hand with respect to the
transcendent freedom of God, and on the other hand with respect
to human free will as well as to natural accidents and vicissitudes."[15]

The light of history is distinct in nature from that of the philosophy of history, however closely related they may be:

> On the one hand, we have *history integrally taken,* in which the his-
> torian moves up, so to speak, from the level of merely factual history
> toward philosophy—without, for all that, reaching the level of philoso-
> phy proper. And, on the other hand, we have the *philosophy of history,*
> in which the philosopher moves down from the level of moral philoso-
> phy toward history, without, for all that, reaching the level of history
> proper. . . .
>
> It is normal for the historian—the real historian—to have a yearning
> for, and a leaning toward, the philosophy of history, as it is normal for
> the physicist or the biologist to have a yearning for, and a leaning to-
> ward, the philosophy of nature. Yet, in both cases the line of demarca-
> tion can be safely crossed, and the yearning in question genuinely
> satisfied, only if one really becomes a philosopher, in other words, if one
> really becomes equipped with a new intellectual virtue.[16]

Collingwood remarks that the work of the historian terminates
in the present and that historical science, as such, knows nothing
about eschatology.[17] But could not the philosopher of history be
interested in the trans-historical ends of history? If he is a believer,
could he not know that the Kingdom of God will be realized not
within history, but beyond history? And can the historian, no
longer directly and as a historian, but at least as a man, fail to have
a philosophical view, whether true or false, of life and of history?

We come now to our last question: does Maritain's philosophy
allow him to come to any conclusions, without undue extrapolations,
as to the meaning of the human adventure, its origins, its destinies?

Christianity has taught us that history has a direction, that it works in a determined direction; that it is not an eternal return and does not move in circles; that time is linear or vectorial, not cyclical; that it is structured; that humanity is united in its origins and its destinies; that there exists a universal history. With the aid of Christian revelation, Saint Augustine will be able to attempt, in his *City of God,* "to bring out the intelligible and, so to speak, transhistorical meaning of history, the intelligible meaning of the sequence or development of events in time."[18]

But on these points, philosophy, as a work of pure reason, is speechless. When it comes to the why and the wherefore of the coming into existence of the world, and to the origins and supreme destinies of the human adventure, what can philosophy do but remain silent and give way to myth? Consequently, how would a philosophy of history which would be anything else than a dream or a lie be possible? The difficulty is evident.

It has appeared insoluble to several good minds accustomed to the theological way of thinking. For them there is but one valid manner of reflecting on history, that of theology. The theology of history can be constructed only in terms of revelation; reason no doubt will have its part to play in it, but as the servant of faith. A Christian philosophy of history, if it means anything else than a theology, appears to them to be a contradiction in terms. Consequently, the sole course for philosophy to take is to give up thinking about history.

The contrary solution is that of Hegel. Instead of abasing philosophy before theology, Hegel undertakes to reabsorb the content of theology into his philosophy. He recognizes the exceptional importance of the revelations of Christianity on Creation, the Fall, the Incarnation, the Passion, the Last Judgment. But they have for him only the value of a myth whose meaning it belongs to the philosopher of history to disengage. It is the Spirit such as Hegel conceives it which in collective Humanity alienates itself, dies, comes to life again and transfigures itself.

From the Judaeo-Christian revelation, not accepted as true, but as the bearer of a myth, Karl Jaspers borrows his fundamental views on the meaning of history: "All men are related in Adam, originate from the hand of God and are created after His image. In the beginning was the manifestness of Being in a present without consciousness. The fall set us on the path leading through knowledge and finite practical activity with temporal objectives, to the lucidity of the consciously manifest. With the consummation of the end we shall attain concord of souls, shall view one another in a loving present and in boundless understanding, members of a single realm of everlasting spirits. All these are symbols, not realities. The meaning of universal history, so far as it is empirically accessible—whether it possesses such a meaning, or whether human beings only attribute one to it—we can only grasp when guided by the idea of the unity of the whole of history. We shall examine empirical facts in order to see to what extent they are in accordance with such an idea of unity, or how far they absolutely contradict it."[19]

Such a conception of history, however weak and insecure it may be, nevertheless marks an advance over the pantheistic views of Hegel and the positions of Kant, according to whom Nature, in the manner in which it governs the world by infrangible laws, governs human history by infallible intentions, making use of the stupidity and of the malice even of individuals for the greater good of the human species, and so as to cause to progress in it, in spite of them, the reign of reason and of liberty: "Nature makes use of selfish inclinations in order to come to the aid of the general will which is founded on reason and which, however respected it may be, is powerless in practice. . . . So that the problem of the constitution of a State can be resolved even for a people of demons."[20]

We see what philosophy comes to when it renounces revelation or thinks to enclose it "within the limits of reason."

Only the notion of "moral philosophy adequately considered," elaborated by Maritain, can provide a solution here, as in other domains, for example, in that of a philosophy of religion:

. . . we have either to accept or to reject the data of Judeo-Christian revelation. If we accept them, we shall have to distinguish between two orders—the order of nature and the order of grace; and between two existential realms, distinct but not separate—the world, on the one hand, and the Kingdom of God, the Church, on the other. Hence, we shall have to distinguish between a theology of history and a philosophy of history. . . . The *theology of history* is centered on the mystery of the *Church,* while considering its relation to the world; whereas the *philosophy of history* is centered on the mystery of the *world,* while considering its relation to the Church, to the Kingdom of God in a state of pilgrimage.

If this is true, it means that the philosophy of history pertains to moral philosophy adequately taken, that is to say to moral philosophy complemented by data which the philosopher borrows from theology, and which deal with the existential conditions of that very human being whose actions and conduct are the object of moral philosophy.[21]

In the light of Christian revelation, the philosopher is able to study the behavior of existential man, of man fallen and redeemed, not directly, as does the theologian, in his relationship to the ultimate ends of eternal life, but directly in his relationship to the infravalent ends of cultural and temporal life. A multitude of problems will thus be illumined.

The parable of the wheat and the cockle, for example, appears valid not only for the kingdom of grace, but also, as the philosopher of history will establish, for the world. It means that the advance of history is a double and antagonistic movement of ascent and descent; that it is a twofold simultaneous progress in good and evil. "This is a law of basic importance . . . if we are trying to interpret human history."[22]

To the paramount questions of the origins, vicissitudes, and destinies of humanity, of the relationships between divine freedom and created freedom, and of the intermingling of good and evil in the formation of history, answers will be given not by an appeal to dreams, to myths, to extrapolations, but by the highest sources of revelation and theology. However, the Christian philosophy of history, always attentive to the human—not to mention the fact that it will reduce to nought such errors as the Comtian law of the three states of humanity—will apply itself to scrutinizing the very mystery of the world and of its impermanence, inasmuch as this mystery is distinct from the mystery of the Church as the things that are Caesar's are distinct from the things that are God's, and inasmuch also as the activities of the world begin to impair the purity of the Gospel in the very interior of societies that believe themselves Christian. In studying in the course of time the relationships of the interaction and mutual influence of Christianity and profane cultures, of the Kingdom of God and the kingdoms of this world, the philosopher of history will open up each day, to the theologian of history himself, fields of investigation as yet unexplored.

NOTES

1. *The Idea of History* (Oxford: Clarendon Press, 1946), Part I, no. 6.
2. *Ibid.*, no. 3.
3. *On the Philosophy of History* (New York: Scribner, 1957), pp. 36-37.
4. *Discours de la méthode, sixième partie.*
5. *Raison et Raisons* (Paris: Egloff, 1948), pp. 53 and 62.
6. *The Range of Reason* (New York: Scribner, 1952), pp. 37-38.
7. *Humanisme intégral* (Paris: Aubier, 1936), pp. 36-37.
8. *On the Philosophy of History*, p. 96.
9. *Poetics*, 1451b.
10. *La foi historique*, in *Les Etudes Philosophiques*, no. 2, April-June 1959, Paris, p. 157.
11. *On the Philosophy of History*, p. 3, n. 2.
12. *Ibid.*, pp. 7-8.
13. *Ibid.*, p. 8, n. 6.
14. *Ibid.*, pp. 29-30.
15. *Ibid.*, p. 34 (italics ours).
16. *Ibid.*, pp. 167-169.

17. *Op. cit.*, Part II, no. 3; Part III, nos. 3 and 7.
18. *On the Philosophy of History*, p. 2.
19. *Von Ursprung und Ziel der Geschichte* (Zurich: Artemis-Verlag, 1949), p. 18; Eng. trans.: *The Origin and Goal of History* (London: Routledge & Kegan Paul Ltd., 1953), p. xv.
20. *Zum ewigen Frieden*, Erster Zusatz, no. 1.
21. *On the Philosophy of History*, pp. 37-38 (italics ours).
22. *Ibid.*, pp. 9-10; 43-49.

Leo R. Ward, C.S.C.

11. Maritain's Philosophy of Education

ANYONE WHO HAS WORKED COMPREHENSIVELY on the other parts of philosophy has already worked on philosophy of education, and we should be able to go through his writings and piece together his philosophy of education. This is because philosophy of education itself pieces together various sections from more standard parts of philosophy: from theory of knowledge, theory of person and society, and general over-all theory of man.

But it happens that Maritain has explicitly worked out his philosophy of education, notably in the Terry Lectures given at Yale in 1943 and in two later articles.[1] What he says most comprehensively in these writings is that philosophy of education depends on philosophy of man, and then that education is, above all, liberation. What is at first most striking about these writings, perhaps, is that liberal education, historically available only to an elite, is said to be naturally, rightly and eternally for all, and in modern times should help all citizens to understand and live "the democratic charter." But what, on a close second reading, is seen to be most novel and striking is that though education in schools is properly taken up with the life of the mind, education both in and out of schools supposes and implies what we may call the synergistic

193

operation of the whole human substance. Maritain means to be following Thomas Aquinas in the main outlines of educational theory, and on the point just mentioned he is particularly Thomist. For, says Aquinas,[2] there is such an interrelation and inter-working among the powers of man that anything happening to the body happens to man and anything happening to the soul affects the body. Even conversion from vice to virtue and from ignorance to knowing, says Aquinas, occurs first in the body.

Maritain takes seriously the inter-linking of all the powers in man. Intellect indeed works, but does not and cannot work all by itself. Man is free and makes free choices and develops in freedom, but his life of freedom does not operate independently of the other powers such as sense powers and intellect and imagination. It is true that education in schools has always been chiefly an education in the intellectual life, and of course that is what it continues to be. It is also true that intellect can never be reduced to will, or will to intellect, or sense to either of them. As Aristotle said, distinct operations imply distinct powers, and we evidently find distinct operations in man: intellectual, volitional, locomotive, sensory, and digestive. They are distinct, but they are not separate nor really separable. When one power, such as the sensory, acts, the others are affected and in some way involved.

This fact of interaction among them we have tried to indicate in the words, "synergistic working." Maritain is fond of this idea and fact of a total human interaction. It forms an important part of his theory of human operation, human being, human knowledge and freedom and education. Let us see how he expresses it.[3]

The life and activity of reason are ordinarily seen as merely "the world of Concepts and Ideas in a state of explicit formation, say, the conceptualized externals of Reason: the world of the workings of conceptual, logical, discursive Reason." Now undoubtedly Reason includes the world just mentioned: this world is reason in the usual and most obvious meaning of the word. But this is not the whole story. The life and activity of reason are also, and perhaps we should say primarily, "an immense dynamism emanating from the very center of the Soul." So too for the life and activity of the imagination. These are twofold. They are of course the world of imagination's achievements as stirred by and centered on the exercise of the external senses and as used for many creative and many practical purposes in the everyday activities of man in his waking state. But secondly, and in a real sense primarily, they are "an immense dynamism working upwards and downwards along the depths of the Soul and terminating in this circle of externals."

Whichever powers we speak of, we have to keep going back to a single root. We may and should call this root "man," but it is the root or source from which this living thing "man" lives and moves and senses and imagines and conceptualizes. Several diverse powers, yes; each with an obvious external achievement, yes; but more radically each also being a great dynamism welling up from the basic center and source of life and rooted in that source.

Yet further, and certainly as important for theory of education, is another fact. A central source and root, and diverse operative powers—that is not the whole of the picture. None of these powers proceeds on its own *laissez-faire* way independent of the others. All are "engaged in common." Man is an almost terrible unity. Engaged in common are the intellect and the imagination and the powers of desire, love, and emotion. This doctrine goes a step beyond the important simple statement of Aquinas: It is man who suffers, and not merely his toe; it is man who sees, using his eyes; it is man who thinks, using his intellect. "The powers of the soul envelop one another, the universe of sense perception is in the universe of imagination, which is in the universe of intelligence. And they are all, within the Intellect, stirred and activated by the light of the Illuminating Intellect. And, according to the order of the ends and demands of nature, the first two universes move under the attraction and for the higher good of the universe of the intellect, and, to the extent to which they are not cut off from the intellect by the animal or automatic unconscious, in which they lead a wild life of their own, the imagination and the senses are raised in man to a state genuinely human where they somehow participate in intelligence, and their exercise is, as it were, permeated with intelligence."

Thus does Maritain express, we might perhaps say begin some stammering expression of, the inter-working of all the powers in man. In their operation they influence each other and involve one another. As Aquinas puts it:[4] "This is the order of nature, this tying together of the powers of the soul in one essence, and the powers of soul and of body in one composite *esse,* so that they mutually influence one another." Edgar Allan Poe spoke of art as "the reproduction of what the senses perceive in nature through the veil of the soul," and Maritain is happy to use Poe as some confirmation of what he is saying. To conclude our use of these pages from Maritain's study of creative intuition and poetry we append the few words in which he says that the external senses, such as seeing and hearing, likewise enter into that "totality or integrity." "As to the life and activity of the External Senses, it takes place, no doubt, at the level of the intuitive data afforded by Sensation— there where the mind is in contact with the external world. But it radiates upwards into the depths of the Soul; and all that it receives from the external world, all things seized upon by sense perception, all treasures from that sapid and sonorous and colorful Egypt, enter and make their way up to the central regions of the Soul."

Maritain is expressing in the pages just used more than a theory of poetic knowledge. It is evident that he is expressing a theory of knowledge in general, of all the various powers in man and of how they are related: (a) to each other, (b) to the soul, and (c) to the composite known to us as man. He is also expressing a theory of the greatest relevance to philosophy of education.

The generalized theory is this: Maritain is attempting to express what goes on in man, what a man does when he performs his characteristic acts such as seeing and loving and reasoning. Any of these acts is done by man using a distinct power or "faculty," but none of them is ever done by a power that exists and operates as a separate entity or in a vacuum. Besides, they come up from what Maritain calls "a deep non-conscious world of activity." From this emerges the ordinary and recognized acts and fruits of consciousness. "Far beneath the sunlit surface thronged with explicit concepts and judgments, words and expressed resolutions or movements of the will, are the sources of knowledge and creativity, of love and suprasensuous desires, hidden in the primordial translucid night of the intimate vitality of the soul."

Maritain is presupposing and he affirms the existence in man of a vital "unconscious or preconscious." What does he mean by this idea, and what does the thing signified mean for philosophy of education?

In his most elaborate study of education,[5] he says that it is important to make clear to ourselves that here we are speaking of a dual reality under the one heading, the "subconscious or unconscious." We are speaking of it in a Freudian sense, but also in a Maritain sense, and we are talking of two different though related things, two "different, though intermingled, fields." One is the field of which the Freudian school makes so much. This is the field of latent images, affective impulses and sensual drives. This Maritain says we may call "the unconscious of the irrational in man." The other is really other, and seems to be missed by Freud and his followers. This is the area of the spiritual powers in the human person, "the field of the root life of those spiritual powers, the intellect and the will, the fathomless abyss of personal freedom and of the personal thirst and striving for knowing and seeing, grasping and expressing—I should call this the unconscious of the spirit in man."

These ideas, inspired by a cross between Aquinas and Freud, are so novel and so vital and basic to theory of education that we repeat Maritain's labels for them. The labels are these two:

> "the unconscious of the irrational in man" and
> "the preconscious of the spirit in man."

We have the custom of allowing to intellect only its conscious acts and manifestations, and to the will only its deliberate conscious choice. But that, according to Maritain, is far from the total picture. We are thus thinking correctly, but inadequately, for there is something far deeper in the life of intellect and of will. The very source of the intellect's and the will's spiritual life is hidden from us. Beneath what we see on the surface as concepts and judgments and words, and the express movements of the will, are the sources of those things that enter into the work of education, namely knowledge and poetry and love and truly human desires. "Before being formed and expressed in concepts and judgments, intellectual knowledge is at first a beginning of insight, still unformulated, which proceeds from the impact of the illuminating activity of the intellect on the world of images and emotions and which is but a humble and trembling movement, yet invaluable, toward an intelligible content to be grasped."

Now consider this preconscious spiritual dynamism of the human person in its relation to the educative process. For one thing, this whole world of the spiritual preconscious is naturally and necessarily and fortunately unknown to the youthful student. What Maritain often calls the "mysterious identity" of the child's soul is of course also unknown to him. It would be a rare teacher who could express such depths and mysteries even to experts or to himself. The teacher can, however, respect this spiritual dynamism and this mysterious identity within each child, and he should do so.

For, says Maritain,[6] a Thomist philosophy prudently aware of itself and its own resources, already knows the following matters basic to theory of knowledge and of the human person and to theory of education. First, the human soul is obscure to itself. Secondly, the intimate nature of its basic tendencies, its powers or faculties escapes introspection. Thirdly, our radical tendencies and those acquired tendencies called *habitus,* some of them virtues or "internal improvements of the faculties," and some of them vices —all these form within us a world of reality whose effects alone reach our waking conscious life.

Regarding Freud, we have to say several things. He is of course
up to this time the great investigator of "the unconscious of the
irrational" in man. He missed the world of the spiritual in man,
even the possibility and conceivability of it. He justly called mankind's attention to a "psychic dynamism" in every man, and this
dynamism, made up of drives, desires, instincts and impulsions, he
rightly saw—continues Maritain—not as mechanical forces, but as
vital energies orientated toward a goal. Tendential dynamism or
dynamism always linked to finality—this radical thing in man is
emphasized by Freud, and perhaps it is to be found in some form in
the whole of nature.

Let us have Maritain say what is the relevance of any doctrine
of the unconscious, above all the spiritual unconscious, for philosophy of education. These two depths of the irrational subconscious and the preconscious are closely related to each other, are
vitally interconnected and can easily get in the way of each other.
Yet they are different worlds, though the two coexist in the one
human person. Our universal human vocation, to be achieved in
school and out of school, is to free the spiritual unconscious from
the irrational unconscious. "In reality that to which we are called
by our genuinely human aspirations is to free and purify the spiritual unconscious from the irrational one, and to find our sources
of life and liberty and peace in this purified preconscious of the
spirit."

Something that is given in the child is to be brought out and
developed—that is the common denominator in all theories of education. It is in Aristotle, who perhaps above all philosophers is in
general dominated by the *is to be*. It is strong in any Christian and
presumably in any theist, and it is strong in Dewey. Man partly is
and wholly hopes to be. There is in man a drive to be. Man is of
his nature demanding a way to fulfillment. As Augustine said, the
end is that man should fully be. Aquinas went farther and said that
everything desires to be, in its own type of being; what each wants
is *esse suo modo*. Maritain starts out by saying that the chief task
of education is to shape man and to guide the evolving dynamism

through which man forms himself as man.[7] Man is to be, and he is to be both thoroughly and fully man. No half man will do, no "underdone" man—and we repeat that the assumption of any educational theorist worth his salt is that man by nature is to be. We may remark that on this natural finalistic or teleological premise are based all theory and practice affirming and defending the rights of man.

Among the rights of the child is the right to be educated, to be brought out of primal night, to get a chance to come out of that twilight state in which he is born. He is human to begin with, and is free, and is by nature orientated toward full humanity and fullness of freedom. It is a long step from the chrysalis stage of humanity and freedom to anything like their fullness. Debutantes are said to be "brought out." Maritain would say that every child of man is naturally a debutante and needs and deserves to be "brought out." The child is to be enlightened and liberated. So Maritain frequently remarks. He holds that the nature of man is good and that the life of instinct itself has an essentially human character, i.e., a natural rightness and goodness.[8] To help us go all the way with this natural-divine rightness and goodness is the work of education.

Learning keeps occurring everywhere in the life of society. But it is of schools and school education that we speak. These are above all, but not exclusively, concerned with the education of man in his intellectual being, and intellectual good is one of the best things in the universe (as Aquinas notes). It is the most proper human good, and though in our circumstance (of being on the way to the fatherland) intellectual good is not so great a good as moral good, in its nature it is the best good available to man in heaven and on earth. This is the good to which schools historically and now are dedicated. To fight shy of intellectual work and life is to try to evade man and his good, and for schools to try to run away from this work and life is to try to dodge the thing that chiefly justifies their existence.

Education turns around two centers, the child who is to know and love, and the object to be known. Newman emphasizes "the value and dignity of liberal knowledge," and his words and ideas make a fundamental sense. In contrast,[9] though Maritain of course defends liberal education, he is much more fond of featuring the child who is being liberated through education. What we must always keep in view is the being who is to be formed into a true human person, "perfecting himself by knowledge and love, and capable of giving himself" with an immense generosity to the kingdom of persons. This being is to achieve rationality and freedom, and to reach these ends he needs to be taught and disciplined in his spiritual life of intellect and will. The primary tendency of any intellectual nature such as man's is toward truth. To seek to know is natural to any man, natural and primary. But in most matters and for almost all men, to go steadily and effectively with this natural tendency to knowledge is something of a task. It is not as easy as falling off a log. It takes discipline and a bending and shaping of the initial promise. That is why we need teachers.

Teachers are far more than referees of play. They are tutors of the spirit. They are secondary and in a true sense instrumental agents, yet essential ones. Youths let go on a kind of perpetual progressivist spree would seize and possess themselves of little if anything out of our rich human tradition and would turn out to be ninnies dispossessed of their heritage. Teaching has the greatest opportunity to encourage, and an ounce of encouragement is worth more than any amount of scolding and the hickory stick. It is a terrible and irretrievable thing to inflict humiliation on a child. As Chief Justice Warren said in the Desegregation Case, forcibly to impose segregation on children might cause in them a feeling of inferiority from which they would never recover. Something freer, something more trustful of the child and of nature and the good of nature in the child—this is always in order in education and in everything else, at home and at school.

The child no doubt is to fear, but "this fear should be respect and reverence, not blind animal dread."[10] The teacher, whose causality, like that of medicine, is only through really "cooperating and assisting," should be full of respect and reverence toward the materials to be used and toward the object to be known and above all toward the child being formed. The teacher is turning the child's face toward being and truth and good and toward "grace-given spirituality, toward a participation in the freedom, wisdom, and love of the saints." Hence the dignity of the teacher's vocation.

Maritain has several times remarked that progressivism in education has brought something important into theory and practice. Quite aside from progressivism, the significance and merit in modern conceptions of education ever since Pestalozzi, Rousseau and Kant, lie in the rediscovery of the old truth, held by Plato and Aquinas, that the principal agent and dynamic factor in education is not anything done or not done by the teacher, but "the inner dynamism of nature" itself and of the child's mind. The teacher is co-operating with the child and with nature, and, so far from being "a tractable and useless attendant," is "a real giver whose own dynamism, moral authority, and positive guidance are indispensable." The authority spoken of is simply the duty of the adult to the freedom of the child.[11]

As for American progressivism proper, Maritain holds that it makes real sense in some of its emphases. Due attention is given to "the unconscious, the instincts, the nonrational elements in the psyche of the child." Also, educational techniques are in process of continually broadening and enriching. We may justly speak of reconstructing the means, so long as we do not make the fundamental error of those who think men may somehow become as gods and proceed to reconstruct the ultimate ends of the human mind and of person and society. The biggest point in favor of progressivism lies in its giving due freedom to the child: "the main thing in this teaching process is that his natural and spontaneous activity be always respected and his power of insight and judgment always fostered." We may hope that the long ages of humiliation for youths in school are past.[12]

Of course, progressivism can go overboard and turn into a baby-ing process. It has often done so, keeping the child in the infantile stage when he should be growing up. The result is that the youth or even the adult is an intellectual jellyfish. He has had little intel-lectual challenge and discipline, and instead of liking a fight in matters of the mind he is likely (so Maritain says[13]) to become indifferent and over-docile and "too passively permeable" to what-ever the teacher says.

A chief incubus burdening many Americans in matters of educa-tion is that their theory has been pragmatized half to death. Learn-ing has its practical side, and it has its theoretic, contemplative side. We must accept and respect both. We must accept the child as the child of man and not "as if he were a child of some simian particularly evolved and supposedly civilized."[14] Empirical method is good, but to make it exclusive is bad. It amounts to the denial of reason itself, a denial which it can attempt only by using reason. An instrumental theory of knowledge runs into a similar difficulty. It is exclusive and one-sided and sees only half the picture. In coming to know, the human person is often affected by stimuli and his thinking is a response to these and to the total situation. Often too, in knowing, he is in the act of solving problems, and Dewey's figure of the man at the forked road, not knowing which way to go, and learning by finding out, is a faithful report (Maritain does not name Dewey in this connection) of many factual occur-rences. Animal knowledge may be merely a matter of action and reaction, but man's knowledge is not. Nor is it merely a matter of problem-solving. Maritain is insistent on the narrowness and in-adequacy of the Dewey position. Genuine human knowledge, he says, begins with insights and intuitions: and by intuition, he says, he means not mere knowledge, but "knowledge into." At the very start, one sees many basic truths a priori; one sees that things are, that being is good, that truth is good, and that the seeking of good is our vocation. We see these truths without noticing that we see them. We do not see them out of need to see them: we just see them. We do not encounter some problem and then, as a happy byproduct of trying to solve it, stumble upon these truths: we know them at the outset. Maritain holds that within the reasoning process itself there are insights or intuitions, and that human thought ends up, as he says, in insights. "Human thought is a vital energy of spiritual intuition grasping things in their intelligible consistency and universal values."

It is obvious that little children are incapable of a depth philosophy and thus they do not know what is primary or what secondary. It is obvious too that they need action and play—their play being perfectly serious to them—in order to get well started in knowing. The philosopher takes account of the fact that a child's life is full of intuitions and insights and full of unqualified seeing, in both a physical and an intellectual meaning of the term. In the daily routine of school, the child can and should learn much by doing. "Learning by doing" makes real sense, so long as it is not pushed too far in theory or practice. Maritain's point is that one also learns by not-doing, by seeing and by what he often calls insights. The child learns that way, and so does the man. Of course, the adult, in knowing, is able to free himself more and more from doing. From first to last, however, child or man learns both in a practical or doing way and also in a speculative or seeing way. A dogmatic exclusive activism is blind in one eye.

In the actual learning process, the child takes many steps prompted by interest and by need and problems. That is evident to all. Nevertheless, in taking those steps the child or the man carries along with him a wealth of insights and intuitions. In his life of reasoning and of controlling, dominating and refashioning so much of the world, he will always continue to be dictated to by trust in truth and an antecedent desire for unlimited good. He did not and could not make this trust or this desire. Each was given a priori to him.

The youth has to learn to bend his mind to truth. He is born to know, in the sense that he has the capacity to know and the inborn desire to know. That is the kind of being he is. But many obstacles stand in his way. Some of these are eternal, and some are his own acquired intellectual and moral vices, and these are built in, so much so that to him and others it may well appear that he was born for anything else but to know. He has after all to learn to make terms with the object and with things. Whether we like it or not, the object to be known, say in science or philosophy or spelling or history, is unyielding. The child has to learn to grasp the object, and that is what school is for—to help him learn to grasp it. The object, we said, is uncompromising.

Getting acquainted with the object, with reality or things, is almost (as Plato would have it) like coming home. Even so, things are strange at first to children, hence the child's endless curiosity, rightly featured by Dewey, and hence, too, his natural and boundless wonder. Looked at rightly, the child seems like the "stout Cortez" of Keats:

> Then felt I like some watcher of the skies
> When a new planet swims into his ken;
> Or like stout Cortez, when with eagle eyes
>
> He stared at the Pacific—and all his men
> Looked at each other with a wild surmise—
> Silent, upon a peak in Darien.

With the help of parents and teachers, the child has to foster right dispositions. These are listed briefly but with care by Maritain as follows:[15] love for knowing the truth which in any case is "the primary tendency of any intellectual nature"; the love of good and justice "and even of heroic feats, and this too is natural to the children of men." A third disposition to be fostered is simplicity and openness in the face of existence. Plato said that the gods took pity on men "born to work" and made a run of feasts and celebrations so that nourishing themselves in festive companionship with

the gods, men would be able "again to stand upright and erect."
Maritain would like to have the sons of men, who are also the sons
of God, exist gladly and stand upright unashamed before being,
as trees and animals in their way also do. "Fear and trembling"
of course go with our status and belong to the great experience
of the soul: but in this Kierkegaardian sense they belong more to
the adult when he is encountering mysteries. The child's attitude is
gladness and simplicity.

Two more dispositions are cited by Maritain. The child needs
to learn at home and at school the sense of cooperation which can
so easily be missed. And he needs to learn how to work, to get the
sense of work well done, "a respect for the job to be done," a feeling of fidelity to it and responsibility for it. If this is marred, an
essential basis of morality is lost.

In educating, we are trying to develop persons. We are helping
the person to be, and of course to be what he was born to be. So
we have already remarked. This "helping persons to be" is a delicate and exacting task. We may not throw children together hig-
gledy-piggledy in masses and expect them automatically to reappear
as really developed and mature human beings. We are above all
preparing the mind to think for itself and also shaping the will to
love, as it naturally wants to do, all the good things of nature and
grace.

"School and college education," remarks Maritain,[16] "has indeed
its own world, which essentially consists of the dignity and achievements of knowledge and the intellect, that is, of the human being's
root faculty. And of this world itself that knowledge which is wisdom is the ultimate goal."

Here we have to respect the fact of that modifier "ultimate." The
child is not yet by a long way up to going for wisdom as a virtue,
or for formed and finished intellectual virtues. These are perfections which just now are too high and advanced for him. He has a
lofty and commanding level on which to operate, the level called by
Maritain that of "natural intelligence."[17] Even in achieving this

first level we have to avoid extremes, one of which is the *simpliste* notion that "encyclopedic inculcation" will do the job; i.e., the notion that all the knowledge acquired by humanity, in history and tradition and in all sciences, can be taken in easy tablet form by the child, and thus he will be "educated." The use of racy and jejune "surveys" would be the means to this supposed end. The other extreme is perhaps just as common, at least in American schools. It is summed up as "nursery accommodation," and the words no doubt speak for themselves. It can only result in a formless mind and at best in "a good-humored childish adult." Each extreme would avoid the hard work and discipline needed for achievement, and the assumption back of them is a denial of the old Greek saying, "Good and lovely things are difficult."

What then is intellectual virtue, and what is the prior state known as natural intelligence? Let us first take intellectual virtue and say that the scientist is possessed of it, and so is the competent professional man such as a doctor or a lawyer, as is the man called a scholar in history or theology. The child does not have this virtue, nor does the schoolboy, and Maritain thinks it would be stretching things to say that the college student ordinarily has intellectual virtue. This virtue is a formed intellectual perfection. It is a good intellectual habit, and habits, which are "inner living energies," give added power to the power called intellect. All can see that a real scientist has such perfection and virtue. As a result he can do what the beginner cannot do. "The intellectual virtues are special energies which grow in intelligence through exercise in a given object, are superadded perfections, superior in quality" to the capacity called natural intelligence, that is to say, "intelligence in its bare nature."

Thus we see two quite different states in two men or in the same man at widely different times. One state is natural intelligence and the other is intelligence perfected by intellectual virtues.

On the one hand we have natural intelligence or intelligence with its native power only. On the other we have intelligence perfected by intellectual virtues, "those acquired qualities or energies which are peculiar to the scientist, the artist, the philosopher." It is evident that an accomplished artist, say in music or painting, has an acquired development and perfection which his son of three lacks and may sometime acquire. In spite of schooling, most of us remain in most fields much like the son: he has native intelligence, and so have we.

The native power is there. It needs a liberation, a development that can come to it as an acquired power or intellectual virtue. But the kindergarten is hardly the place to develop it. Maritain thinks the high school or even the college is not the place where we can reasonably hope to develop outstanding intellectual virtue. His position is that liberal education in high school and college is not called upon to go through the "terribly exacting" and absorbing special training needed to achieve the virtues of scientist or artist.

What then in his view would high school and college advisedly do? They should attempt to be seats primarily of liberal education. In any ordinary case, the child should not be expected to be a minor composer or a minor scientist. He wants to get in school and college a sense of what music is and of what science is. He wants to begin to appreciate each and to form, perhaps without knowing it, some criteria of beauty and good and truth. Great masses of information in sociology and history will not give him this sense of the science, and of truth and beauty, nor will a complete coverage of theology and philosophy. In high school the mode of teaching should be adapted to the freshness, spontaneity and curiosity of the child whose reason is budding though still somewhat in the chrysalis stage and is naturally "stirred and nourished" by imagination. In college the youth is beginning to come into another stage; his natural intelligence is in a state of growth and is aspiring toward universal knowledge; the youth is now, likely as not, in movement toward the development of some intellectual *habitus*. We do not think of him as about to be or even going to be either an artist or a scientist. That would be quite the exception. He is still getting that freedom-making thing, a liberal education, though he may at the same time be looking with some effectiveness to or perhaps developing in the *habitus* of a profession. Most youths, of course, will have to be looking toward skills to be acquired on the job.

That sums up Maritain on nature, intelligence, and intellectual virtues. His views on liberal education are also of much interest.[18] As a believer in God and in intelligence, he holds that the good of a liberal education is for all and not merely for an aristocratic elite. His two reasons for this view are compelling though simple. First, government of the people, by the people and for the people is impossible if the people are undeveloped, intellectually immature and like children in the face of great social problems. People need to be able to make judgments on the most human matters, such as those relevant to helping to rule the tribe. Otherwise, as events have shown us for over forty years, we will be ruled, and it will not be a rule for the people.

The second reason is more basic. Man is made to know, and liberal education better than any other opens up and liberates the mind of man. As Newman so persuasively argued, liberal education is a great natural good. But is it good merely for a chosen few, the privileged? That is what those few have always liked to think, and, generally in a position to rule the masses, those few have had the power and prestige to enforce their views on the people in this as in other matters. But this "liberal education only for an elite" view is far out of date, and in fact, if we inspect natural law, we will see that the enrichment and enlargement proper to liberal education are values that naturally belong to the human person. As believers in man and as believers in nature, we cannot settle for less than this—liberal education for all.

How this could be is considered too by Maritain, though we must omit this point, with the one remark that Western man now has the resources and leisure to achieve the good of liberal education for all. Leaders in New York State for example are already saying that "college education" should be available to everyone.

Maritain says that the study of sciences is integral to liberal education, since it provides us with a vision of the universe and with a sense of "the sacred, exacting, unbending objectivity of the humblest truth."[19] Youth does not need a mass of books, much less a mass of rubbishy textbooks, but a few great books "seriously and lovingly scrutinized," and a personal wrestling, not with an abstraction, but with a real man in a book. Nothing can justly be substituted for "the pure reading of a pure text."

Any genuine human education in childhood and through high school and college, Maritain keeps saying, implies the working of head and hands together. This cooperation is good, for four reasons:[20] it is good for psychological equilibrium, it furthers "ingenuity and accuracy of the mind," it is a radical basis for artistic activity and making things, and is in line with the world of tomorrow where "the dignity of work will probably be more clearly recognized, and the social cleavage between *homo faber* and *homo sapiens* done away with." Open to the whole of nature and the whole of the human person, Thomist philosophy "heartily approves of the general emphasis put by progressive education on the essential part to be played in the process by the senses and the hands and by the natural interests of the child."[21] In assuring liberal education for all, we would have to take account of the fact that some persons learn best, so far as they can learn, through curricula largely made up of matters such as handicraft and drama. Linked to these and their like is the life of play for the child in elementary school and the youth in high school and college. Play has an essential though secondary part in school life, with a value of its own as affording free expansion and a gleam of poetry.

In the life of the will, Maritain thinks that schools and education, above all on the liberal level, have two chief functions to perform, the two coming to one: namely, a liberation of man's powers. The two are these. The school has to furnish the rational basis and understanding of the good life, of the rightness and true character of nature and the universe, and of virtue and the moral order. Sec-

ondly, the school has to help us to understand and even to adopt
the democratic charter. In a nation such as ours, we have groups
of many faiths and of divers ways of claiming to justify democratic
values; e.g., truth and intelligence, human dignity, freedom, brotherly love and the absoluteness of moral good. Such values make up
the "charter" in question. The body politic has the right and duty
to promote those values and that charter. It does so largely through
schools, private and public, and neither they nor it may renege on
this work of promotion.[22]

On Christian education as such, Maritain has given a few invaluable suggestions.[23] Let us put them down in numbers. 1. He
agrees with Christopher Dawson that liberal education in a Christian college must deal even more than does that in a secular college
with the whole of culture. Christianity has a universality more truly
than has paganism or any non-Christian religion; its scope is nature
and man, the totality of this world, as well as beyond this world.
2. The Christian school is, if it knows its business, "illumined by
Christian inspiration." The meaning is not that there is a Christian
astronomy or a Christian engineering. The meaning is that if the
teacher himself has Christian wisdom and if his teaching wells up
as an overflow from his life of contemplation, then the way in which
he teaches, "the mode or manner in which his own soul and mind
perform a living and illuminating action on the soul and mind of
another"—this mode or manner will awaken in the youth something beyond astronomy or engineering: namely, a sense of these
learnings in the universe of learnings, and an unspoken intimation
of the value of truth and of the rational laws and harmony at work
in things.

Intelligence being, according to Clérissac, the very basis of Christianity, the school has a sacred obligation: a) to keep alive in the
student the sense of truth; b) to respect his intellectual and spiritual
aspirations and any beginning of creative life in him and personal
coming-to-terms with reality; c) as St. Thomas said, never to dig a
ditch in front of youth without filling it up; and d) appealing to his

intuitive power, to offer him "a unified and integrated universe of knowledge."

Among residual difficulties and unfinished tasks, the following may be mentioned.

First. A theory of how taste and the feelings are educated should be developed in general theory of education, and this in spite of the delicacy and obscurity of the subject. It seems to us that Maritain assumes a theory in this regard but does not state it.

Second. Within a highly pluralistic democracy, education in theory and practice must do two things at once. It must respect and work toward knowledge and love of the democratic charter. It must also, as Maritain says,[24] take full account of the religious and philosophical traditions and schools within the given society. We would like to see Maritain give more attention than he has done to the ways in which this latter "must" can be effected.

Third. In general, Maritain's theory, declaring itself of course for man, gives a proper secondary place to the humanities and the classics; in one glowing passage[25] Maritain says that the youths of Europe, still going for the old classics, seem to be stumbling among tombstones. Yet in a few places he himself might appear to be emphasizing "the humanities" and putting man second.

Fourth. The distinction between "natural intelligence" and "intellectual virtue" is not common currency in America and no doubt we will keep missing it or regarding it as unimportant. For his part, Maritain may be seeing the distinction as too absolute, and as too simply dividing school and college from post-college studies and skills.

Fifth. We just saw that Maritain has given in *The Christian Idea of Education* some clear suggestions toward the meanings of "Christian intelligence" and "Christian education." These suggestions, though not greatly developed, seem to be in line with his idea of "Christian philosophy." At the outset of his work on the latter subject, he said a few words to the effect that a problem like that encountered by the Christian philosopher is met up with, though in different terms, in the case of others such as the artist, the historian and the exegete.[26] The idea seems particularly fertile and we think that if carried out it might help us to understand the being and *raison d'être* of Christian—and Jewish—education, school and scholar. We would like to see a full-length development of it.

On the positive side we would put down the following as in sum the most remarkable points in Maritain's theory of education.

First. It is a synthesis of many good things from many sources. Based on the philosophy of Aquinas, it also uses ideas from modern educators, including pragmatists, and from Bergson and Freud.

Second. Maritain's theory regarding the preconscious of the spirit is most arresting and is so novel that perhaps it has not yet received the attention it deserves.

Third. For his part, Maritain would no doubt take as most important his insistence on the child and person. The object must be accepted and respected. But the child must in a way be more respected, the person in the child, his freedom and spontaneity along with any spark of creativity he shows. The child's own intuitions, his personal grasping of ideas and problems, his own free even if inchoate expression, and his "mysterious identity"—these are prime considerations with Maritain.

NOTES

1. *Education at the Crossroads* (Yale University Press, 1952). (Hereafter referred to as *Crossroads*.) "Thomist Views on Education," pp. 57-90 of *Modern Philosophies and Education,* ed. by Nelson B. Henry (Fifty-fourth Yearbook of the National Society for the Study of Education. Distributed by University of Chicago Press, 1955). (Hereafter referred to as "Thomist Views.") "On Some Typical Aspects of Christian Education," pp. 173-198 of *The Christian Idea of Education,* ed. by Edmund Fuller (Yale University Press, 1957). (Hereafter referred to as "Typical Aspects.")

2. *De Veritate*, q. 26, a. 3, ad 12.
3. Jacques Maritain, *Creative Intuition in Art and Poetry* (New York: Pantheon, 1953), pp. 106-111.
4. *De Veritate*, q. 26, a. 10.
5. *Crossroads*, pp. 40-42, 63.
6. Maritain, *Scholasticism and Politics* (New York: Macmillan, 1940), pp. 146-147, 158-159.
7. *Crossroads*, p. 1.
8. *Scholasticism and Politics*, pp. 165-166, 152.
9. Cf. Irène Ramon-Fernandez, "Newman et Maritain," in *La France va-t-elle perdre sa jeunesse?* (Paris: Librairie Arthème Fayard, 1954), pp. 62-63.
10. "Typical Aspects," p. 175.
11. *Crossroads*, pp. 32-33.
12. "Thomist Views," pp. 64-65, 71.
13. *Crossroads*, p. 32.
14. *Crossroads*, p. 13; and "Typical Aspects," pp. 58-59, 67.
15. *Crossroads*, pp. 36-38.
16. *Crossroads*, p. 28.
17. "Typical Aspects," pp. 81-82; and "Thomist Views," pp. 182-184.
18. *Crossroads*, pp. 64-65; "Typical Aspects," pp. 191-197.
19. "Thomist Views," p. 78.
20. *Crossroads*, pp. 45-46.
21. "Thomist Views," p. 60.
22. Maritain, *Man and the State* (University of Chicago Press, 1951), pp. 111-112.
23. "Typical Aspects," pp. 177-180.
24. "Typical Aspects," p. 73.
25. Maritain, *Primauté du Spirituel* (Paris: Librarie Plon, 1927), pp. 154-155.
26. Maritain, *An Essay on Christian Philosophy*, trans. by Edward H. Flannery (New York: Philosophical Library, 1955), Preface, p. ix.

Joseph W. Evans

12. Jacques Maritain and the Problem of Pluralism in Political Life*

THE PROBLEM OF PLURALISM in political life causes contemporary man much anguish. Many and varied, difficult and challenging are the peculiar problems posed by the hitherto unrivalled heterogeneity within present-day political life. These problems have to be *lived* daily by every man at the level of prudence. And they must be continually examined and sifted by social scientists and philosophers. The social scientist must pursue them with his empiriological or phenomena-minded analysis, that is, an analysis that is primarily concerned with the controlled observation of the facts, and with the formulation of hypothetical generalizations based on presumed facts; the philosopher must pursue them with his ontological or being-minded analysis, that is, an analysis that is primarily concerned with the fundamental principles that must guide the resolution of the problems. Among contemporary philosophers who have grappled with these problems, Jacques Maritain, the distinguished Thomist philosopher, is surely one of the most discerning and illuminating. I wish to consider in this essay some of the main tenets in Maritain's position *vis-à-vis* the problem of pluralism in political life, with particular attention to his views on the problem posed by religious pluralism.

A fundamental principle of Maritain in tackling the problem of pluralism is that principle so aptly and succinctly stated by Aristotle in challenging Plato's premise that "the greater the unity of the state the better."[1] "Is it not obvious," Aristotle asks,

> that a state may at length attain such a degree of unity as to be no longer a state?—since the nature of a state is to be a plurality, and in tending to greater unity, from being a state, it becomes a family, and from being a family, an individual; for the family may be said to be more one than the state, and the individual than the family. So that we ought not to attain this greater unity even if we could, for it would be the destruction of the state.[2]

Maritain certainly wants unity in political life, and thus he is strongly opposed to bourgeois liberalism's anarchical atomization of society. But he also knows, metaphysician that he is, that unity is an analogical value, just as being is: the unity that belongs to a being, goes hand in hand with the being that belongs to it, that is, with the kind of being it is cut out to be. For Maritain, political society, that being that is human persons be-ing together with the super-added existence that is the intellecting and willing of the good human life in all its totality, is a being that admits of, indeed calls for, much plurality and diversity. Thus he is strongly opposed to any kind of totalitarian usurpation of the positive liberties of social groups within the body politic. He holds that the human person's attaining to his full freedom of autonomy normally requires his living in a plurality of communities. He sees this plurality as issuing not only from the person's needs, but also from his abundance and root generosity—a basic truth for Maritain: communing, and sharing, and the giving of self go hand in hand with the kind of dynamic, active, and superabundant being that man is. And he asks that the body politic respect the rights, liberties, and authority of the diverse groups assembled within it. Maritain likes to quote, in this matter of societal pluralism, the words of an early and brilliant student of his, Professor Yves R. Simon:

The tendency to restrict the attributions of the State—disquieting and dangerous as long as it is accompanied by any sort of hostility regarding the temporal supremacy of the State—becomes purely and simply salutary, as soon as the just notion of the State and its supremacy is duly re-established. This restrictive tendency then only expresses the fundamental idea of all philosophy of autonomy, to wit, that in a hierarchic whole, every function which can be assumed by the inferior must be exercised by the latter, under pain of damage to the whole. For there is more perfection in a whole, all of whose parts are full of life and of initiative, than in a whole whose parts are but instruments conveying the initiative of the superior organs of the community.[3]

In this vein Maritain himself writes: "Since in political society authority comes from below, through the people, it is normal that the whole dynamism of authority in the body politic should be made up of particular and partial authorities rising in tiers above one another, up to the top authority of the State."[4]

Societal pluralism within the body politic, then—that is, a multiplicity of other particular societies which proceed from the free initiative of citizens and which should be as autonomous as possible—would for Maritain belong to the *essence* of a truly political society. Religious pluralism, on the contrary—that is, a multiplicity of spiritual families with different ways of conceiving the meaning of life and modes of behavior—does not for Maritain belong to the essence of political society. No, but it does belong *de facto* to the *existent* that is contemporary political life. And Maritain is a most existential thinker! He is admirably attentive to essences, to natures, to intelligible structures. But his thought is always centered on existents, on *essences existing,* and consequently he is also attentive to the *existential state* or the *ensemble of existential conditions* in which these essences are actualized or realized. In *Humanisme intégral,* Maritain writes:

. . . Political and social life takes place in the world of existence and contingency, not of pure essences; and God knows to what adventures essences are there exposed, those essences that the philosopher considers apart. In the end, if history were nothing more than an unrolling of logical necessities, the automatism of essences would suffice for it, and the government of God, the free master of all free agents, would become superfluous. . . . In history . . . it is not theses that confront one another, as in a book or in an academic discussion, where everything is concluded to the inmost and meritorious satisfaction of the one who is right and who has shown that he is right; it is rather concrete forces charged with humanity, heavy with fatalities and with contingencies, and which are born of the event and move towards the event, and the existential significance of which politics has to take into account.

Now one of the most existential facts of the contemporary body politic is the religious pluralism within it. Maritain gazes at this existential fact, and with his keen sense for the complexity of things and his great sense of history he sees many, to my mind, incontrovertible and extremely fruitful truths. In itself religious pluralism is for Maritain something unfortunate. But it need not be politically divisive. Furthermore, he knows well that error is often the usher of truth in the human mind: the division of men about *spiritual* being may well have been the occasion and the stimulus for man's latching onto new and deeper truths about *political* being. At any rate, Maritain has no nostalgia for the body politic of the Middle Ages. This body politic, good as it may have been—and it is better in our imagination than it was in reality—has definitely had its day. Time marches on, man goes on *becoming what he is,* the human intellect progressively ferrets out new secrets of social and political being.[6] Consequently, Maritain sees political man as passing under different historical constellations, and he holds that the moral physiognomy of these is far more profoundly different than is ordinarily believed. This tenet is well expressed in the following passage:

Time, the time of human history, has an inner structure. Time is not simply a garbage can in which practical men would have to pick up

more or less profitable opportunities. Time has a meaning and a direction. Human history is made up of periods each of which is possessed of
a particular intelligible structure, and therefore of basic particular requirements. These periods are what I have proposed calling the various
historical climates or historical constellations in human history. They
express given intelligible structures, both as concerns the social, political and juridical dominant characteristics, and as concerns the moral
and ideological dominant characteristics, in the temporal life of the
community.[7]

What, then, is for Maritain the "particular intelligible structure"
of our period in human history? What are some of the new and
deeper truths about political being that he sees modern political man
as having latched onto, and that he as a philosopher would defend
as genuine acquisitions? Well, a first one, and for Maritain a most
fundamental one, is this: the common good of political life is a
genuine end in itself. We find Maritain constantly insisting on this.
The common good of political society may be ordered, indeed it
must be ordered, to something higher, to a something higher that is
not itself in the temporal order. But it is ordered to this, not simply
as a means is ordered to an end, but as an end of a legitimate but
subordinate order is ordered to the end of a legitimate and absolutely superior order. In Book I of his *Ethics* Aristotle speaks of
some ends that are desirable both in themselves and for the sake of
some other thing. For Maritain the common good of political society is such an end—it is an end desirable in itself, and quite capable of being the very *raison d'être* of the communal activity of
human persons in a society to which they naturally belong; it is, in
fact, an ultimate end in a certain respect, the ultimate end in the
temporal order. It is, then, for Maritain—and I wish to stress this
particularly—able to unite in a *same* political activity men belonging to *diverse* spiritual families and traditions; it can be the rallying
ground in the temporal order for men so opposed in the spiritual
order. Religious differences need not divide men politically.
Here I would quote a sentence from Heraclitus, a sentence that,

to my mind, expresses genuine political wisdom, if we relate it to this tenet of Maritain's about the proper finality and desirability of the political common good. Heraclitus wrote: "Those who are awake have a common world, but those who sleep turn aside, each into his own particular world."[8]

So important is this tenet in Maritain, so determinative is it of so much of his thinking on the problem of pluralism in political life, that I would now point briefly to the metaphysical insight that grounds and quickens it. To put it simply, it is this: *being is good, being is to be revered, being is to be cared for.* For Maritain things are *good* insofar as they are (they are *bad* insofar as they are not all they ought to be, that is, insofar as they lack some *due good*). A thing, then, may be at one and the same time both a *means* (as regards some other good) and an *end* (by reason of its own being, goodness, and desirability). And for Maritain it is good for man to see things not only as the means that they are, but also as the ends that they are in themselves, that is, it is good for man to see, and really to live, the being, goodness, and desirability of things. In particular, it is good for man to see, and really to live, the being, goodness, and desirability of man and of human things, and therefore of political society, wherein men pursue together the fullness of personal being in the temporal and terrestrial order.[9] Thus it is good for man to see that the *good* of political society, while it is a means as regards man's supra-temporal fulfillment, is yet a genuine end in itself, and even a *relatively* ultimate end, the ultimate end in the temporal and terrestrial order. It is good for man to see that the good of political society is something intently to be pursued; it really matters. And it is normal for men, before realizing their supra-temporal and supra-terrestrial fulfillment, to realize their *temporal and terrestrial* fulfillment, that is, to bring to actuality all the potentialities of the rational animal for terrestrial and political being and activity.

An immediate corollary, for Maritain, of this principle of the common good of political society as an ultimate end, and as *the* ultimate end in the temporal order, is the distinction between Individual Ethics and Political Ethics. Thus he writes:

. . . political hypermoralism is no better than political amoralism and, in the last analysis, serves the very purpose of political cynicism. Politics is a branch of Ethics, but a branch specifically distinct from the other branches of the same stem. For human life has two ultimate ends, the one subordinate to the other: an ultimate end *in a given order,* which is the terrestrial common good, or the *bonum vitae civilis;* and an *absolute* ultimate end, which is the *transcendent,* eternal common good. And individual ethics takes into account the subordinate ultimate end, but *directly aims* at the absolute ultimate one; whereas political ethics takes into account the absolute ultimate end, but its *direct aim* is the subordinate ultimate end, the good of rational nature in its temporal achievement. Hence a specific difference of perspective between these two branches of Ethics.[10]

Note well that Maritain is not holding for two substantially different Ethics here. For him political being asks to be woven according to the same laws of integrity, justice, and love of neighbor that preside over the weaving of our own private personal being. As they apply to the person in his direct person-to-person relations with other persons and with his God, or to persons as forming a people pursuing together the good human life in all its fullness, these laws have the same substances and the same meanings, but they have different modalities. Maritain would have us keep this truth constantly before our eyes. In a society like ours, with its great diversity of spiritual families, it is vitally important that we recognize the different *perspectives* of Individual Ethics and Political Ethics, and the different modalities that moral principles can take on. Thus we would be better prepared, for example, for the toleration of certain evil deeds by the law, and for the application of the principle of the lesser evil. Much anguish, turmoil, and social unrest, much sapping of internal energies would thus be avoided. We could get on with the positive task of building up the community of the free.

A second truth that modern political man has slowly come to know, however ambiguously, and that Maritain is constantly defending and elucidating, is the value of the human self.[11] For Maritain, again, we must revere being, and we must particularly revere the being of the human person. Maritain *loves* persons, and he would have us love them. He has a profound grasp of what it means *to be* a person; he knows what it is *to be* endowed with intellect and will, *to be* capable of understanding and of loving, *to be* capable of knowing and deliberating about ends, *to be* called to the conquest of freedom. And he would have us appreciate more the implications of the being of man for the fellowship and cooperation of men of different creeds. We who live in a pluralistic society should ponder these words of Maritain:

> . . . it happens that we are men, each containing within himself the ontological mystery of personality and freedom; and it is in this very mystery of freedom and personality that genuine tolerance or freedom takes root. For the basis of good fellowship among men of different creeds is not of the order of the intellect and of ideas, but of the heart and of love. It is friendship, natural friendship, but first and foremost mutual love in God and for God. Love does not go out to essences, nor to qualities nor to ideas, but to persons; and it is the mystery of persons and of the divine presence within them which is here in play. This fellowship, then, is not a fellowship of beliefs but the fellowship of men who believe.[12]

However much we may disagree with the ideas and beliefs of another man, we must never lose sight of, we must respect and love, his *being*—his *person*.

And Maritain insists that such a fellowship among men of different creeds—a fellowship accomplished on the religious and spiritual level itself, but without any doctrinal compromise or diminution of what is owed to truth—should extend, on the temporal level, to common action (doubtless not completely free from all opposition and conflict), to a real cooperation for the good of temporal society.

He knows that men of various creeds are engaged in the common temporal task not as believers, but rather as social and political beings pursuing in society a common good which is a true end and not a mere means. But even here spiritual and ethical values are involved, and these certainly concern the believer as such. Some citizens, for example, will pursue the good of society for what it really is, that is, an intermediate or infravalent end, though admittedly the ultimate end in the temporal order. Other citizens will pursue the good of society as the purely and simply ultimate end. In the common temporal task, then, Maritain considers that friendship will also play an important role: ". . . in this common temporal task itself, an efficacious element of first importance (I say first, I do not say sufficient of itself) for the peaceful existence of men, is mutual good will and friendship. . . ."[13] In short, just as, on the religious and spiritual level itself, friendship is the very basis of good fellowship among men of different creeds, so also, on the temporal level, friendship is an essential requisite for the cooperation of men of different creeds in the pursuit of the common good of civil society. Those citizens, for example, who are pursuing the good of society as an intermediate end, must in friendship cooperate with those citizens who are pursuing this good as the purely and simply ultimate end. Maritain holds that friendship has a vital role to play in any civil society, but that it is all the more vital, that it is all the more of an indispensable bond, in a society in which men of different creeds must pursue a common good of a temporal order. Communal activity in such a pluralist society would be inconceivable if men holding different spiritual points of view did not work together in mutual good will and friendship.

A third fundamental tenet of Maritain's views on pluralism has to do with the common principles, the certain basic community of doctrine, that must ground communal activity—for, again, friendship is not sufficient of itself. Maritain insists that "a genuine democracy implies a fundamental agreement between minds and wills on the bases of life in common; it is aware of itself and of its principles, and it must be capable of defending and promoting its own conception of social and political life; *it must bear within itself a common human creed, the creed of freedom.*"[14] But he also insists that this common creed or faith is not a religious, but rather a *civic* or *secular* one; it is not of the order of religious and eternal life, but rather of the order of secular and temporal life.[15] And he insists, too, that this creed is not at all a set of universally proclaimed theoretical conceptions, but rather a set of practical tenets, that is, a set of "practical conclusions" or of "practical points of convergence."[16] Maritain's confidence that men divided in their philosophical or religious convictions can still agree on a set of "practical conclusions" or "practical points of convergence" is rooted in the fact that all men have the same human nature. There is among us all a unity more fundamental than any unity of thought or doctrine, and this is the unity of human nature and of its primordial inclinations taken in their very extra-mental reality. This unity does not suffice to assure a community of action, since we act as thinking beings and not merely by natural instinct. But it underlies the very exercise of our thought, and it is the unity of a rational nature, subject to the intelligible attraction of the same primordial objects, and it is the first ground of the similarities that our principles of action, however different otherwise, can have among themselves.[17] Moreover, this knowledge through connaturality of the practical tenets of democratic life has been quickened by the Gospel leaven.[18] Maritain's thought here is best expressed by this passage from *Man and the State:*

The secular faith in question deals with the *practical* tenets which the human mind can try to justify—more or less successfully, that's another affair—from quite different philosophical outlooks, probably because they depend basically on simple, 'natural' apperceptions, of which the human heart becomes capable with the progress of moral conscience, and which, as a matter of fact, have been awakened by the Gospel leaven fermenting in the obscure depths of human history.

Thus it is that men possessing quite different, even opposite meta-physical or religious outlooks, can converge, not by virtue of any identity of doctrine, but by virtue of an analogical similitude in practical principles, toward the same practical conclusions, and can share in the same practical secular faith, provided that they similarly revere, perhaps for quite diverse reasons, truth and intelligence, human dignity, freedom, brotherly love, and the absolute value of moral good.[19]

And Maritain would have each philosophical or religious school of thought assert its belief with fullness and integrity. For him it is but normal that in a democratic society the different philosophical and religious schools of thought which, in their practical conclusions, agree as regards the basic common democratic convictions, and which claim to justify them, should enter into free competition. The resulting reciprocal tension, he holds, would enrich rather than harm the common task.[20] Indeed, a democratic society simply must promote and defend, mainly through education, the practical tenets that are its very bases, and this cannot be done apart from the philo-osophical or religious convictions that ground and quicken these tenets in the thought of each citizen. In an essay entitled, "Thomist Views on Education," which appears in *Modern Philosophies and Education,* Maritain writes:

For the very sake of providing unity in the adherence to the demo-cratic charter, a sound pluralism must obtain in the means. Inner dif-ferentiations must come into force in the structure of the educational system, which must admit within itself pluralistic patterns enabling teachers to put their entire convictions and most personal inspiration in their teaching of the democratic charter.[21]

He goes on to propose three ways to which prudential wisdom might have recourse in order to effect this pluralism in the teaching of the democratic charter. First, as regards communities homogeneous in their spiritual traditions, teachers of the charter could be allotted according to their own wishes as well as to the moral geographies of the local communities, so that their own deepest philosophical and religious convictions would roughly correspond with those prevailing in the social environment. Secondly, as regards communities heterogeneous in their spiritual traditions, a few different teachers might be allotted to the teaching of the charter, so that each teacher's own deepest philosophical or religious convictions would roughly correspond with those of the particular group of students he would be teaching. Thirdly, a new discipline might be introduced —one putting less emphasis on theoretical principles, and yet still giving free rein to personal inspiration—and which would bring to the study of the practical tenets of the democratic charter, pursued against the background of national history and the history of civilization, the light of the great poets, thinkers and heroes of mankind.[22]

In my opinion, Maritain's insistence on the need for this pluralism in the teaching of the democratic charter, as also his proposals for the implementing of this pluralistic teaching, bear witness to his real wisdom. "It belongs to the wise man to order"—it belongs to the wise man to *see* order, and to see different *orders*; it belongs to the wise man to *distinguish in order to unite*. That is what Maritain is doing here: the philosophical order is one order, one universe, one frame of reference for man; the religious or theological order is another order, another universe, another frame of reference; and the political order is still another order, still another universe, still another frame of reference. They are distinct, yes; but they must not be cut off from each other. Political life is something temporal, something terrestrial, something practical. But it must be quickened by the sap that flows into it from above—from the above that is the philosophical, from the above that is the religious and the theological. And if a man as a philosopher, if a man as a religious man or as a theologian, differs with the philosophical and religious convictions of his fellow men; and if he will try, through the power of his demonstrations and the testimony of his love, to lead others to the truth as he sees it—nevertheless, as a political man in a democratic society that has within it great philosophical and religious diversity, he must not only tolerate, he must see as a good, a political good, the life-manifesting and life-giving efforts of the various philosophical and spiritual families to promote, defend, and critically elucidate the practical tenets that are the temporal and terrestrial faith by which they live.

Another fundamental tenet of Maritain's views on pluralism is the principle that immutable principles call for analogical applications in different existential situations. For Maritain, beings are beings *analogously,* that is, in ways that are only proportionately the same: the essence-existence polarity that the very notion of being implies, is in beings proportionately—each being exercises the act of existence in proportion to its nature or essence. This is a basic insight of Thomistic metaphysics. A real contribution of Maritain's, I suggest, has been to show the relevance and the fecundity of this insight in political philosophy. In particular, he has shown its relevance and fecundity when it comes to the problem of the relationship between the Church and the State—a crucial problem at any time, but an especially crucial one in a body politic that has within it a great diversity of spiritual families. For Maritain, political beings, that is, political societies, are political beings analogously—they exist in ways that are only proportionately the same. Consequently, if the guiding principles are immutable, owing to the immutable essential and hierarchical structures of man and the universe of being, their realizations and applications in different political beings are analogical, owing to the different existential situations. Thus Maritain writes:

In our opinion, the philosophy of culture must avoid two opposed errors, one of which brings all things together as if univocal, while the other separates all things as if equivocal. A philosophy of *equivocity* will imagine that with a change in time historical conditions become so different that they depend on supreme principles which are themselves heterogeneous: as though truth and right, the supreme rules of human action, were mutable. A philosophy of *univocity* would lead us to believe that these supreme rules and principles always apply in the same way, and that in particular the way in which Christian principles are proportioned to the conditions of each age and are realized in time should not vary at all. The true solution is found in the philosophy of *analogy*. The principles do not change, nor the supreme practical rules of human life. But they are applied in ways essentially diverse, ways answering to the same concept only according to a similitude of proportion.[23]

Thus for Maritain different existential situations call for analogical applications of immutable principles. But we must clearly understand that by "different existential situations" Maritain does not simply mean different congeries of empirically ascertained facts. Rather, he means the different historical climates or historical constellations in human history, in other words, the different ensembles of ideological, moral, social, political, and juridical dominants or guiding stars of the different phases of human history. And these different historical climates or historical constellations in human history can be determined only by submitting the different congeries of empirically ascertained facts to a genuinely philosophical analysis and interpretation, only by seeing them in the light of a genuine philosophy of history.

Now it is Maritain's view, as I have already indicated briefly, that the historical climate of the modern world is quite different from that of the medieval world. For him, medieval civilization was a "sacral" civilization, and by this he means that the historical ideal of the Middle Ages was principally controlled by two dominants: on the one hand, the idea or myth or guiding star of fortitude in the service of God—the lofty aim was to build up a fortress for God on earth; and on the other hand, this concrete fact that temporal civilization itself had largely a ministerial role as regards the spiritual—the body politic was to a great extent a function of the sacred, and imperiously demanded unity of religion. On the contrary, modern civilization is for Maritain a "secular" civilization, and by this he means that the historical ideal of modern times is principally controlled by two dominants: on the one hand, the idea or myth or guiding star of the body politic as being by nature something of the natural order and something directly concerned therefore only with the temporal life of men and their temporal common good; and on the other hand, this concrete fact that in pursuing this temporal common good modern man is most intent on the conquest of freedom and the realization of human dignity, and this in social and political life itself.

As a result, Maritain holds that the supreme principles governing the relationship between the Church and the State—such principles as *the freedom of the Church to teach and preach and worship,* or *the superiority of the Church over the body politic or the State,* or *the necessary cooperation between the Church and the body politic or the State*—Maritain holds that these principles ought to be applied differently today from the way in which they were applied in the "sacral" civilization of the Middle Ages. Thus he writes:

Given such an existential frame of reference, what can be the ways of applying and realizing, in our historical age, the supreme principles that hold sway over the relationship between Church and State? Let us say that in a new Christianly inspired civilization, as far as we are able to see it, those principles would in general be applied less in terms of the social power than in terms of the vivifying inspiration of the Church. The very modality of her action upon the body politic has been spiritualized, the emphasis having shifted from power and legal constraints (which the Church exercises, now as ever, in her own spiritual sphere over her own subjects, but not over the State) to moral influence and authority; in other words, to a fashion or "style," in the external relations of the Church, more appropriate to the Church herself, and more detached from the modalities that had inevitably been introduced by the Christian Empire of Constantine. Thus the superior dignity of the Church is to find its ways of realization in the full exercise of her *superior strength of all-pervading inspiration.*[24]

The mode in which the body politic would today cooperate with the Church would likewise be different. Instead of the cooperation of the body politic with the Church which prevailed in the Middle Ages, and which consisted in the extensive use of the external and visible means of the temporal order, and even in the use of force in various degrees, we would now have, for example, that most general and indirect form of cooperation—on the part of both the body politic and the State[25]—which would consist in their being more fully what they are cut out to be, that is, in their striving to realize more fully their own ends, in their own regard for the natural law, and in their organizing of society according to the demands of justice. A *good* political order will indirectly aid the Church, so far as it indirectly assists the human person with regard to his eternal destiny.[26] In addition, we would now have, to cite another example, that positive cooperation between the body politic and the Church which would consist in the body politic's "*asking the assistance* of the Church for its own temporal common good." As Maritain puts it,

. . . the body politic, its free agencies and institutions, using their own freedom of existential activity within the framework of laws, would ask more of the Church. They would ask, on the basis of freedom and equality of rights for all citizens, her cooperation in the field of all the activities which aim at enlightening human minds and life. They would positively facilitate the religious, social, and educational work by means of which she—as well as the other spiritual or cultural groups whose helpfulness for the common good would be recognized by them—freely cooperates in the common welfare. By removing obstacles and opening the doors, the body politic, its free agencies and institutions, would positively facilitate the effort of the apostles of the Gospel to go to the masses and share their life, to assist the social and moral work of the nation, to provide people with leisure worthy of human dignity, and to develop within them the sense of liberty and fraternity.[27]

The Church, asked by the temporal to give more assistance to the temporal, would thereby be itself assisted in the realization of its own spiritual task.

Finally, I would turn for a moment to Maritain's views regarding the kind of notions legislation would call into play in such a pluralistic society, when it comes to matters involving at once a civil and a religious aspect. He maintains that the widespread religious diversity of the modern world requires that the State should someday grant, in such matters, different juridic systems to different religious groups.[28] It would belong to the State, in its political wisdom, to accord to different institutionally-recognized religious groups the juridic systems best adapted, on the one hand, to their condition, and most consonant, on the other hand, with the general line of legislation leading to the virtuous life and the prescriptions of the moral law, to the attainment of which the State should direct as much as possible the diversity of religious groups.[29] In keeping with this, Maritain writes:

. . . we have to maintain that the legislation of the Christian society in question could and should never *endorse* or *approve* any way of conduct contrary to Natural Law. But we have also to realize that this legislation could and should *permit* or *give allowance to* certain ways of conduct which depart in some measure from Natural Law, if the prohibition by civil law of these ways of conduct were to impair the common good, either because such prohibition would be at variance with the ethical code of communities of citizens whose loyalty to the nation and faithfulness to their own moral creed, however imperfect it may be, essentially matter to the common good, or even because it would result in a worse conduct, disturbing or disintegrating the social body, for a great many people whose moral strength is not on a level with the enforcement of this prohibition . . . .[30]

As I see it, Maritain is primarily suggesting that civil legislation might tend to coincide with church regulations in such matters as marriage, education, domestic responsibility for children, freedom of succession, etc. Thus, civil legislation might permit divorce for those religious groups which believe in it. Thus, too, I suggest, civil legislation might permit—as it finally did in the New York controversy recently—birth-control therapy in public hospitals, provided, of course, that the views of those who object to it, whether patients or doctors or nurses, would be fully respected.

Maritain cannot share the optimism of those who foresee religious unity in the near future. These people are prone to consider the socio-religious problem, with which Maritain is dealing, as a speculative rather than a practical problem. They would deal with it in such a way that they would hope for a solution through an analysis of religious concepts and the deduction of a universally valid judgment rather than through the consideration of actual conditions in which adjustments must be made. Maritain's position in this matter is an existential solution offered as the most that can be hoped for in a society in which there is religious disunity either indeterminately or certainly for a very long time. He is viewing the matter in the perspective of Political Ethics; he is taking into account the absolute ultimate end, but his direct aim is the ultimate end *in a given order,* the terrestrial common good, the good of civil life, the good of rational nature in its temporal achievements.

Jacques Maritain is a philosopher who really *sees*—he goes beyond phenomena and signs, he comes to grips with the deepest dimensions of things. I suggest that this is nowhere more evident than when he turns his philosophical gaze to the problem of pluralism, especially the problem of religious pluralism, in political life. He is seeing much, he is saying much, about the deepest dimensions of this problem. He is seing the dimension that is *essence*—he is seeing essences, natures, intelligible structures, the exigencies of the object. And he is seeing the dimension that is the *existent*—he is seeing time, adventure, freedom, the exigencies of human subjectivity. He holds these different dimensions in a living unity, and it is thus that he can speak so well about unity and diversity in political life.

love at the price of truth and to dissolve all knowledge into eclec-
ticism, agnosticism, skepticism, or relativity. Genuine love is born
in faith in truth and remains in this faith, while at the same time it
reaches out to those who do not have the same convictions. As a
result it inevitably carries with it a sort of heartrending, attached
as is the heart at once to the truth we love and to the neighbor even
when he is an enemy of that truth. It is accompanied, with regard
to ourselves, by a humble compunction and soul's sorrow, for it
is supra-subjective though not supra-dogmatic, making us go not
beyond our belief but beyond ourselves and beyond the shell of
egotism in which we instinctively tend to enclose the infinite truth
itself. With regard to our neighbor, on the other hand, it must
contain a kind of forgiveness, not of his ideas—ideas deserve no
forgiveness if they are false—but of the person whose innermost
heart we cannot judge and can only commend to divine mercy. One
who loves genuinely is prepared to give up his life but not his truth
for his fellow men.[12]

C. *Love must be genuine.*

For genuine love goes first to that Goodness who is also the
Truth. Love for God is the natural and universal *eros,* the very
power and innermost vitality in which all beings desire and act.
God is the only person whom human love can fly to and settle in
so as to find that freedom to which it aspires. The very perfection
of human life, which is a perfection not so much of our self as of
our love, primarily consists in a ceaselessly increasing love between
the Uncreated Self and the created self. Only such love, which
unites us, above being, to the principle of being, can realize the
integration of the person within himself and with others. Thus a
theo-centric humanism of the heart is the only practical solution
of life. The practical-mindedness of Americans grasped this crucial
truth and built a strong United States by making her "the only
country of the West in which society is conceived as being basically

a religious society." For the animal which is by nature rational is by nature also, and even more fundamentally, religious.[13]

After love has risen to the Absolute Good as its primary object and so rectified itself by making the true God its God, it then descends again upon all creatures insofar as they participate in Goodness. It now embraces all in the Good, and the Good in all, including the self, without injuring the native privileges of any, wishing well even to enemies. It thaws coldness and shatters obstacles, for it confronts creation no longer as its slave but with the dignity of a freedman endowed with divine power and mercy.[14]

II. *The Nature of Love*

But by what right can one say that this is the only genuine love? How can love, which is the very paradigm and source of all freedom, be itself bound in conformity to a pattern?

The reason is that even love must to its own self be true. It possesses a nature by which it is what it is and not anything else. It is free indeed, even to go contrary to its nature, but only to its own detriment. Only by freely actuating the potentiality of that nature can it attain its perfection and its true liberty, peace, and joy.[15]

A. *Known by intuition.*

That nature of love is rooted in being; and, although we cannot fully comprehend its mystery, nevertheless its general structure can be discovered; and it is discovered most fundamentally in our knowledge of being. For when the intuition of being takes place in us it normally carries along with itself an intuition of one's own existence or the self, an obscure, immediate knowledge of subjectivity as subjectivity. Now subjectivity as such is not an object conceptualized before thought but rather the very well-spring of thought. It is a deep and living center which exists and superabounds in knowledge and love. The self possesses itself and holds itself in hand; and to what purpose does it so dispose of itself, if not for what is better, or to give of itself? Existence as giving itself, its very superabundance, is its love. Thus a man discovers the basic generosity of existence and realizes that love is the supreme perfection of being.[16]

Together with his awareness of subjectivity, he also begins to see two conflicting images: that of himself as subject, and that of all others in the world who are presented to him as objects of his thought but who are also in themselves similar sacred subjectivities. These two perspectives, that of himself as subject and that of his situation in respect to other objects, will not coincide. He usually oscillates rather miserably between them. If he abandons himself to the perspective of subjectivity, he absorbs everything into himself and, sacrificing everything to his uniqueness, is riveted to the absolute of selfishness and pride. On the other hand, if he abandons himself to the perspective of objectivity, he is absorbed into everything and, dissolving into the world, is false to his uniqueness and resigns his destiny. The antinomy can be resolved only from above. God is the true center, not in relation to a certain particular perspective, like that in which each created subjectivity is the center of the universe it knows, but speaking absolutely, and as transcendent subjectivity to which all subjectivities are referred. In God I can know both that I am without importance and that my destiny is of the highest importance. I can know this without either falling into pride or being false to my own uniqueness. For, loving the divine Subject more than myself, I *will* my own destiny in His Will and embrace in Him and for Him all subjectivities, which become a "we" called to rejoice in His life.

B. *Further understood by metaphysical analysis.*

In other words, every creature by its nature loves God more than itself, as a part loves the whole more than itself. This doctrine of St. Thomas Aquinas is central to M. Maritain's thought, not merely as a pious or moral ideal or exhortation, but as his view of the basic ontological structure of love. This structure appears in the intuition just described which he further develops and supports by a metaphysical analysis that we shall now summarize.

It should be noted at once that the nature of love is in some important respects similar to that of knowledge. Both are spiritual superexistences. That is to say, in both, the finite self transcends the limiting individuality of its own entitative substantial being in order to be enriched with another being which now exists within it as known or loved. To be knowing or loving something is first of all, therefore, a metaphysical accident when it is considered according to its being of nature. It is superadded to the substance as a distinct actual perfection which exists in the substance but which can come or go without entailing a substantial change. In other words it is an *esse* or, more precisely, an *inesse reale accidentale.* A second characteristic common to knowledge and love is the fact that they are also intentional being, *esse intentionale;* for the thing which is being understood or loved exists within the act of knowledge or love, not, of course, with its own unique extra-mental entitative existence, but with a numerically distinct intentional existence peculiar to the actually known or beloved as such.

1. *Intentional being.*

Thus the mystery of love compels the philosopher to conceive it as immaterial intentional being, which resembles knowledge, but which also crucially differs from knowledge. The immaterial activity of knowing receives the known into itself, so that the knower becomes the other (the known) insofar as it is other. The known now exists as object within the knower; and since whatever is received is received according to the mode of the recipient, the known exists according to the mode of existence of the knower. Knowledge essentially pertains to the absolute perfection of the knower as it is in itself, rather than to its relation to others, for its proper intentionality is an assimilation of the known in the mode of immaterial identity. Consequently, the true, which is the formal object of knowledge, is within the intellect; speculative knowledge of evil is not evil; and the first object naturally known by a creature is another creature on its own level, while God is known only last, by rising through creatures to Him.

Love, on the contrary, is the other way about. Knowledge receives the other into itself. Love gives itself to the other. The cause as well as the term of love is the good, which is in things as they exist in themselves. The formal aspect of the good is in fact the very perfection of things; and since existence is the perfection of all perfections, the good is the fullness of the perfection of existence itself. The good attracts the appetite to itself precisely insofar as it is existing outside the appetite; and love, the first act of appetite, gives itself to that other as good. The intentional being of love, therefore, is not an *esse* in virtue of which, as in knowledge, the subject (knower) becomes the other (the known); rather contrariwise, it is an *esse* in virtue of which the other (beloved) becomes to the subject (lover) another self. "The immaterial activity of love is to lose oneself in the other as the self, to alienate myself in the reality of the other to the extent that he becomes more me than I am myself. It is in this that love is 'ecstatic' . . ., and is the cause of everything the lover does."[18] The immateriality of love, though no less pure than that of knowledge, is therefore less separated from things and wholly turned toward their concrete state. The spiritual presence of the beloved within the appetite of the lover is as a weight drawing the love outward into the thing in itself. The beloved as it exists in itself is thus mysteriously impressed upon the affections of the lover; and love is more unitive than knowledge in uniting with things in the very subjectivity of their existence.

One consequence of this intentional presence of the beloved within the act of love is that the love itself (as well as the subsequent appetitive acts, which participate in its nature) can become a medium of a more intimate knowledge of what is loved.[19] M. Maritain calls this a knowledge by connaturality, since the appetite is made consonant with the subjectivity of the beloved; and he gives it a prominent role in his philosophy, especially in the fields of art,[20] morality,[21] and mysticism.[22]

Another consequence pertains more directly to the nature of love itself (and so to our present study). Because love is an inclination to being as it is in itself, it goes first to God, the First Being, and secondarily to creatures. Although some distinctions and precisions will have to be made, the general motion of love in creatures, therefore, is contrary to that of knowledge, which naturally attains God only through creatures; and we are brought back again to the principle that every creature naturally loves God more than itself or anything else.

2. *"Natural" (as distinguished from "supernatural") love.*

Before following M. Maritain into a more profound analysis of this principle it now becomes necessary to note that he is giving to the word "love" a meaning which is both more restricted and more extended than its common usage in modern languages. He restricts it first of all in the sense that, by virtue of its possessing a nature, true love is distinguished from false love, as normal individuals of a species can be distinguished from monstrosities. True love is for him, as for St. Augustine, love for God above all; and false loves have the common characteristic of being a love of a creature above God. Moreover, he also distinguishes love in the natural order from charity in the supernatural order of grace. St. Thomas made the same distinction; but St. Thomas did not fully develop the concept of natural love by explicitly studying the hypothesis of nature considered in abstraction from the gifts of grace. M. Maritain, by making an explicit study of natural love in this more restricted sense, offers a considerable development of the doctrine.

3. *"Love-of-nature" (as distinguished from "love-of-free-option").*

In another sense M. Maritain also enlarges the meaning of "love" beyond the common contemporary usage, in order to give it, with St. Thomas, an analogical extension as ample as that of being itself. Every being, even inanimate, in their view, "loves" the good and the end to which it tends by the very necessity of its nature. "Nature" here means "determined to one," and is contra-distinguished from freedom with its indetermination and active self-determination (both of which are found in the natural as distinguished from the supernatural order). In an attempt to avoid confusion of terminology which might arise from making "natural" carry the double distinction from both the supernatural and the free, he calls this necessary love the love-of-nature as distinguished from the love-of-free-option or choice.[23]

Love in the created will, then, possesses two moments. The first and fundamental moment is its love-of-nature, the moment preeminently of necessity. The second, which flowers out of the first, is its love-of-free-option, preeminently the moment of liberty.

The will's love-of-nature, in turn, is fourfold: (1) an *ontological love-of-nature* for its own proper good, and on beyond for God above all; (2) an *elicited love-of-nature* for its own good, which contains the *intra-elicited ontological love-of-nature* for God above all; (3) an *elicited love-of-nature for God* above all; and (4) a *natural inclination towards a love-of-free-option for God above all.* We shall briefly consider each.

a. *Ontological love-of-nature for universal good and for God above all.*

The *ontological love-of-nature* is analogously present in all, even inanimate, beings and in all their parts, for it is identical with being itself. It is being in its dynamic aspect, as tending with spontaneous *élan* toward what is suitable for it. Every being not only is what it is at any moment, but also loves to be. It tends to communicate its existence on into the next moment, to resist destruction. Because of this radical tendency existence gushes forth into other times and places, superabounds everywhere, communicates its perfections in profusion. This basic generosity or love of existence itself is the intrinsic source of all the vast activity of the universe. As the principle of finality expresses it, being in act acts out of love for a good and an end.[24]

That law of finality in turn rests upon the law of hyperfinality, which states that every creature tends to its proper end in virtue of its love for the supreme End. Every creature loves to be in some limiting form because it loves To Be. It loves something as possessing goodness because it loves Goodness. It loves a perfection which is limited in such a way as to be proximately proportionate and suitable to its own limited being, not by reason of the limitation, but by reason of the perfection. Creatures are, and are perfect and good, only by participating in God who is Pure Existence, Perfection, and Goodness; and the ontological love-of-nature loves things as they are. Consequently, as the part loves the whole (in which alone it exists) more than itself, so every creature loves the Supreme Whole more than itself. Under the aspect of specification by the object this love goes first to the end proper to the created agent and then extends on through that good to God, while under the aspect of intensity of exercise it goes first (with priority of nature) to God and then to the limited good. Since the order of exercise and existence enjoys primacy over that of specification and essence, love primarily tends first to God.

Now the will is the appetite of the person as person, the intellectual appetite of the intellectual creature; and the intellect knows the universal. By nature, therefore, the will is an appetite for the universal good and its possession in happiness as for its proper good. Consubstantial with the being of the will as it stands forth

from the creating, conserving, and moving First Cause, its ontological love-of-nature immediately bursts forth as an actual *élan*
toward the universal good and happiness and on beyond toward
God above all as Supreme Whole and Common Good.[25] This love
does not proceed from any knowledge other than that which belongs
to the Author of nature. It is necessary, not free. It could only be
lost by the will's ceasing to be, which is impossible; so it remains
even in a will which rejects God by subsequent free option.

b. *Elicited love-of-nature for universal good together with intra-
elicited ontological love for God above all.*

The second love-of-nature discovered in the will is elicited. By
elicited love is meant a love which bears upon an object *as first
known* because the love emanates from an appetitive power (sense
appetite or will) insofar as it is itself rooted in a cognitive power
(sense or intellect). When the intellect presents to the will the good
in general and happiness as known, a spontaneous love is necessarily elicited by the will for this, its proper object. This love-of-
nature for the good in general and happiness is necessarily present
within all the will's operations of willing any good whatsoever, for
it cannot will anything except in the light of the common notion
of the good. The previous ontological love for God above all also
remains within this elicited love for good in general; but since there
is at this point no knowledge properly so called of God (all wills,
even of atheists, possess this love), M. Maritain calls this an intra-
elicited ontological love for God above all as Supreme Whole and
Common Good who is the *de facto* source of all good. "Just as
nature cannot tend toward any end whatsoever without tending
still more toward the supreme Whole through each of its single
particular ends, so the will cannot love any good whatsoever without loving still more the supreme Whole, through the good in
general and happiness, of which our intellect has an idea, and which

we will and love in all that we will."[26] This *elicited love-of-nature for good in general and happiness* together with its *intra-elicited love-of-nature for God above all* is necessary, and cannot be lost even in a will which turns away from God in its subsequent love-of-free-choice.

c. *Elicited love-of-nature for God.*

Thirdly, the will produces an *elicited love-of-nature for God above all*. When the intellect knows the Absolute Subsisting Good who is the Common Good and Principle of all goods, an immediate indeliberate movement of love for It spontaneously bursts forth in the will. This love is analogous to the indeliberate movements of sense appetite which arise from sense knowledge of an object as pleasant to sense. Although this love is necessary in its mode of emanation from the will, it depends extrinsically and indirectly upon free choice in the sense that the (ontologically) subsequent free option against God can prevent its actuation.

d. *Natural inclination to love-of-free-option for God above all.*

The fourth and last of the great natural loves in the will is a *necessary inclination towards a love-of-free-option for God above everything else*. This love is determined but not determining. It is determined in the sense that it necessarily inclines the will towards a love-of-free-option for God as primary object rather than towards a love-of-free-option for anything else as primary object; but it is not determining, because the love-of-free-option remains essentially and intrinsically free in its mode of emanation from the will. Hence the love-of-free-option can rest primarily in something other than God; but if it does so, it cannot escape the fact that it is thereby going contrary to its own natural inclination, contrary, in fact, to that entire nature, that first moment of love whose four elements we have now seen.

Now none of these four loves-of-nature, either separately or together, establish the moral life, the adult life of the person as person.
Only the love-of-free-option, the second and completing moment of
love, establishes the moral life; and a right and good moral life is
established only by a *love-of-free-option for God above all*.

4. Love-of-free-option.

The reason for this lies in the Transcendence of God and the
nature of love-of-free-choice. For the Good is not just the Common
Good and Supreme Whole. He is also the Transcendent Good, infinitely distinct and elevated above all else in the absolute singularity of His Essence. To us who do not as yet see Him immediately
in the Beatific Vision but know Him only in the mirror of creatures,
He appears as one limitedly known good among other goods. Conflict arises in our affections, therefore, between those goods which
we can comprehend and that Good which surpasses our understanding because it is so much other that every similarity with our
familiars fades before the dissimilarity. To love that Good above
all as the end and rule of our very life, then, means for us *to choose*
between that good which is The Good and other goods which are
not He. It is to throw oneself into the darkness of the Incomprehensible, to will the Good no matter what unknown sacrifice of
self this may imply.

Only the full self-determining force of the love-of-free-option can
so cross that infinite abyss between the created and the Uncreated.
Those prior loves-of-nature attained God merely as Common Good
through the specifying mediation of a creature. Love-of-free-option
alone gives itself directly to the Good as an Act apart; it alone without intermediary attains the Transcendent Person. For the love-of-
free-choice is *not of this world*. It transcends creation. That is why
no creature (not even angels who know all that belongs to the created universe) can understand the secrets of hearts. Even though a

person's intellect be without ignorance or error, and his nature without blemish, his love is still free to reject or to accept the Good. Such is the mystery and the, in a way, infinite power of love. This crucial decision belongs solely to love, and is its unavoidable and supreme crisis, its splendor or tragedy, and its eternal value. Either it gives itself to the Good or it does not.

a. *Option against the Good.*

If it does not, it nihilates the inclination of its own nature and of the Author of nature, becoming a first cause in the order of nothingness. The person who thus chooses some creature for himself basically loves himself above all; but with a love which is not true love, with a love which is striving to be what it is not and becoming thereby a twisted monster, an explosive ontological contradiction that is simultaneously a hatred of its own nature and its Author. Its hatred cannot succeed, however, in destroying that *ontological love-of-nature,* for the good in general and happiness and for the Good above all, which is identical with the being of the will. Neither can it destroy the *elicited love-of-nature* for good in general and happiness within which endures the *intra-elicited ontological love* for God above all as Supreme Whole and Common Good. An inescapable conflict and torment consequently arises from this implacable necessity always to love, in each particular act as well as in the constant tendency of the will, that same Good who is freely detested. The *elicited love-of-nature* for God above all is thwarted. The *necessary inclination towards a love-of-free-option for God* is enfeebled and frustrated. Instead of the Good for which it was made, this will chooses as its own awful beatitude a solitary confinement within itself as first cause of negation and evil, with resulting emptiness, nausea, and anguish of despair. Pride and envy and endlessly proliferating errors and sins make up this moral life whose first rule is self.

b. *Option for the Good.*

The other basic alternative of love is to give itself to the Good. Here love does not say "no" to its nature's necessary drive towards the Good which is Transcendent. To the question of crossing the abyss between its own proper universe and the Incomprehensible Uncreated, this love freely says "yes." It gives itself to Infinity.

Then (the mystery of love), in giving all, it gets All—Something worth living for.[27] Radical satisfaction comes to the ontological and elicited loves-of-nature for the good in general and happiness, together with the ontological and intra-elicited love for God above all. Even though the intellect may be in speculative ignorance or error about the existence of God (in pseudo-atheism or agnosticism), the will, nevertheless, in choosing any moral good out of love for goodness, *de facto* extends its love on to the True Good;[28] and thereby it carries the practical intellect along with it to an obscure practical knowledge of the Good, even as salvific.[29] The elicited love-of-nature for God above all, therefore, can now be fulfilled. The natural inclination towards a love-of-free-option for God above all, in fact the total nature of love, realizes its inner order and perfection, with consequent peace and joy. Only now is happiness attained; for love, as well as knowledge, is an essential constituent of any beatitude this side of the Beatific Vision. Even the loftiest contemplation of God (always excepting that supernatural Vision) can beatify only by manifesting an object which is not abhorred but loved. Thus M. Maritain preserves the Greek ideal of contemplation, but as purified of its exclusive reservation to a few leisured intellectuals and of its contempt for the common man and for his work.[30] By making the end of human nature consist in the conjoined activity of knowledge and love and by insisting that here below the love of God is better than knowledge, he makes perfection accessible to all men.[31] All virtues can be generated by the intrinsic dynamism of love for the Good which is natural to the human heart. Since love is the principle of all operation, and affective contemplation issues in action, even the lowliest labor of man assumes dignity, and moral perfection can permeate our entire emerging civilization.

5. *The Exemplar and Source: "God is Love."*

In spite of his exalted view of the nature of human love, however, M. Maritain is no Rousseauistic optimist about the actuation of that nature. God alone can be the first source (efficient and exemplary cause) of both the nature and its actuation. As a matter of fact, it is *because* He is the first source of love that He is its first term (final cause or end).

"It is necessary to make clear that the spiritual dynamism at work in human culture implies a twofold movement. First, there is the movement of descent, the movement by which the divine plenitude, the prime source of existence, descends into human reality to permeate and vivify it. For God infuses in every creature goodness and lovability and love together with being and has the *first* initiative in every good activity. Then there is the movement of ascent, which is the answer of man, by which human reality takes the *second* initiative, activates itself toward the unfolding of its energies and toward God. From the point of view of the Absolute, the first movement is obviously what matters most; to receive from God is of greater moment for man than to give to God, and man can only give what he has received."[32]

What does man receive? He receives being which imitates the Divine Being; and the ultimate name of the Divine Being is Love. The rediscovery of love in creatures as superabundance and melioration leads to the rediscovery of Love in God as pure superabundance without melioration. The most resplendent manifestation of the Divine Glory within the scope of our natural reason is that love, which presupposes understanding and is a gift of spiritual life, is in God identical with His essence and His existence. Before any creature was, He is and joyously loves To Be. The deepest secret of the

Divine Nature is His appetitive approval and willing granting of its Goodness to the Good as it is in Itself. And why does He create, as well as continually conserve and activate creatures, except out of the sheer generosity of that same Love of Goodness, now as to be communicated *ad extra*? The ultimate reason that the innermost nature of creatures is a love of The Good is that they are participations in Him who is Love of the Good.[33]

Supernatural faith further accepts the revelation that the Infinite Superabundance communicates itself so completely that a Trinity of Divine Persons lives in the Unity of Divine Nature. Furthermore, the Second Person also gives His Divine Personality to a human nature; and from Him the gift of grace continually flows into every human being in order to heal its wounds, particularly in the sphere of its love, and also in order to elevate it even to the level of divine life and to that supernatural perfection of love which is charity. In the existing order, therefore, charity is the efficacious actuation and super-actuation of all the aspirations of love. The most perfect states of charity, in turn, are those of mysticism, a point on which M. Maritain agrees with Bergson. And the most perfect mystical state, finally, is that of mystical espousal in which the soul and God become two natures in one spirit of love. Love's natural and obediential potency and thirst for union with the Beloved as it is in Itself are here realized fully. Although the human will remains infinitely distinct from God as regards its entitative being, still as regards the intentional being proper to love it becomes one with Him, loving Him as He loves it, loving Him in fact as He loves Himself, with His own Love. Because the Beloved dwells as Gift within the love, that love attains Infinity not only as Term but also as Giving Itself. By true love man becomes truly like God.[34]

These further aspects of love, however, carry us beyond our allotted confines. We shall simply have to admit, in conclusion, that this is an inadequate survey of M. Maritain's thought on love and that to make a complete study is one of the tasks awaiting willing hands. In this, as in other subjects, he has brought perennial wisdom into the dialogue of contemporary culture, and in the process, has added his own development of that wisdom. That has been a good work which has made a good life; and with love's own generous impulse he wishes to share his good with others, particularly with those who welcome suggestions about what to do. Words he wrote some years ago are pertinent here: "The great Thomists have admirably deepened and developed the questions concerning the being of knowledge; fruitful principles for a similar development concerning the intentional being of love and the spiration of love can also be found in their works . . . . But this development itself is yet to be made."[35] He himself has carried that development part of the way. Among the many gifts he has left to those who follow him are two tasks: to study his contribution exhaustively and to carry the development on.

NOTES

1. Edited by Clifton Fadiman, Simon and Schuster, New York, 1939, "Jacques Maritain," pp. 197-210.
2. Edited by Ruth Nanda Anshen, Harper, New York and London, 1947, Ch. XIV, "A New Approach to God," by Jacques Maritain, pp. 280-295.
3. Newman Press, Westminster, Maryland, 1959.
4. Scribner, New York, 1959, Ch. VI, "Mystical Experience and Philosophy," pp. 247-290, and Ch. IX, "Todo y Nada," pp. 352-383.
5. Sheed and Ward, New York, 1948, pp. 95-97.
6. *Our Emergent Civilization,* pp. 281-282; cf. *ibid.,* pp. 285-286; also, *The Angelic Doctor* (Sheed and Ward, New York, 1931), pp. 72-73.
7. *I Believe,* p. 210; cf. *Our Emergent Civilization,* p. 295; *Education at the Crossroads* (Yale University Press, New Haven, 1943), pp. 7-11; *True Humanism* (Scribner, New York, 1954), pp. 83-84; *The Rights of Man and Natural Law* (Scribner, New York, 1943), pp. 1 ff.

8. *Truth and Human Fellowship* (Princeton University Press, Princeton, New Jersey, 1957), p. 24; cf. *ibid.*, p. 21 and pp. 23-32; *Ransoming the Time* (Scribner, New York, 1941), Ch. V, "Who is My Neighbor," pp. 115-140; *The Range of Reason* (Scribner, New York, 1952), Ch. XIII, "The Possibility for Co-operation in a Divided World," pp. 172-184; *A Christian Looks at the Jewish Question* (Longmans, Green and Co., New York, 1939), p. 80 ff.
9. *I Believe*, pp. 209-210; *Truth and Human Fellowship*, p. 8.
10. *I Believe*, p. 205; cf. *Reflections on America* (Scribner, New York, 1958), Ch. XVI, "Marriage and Happiness," pp. 137-145; *The Angelic Doctor*, pp. 77-81; *Education at the Crossroads*, pp. 23, 35, 95-96.
11. *True Humanism*, p. 48; cf. *ibid.*, pp. 48-53, 83-84, 197-198, 275-286; *An Essay on Christian Philosophy* (Philosophical Library, New York, 1955), pp. 17-18, 24-28.
12. *Christianity and Democracy* (Scribner, New York, 1944), pp. 44-56.
13. *Reflections on America*, pp. 174-191; *The Person and the Common Good* (Scribner, New York, 1947), pp. 5 ff.
14. *Art and Faith* (Philosophical Library, New York, 1948), pp. 104-114; *The Range of Reason*, pp. 196-199; *The Angelic Doctor*, pp. 130, 147-148.
15. *Freedom in the Modern World* (Scribner, New York, 1936), pp. 3 ff.
16. *Our Emergent Civilization*, p. 285; *Existence and the Existent* (Pantheon, New York, 1948), pp. 82-84.
17. *Existence and the Existent*, pp. 58, 75-76.
18. *The Degrees of Knowledge*, pp. 368-369; cf. *Existence and the Existent*, p. 40.
19. *The Range of Reason*, Ch. III, "On Knowledge Through Connaturality," pp. 22-29.
20. *Creative Intuition in Art and Poetry* (Pantheon, New York, 1953), pp. 117-145.
21. *Neuf Leçons sur les Notions Premières de la Philosophie Morale*, (Téqui, Paris, 1951), pp. 47-66; *Man and the State*, (University of Chicago Press, Chicago, 1951), pp. 90 ff.
22. *The Degrees of Knowledge*, pp. 260 ff.; *Ransoming the Time*, Ch. X, "The Natural Mystical Experience and the Void," pp. 255-289.
23. *The Sin of the Angel, passim.* This part of the present essay is based upon this recent work of M. Maritain. In it he gives the most

fully developed and precise expression of his thought on this aspect of love.

24. Cf. *Existence and the Existent,* pp. 42-45; *A Preface to Metaphysics,* pp. 110-131.
25. Cf. *Neuf leçons,* pp. 19-22, 26 ff., 36-40; *Three Reformers* (Scribner, New York, 1936), pp. 22 ff.
26. *The Sin of the Angel,* p. 21.
27. *The Range of Reason,* Ch. XV, "A Faith to Live By," pp. 200-204.
28. Cf. *The Range of Reason,* Ch. VI, "The Immanent Dialectic of the First Act of Freedom," pp. 66-85.
29. Cf. *The Range of Reason,* Ch. VII, "A New Approach to God," pp. 86-102, and Ch. VIII, "The Meaning of Contemporary Atheism," pp. 103-117; *Approaches to God* (Harper, New York, 1954), pp. 84 ff.
30. Cf. *The Things That Are Not Caesar's* (Scribner, New York, 1931), pp. 110 ff.
31. Cf. *Prayer and Intelligence* (Sheed and Ward, London, 1928), pp. 11 ff. and *passim; Scholasticism and Politics* (Macmillan, New York, 1940), pp. 170-178, 190-193; *I Believe,* pp. 201-202; *Our Emergent Civilization,* p. 295.
32. *Our Emergent Civilization,* p. 289; cf. *True Humanism,* p. 197.
33. *A Preface to Metaphysics,* pp. 95-97; cf. *Existence and the Existent,* pp. 49-50.
34. *The Degrees of Knowledge,* Ch. VI and IX (see note 4 *supra*); cf. *An Essay on Christian Philosophy,* p. 100; *The Angelic Doctor,* p. 52; *Ransoming the Time,* Ch. IV, "The Bergsonian Philosophy of Morality and Religion," pp. 84-114 (the same appears in *Bergsonian Philosophy and Thomism* (Philosophical Library, New York, 1955), Ch. XVII, pp. 325-345); *Christianity and Democracy,* pp. 64 ff.
35. *The Degrees of Knowledge,* p. 369, n. 6.